Feminism and the Power of Love is a crucial addition to the rapidly expanding field of Love Studies. Too few books tackle the problematic status of 'love' in feminist theory, but even fewer address the central theme of this book, namely the tension between two indisputable facts: love plays and replays sex and gender relationships of power; but it is also a vital source of human enhancement and energy. Understanding this tension through a variety of disciplines and methodological lenses, this book represents an important advance of feminist theory.

Professor Eva Illouz, author of *Why Love Hurts*

Politics, economy, revolution, history: what's love got to do with these? Everything, or so the provocative essays collected in *Feminism and the Power of Love* claim. Whether you find love a distinctly patriarchal invention or a necessary affect for utopian transformations, the conversations arrayed here will convince you of the value of love studies for contemporary feminist theory.

Professor Robyn Wiegman, Duke University

The contribution that *Feminism and the Power of Love* has been making to the wider field of Love Studies has been transformative. The contributors to this book look critically at love as a site where emotional and reproductive labor are distributed unequally – whilst acknowledging the crucial function of loving care in human bonding. This approach throws a much needed light on the complexity of love as a manifestation of interconnected desires, emotions, social relations and cultural modes of expression. If you are interested in intimacy, love or relationships you will find this book indispensable for your study and research whether you agree with its premises and outcome or not.

Professor Michael Gratzke, Hull University,
Convener of the Love Research Network

What might be cutting-edge concepts of love? Transformative intimacies? Anti-ownership possibilities? Non-oppressive bonds? *Feminism and the Power of Love* breaks new grounds as it introduces feminist love studies, arguing that while love is an intimate affair, it also has a huge influence on public and political life. Showcasing creative energies and diverse methodologies, the volume historicizes love, teases out the contradictions of love, and calls on feminist theorists to shape the field of love studies.

Katarzyna Marciniak, Ohio University

Feminism and the Power of Love

The power of love has become a renewed matter of feminist and non-feminist attention in the twenty-first century's theory debates. What is this power? Is it a form of domination? Or is it a liberating force in our contemporary societies?

Within *Feminism and the Power of Love* lies the central argument that, although love is a crucial site of gendered power asymmetries, it is also a vital source of human empowerment that we cannot live without. Instead of emphasizing 'either-or', this enlightening collection puts the dualities and contradictions of love centre stage. Indeed, by offering various theoretical perspectives on what makes love such a central value and motivator for people, this book will increase one's understanding as to why love can keep people in its grip – even when practised in ways that deplete and oppress. In light of such analyses, the contributions within *Feminism and the Power of Love* present new perspectives on the conditions and characteristics of non-oppressive, mutually enhancing ways of loving.

Bridging the gap between Feminist Affect Studies and Feminist Love Studies, this book will appeal to undergraduate and postgraduate students, including postdoctoral researchers, interested in fields such as women's and gender studies, sociology, political science, philosophy, cultural studies and sexuality studies.

Adriana García-Andrade is Professor in the Department of Sociology, Universidad Autónoma Metropolitana (UAM), México.

Lena Gunnarsson is a Researcher and Teacher in the Department of Gender Studies, Lund University, Sweden.

Anna G. Jónasdóttir is Senior Professor at Örebro University, Sweden.

Routledge Advances in Feminist Studies and Intersectionality

Routledge Advances in Feminist Studies and Intersectionality is committed to the development of new feminist and pro-feminist perspectives on changing gender relations, with special attention to:

- Intersections between gender and power differentials based on age, class, dis/abilities, ethnicity, nationality, racialisation, sexuality, violence, and other social divisions.
- Intersections of societal dimensions and processes of continuity and change: culture, economy, generativity, polity, sexuality, science and technology;
- Embodiment: Intersections of discourse and materiality, and of sex and gender.
- Transdisciplinarity: intersections of humanities, social sciences, medical, technical and natural sciences.
- Intersections of different branches of feminist theorizing, including: historical materialist feminisms, postcolonial and anti-racist feminisms, radical feminisms, sexual difference feminisms, queer feminisms, cyber feminisms, post-human feminisms, critical studies on men and masculinities.
- A critical analysis of the travelling of ideas, theories and concepts.
- A politics of location, reflexivity and transnational contextualising that reflects the basis of the Series framed within European diversity and transnational power relations.

Core editorial group

Professor Jeff Hearn (managing editor; Örebro University, Sweden; Hanken School of Economics, Finland; University of Huddersfield, UK)
Dr Kathy Davis (Institute for History and Culture, Utrecht, The Netherlands)
Professor Anna G. Jónasdóttir (Örebro University, Sweden)
Professor Nina Lykke (managing editor; Linköping University, Sweden)
Professor Elżbieta H. Oleksy (University of Łódź, Poland)
Dr Andrea Petö (Central European University, Hungary)
Professor Ann Phoenix (Institute of Education, University of London, UK)
Professor Chandra Talpade Mohanty (Syracuse University, USA)

Feminism and the Power of Love

Interdisciplinary Interventions

Edited by
Adriana García-Andrade, Lena Gunnarsson
and Anna G. Jónasdóttir

Routledge
Taylor & Francis Group

LONDON AND NEW YORK

First published 2018 by Routledge

2 Park Square, Milton Park, Abingdon, Oxfordshire OX14 4RN

52 Vanderbilt Avenue, New York, NY 10017

Routledge is an imprint of the Taylor & Francis Group, an informa business

First issued in paperback 2019

British Library Cataloguing in Publication Data
A catalogue record for this book is available from the British Library

Library of Congress Cataloging in Publication Data
Names: García Andrade, Adriana, editor. | Gunnarsson, Lena, editor. |
    Anna G. Jónasdóttir, editor.
Title: Feminism and the power of love : interdisciplinary interventions /
    [edited by] Adriana García-Andrade, Lena Gunnarsson and
    Anna G. Jónasdóttir.
Description: Abingdon, Oxon, New York, NY : Routledge, 2017. | Series:
    Routledge advances in feminist studies and intersectionality ; 23 | Includes
    bibliographical references and index.
Identifiers: LCCN 2017053568 | ISBN 9781138710054 (hardback)
Subjects: LCSH: Feminist theory. | Love. | Feminism.
Classification: LCC HQ1190 .F44124 2017 | DDC 305.4201–dc23
LC record available at https://lccn.loc.gov/2017053568

ISBN: 978-1-138-71005-4 (hbk)
ISBN: 978-0-367-35099-4 (pbk)

Typeset in Times New Roman
by Taylor & Francis Books

Contents

List of figures

Contributors

Ann Ferguson is Professor Emerita of Philosophy and Women, Gender and Sexuality Studies at the University of Massachusetts Amherst, USA. She is author and co-editor of five books and many other publications on feminist philosophy, feminist theory, the affective economy, and feminist love studies. She is also a socialist-feminist activist. Recent publications include *Love: A Question for Feminism in the Twenty-First Century*, co-edited with Anna G. Jónasdóttir (Routledge, 2014), and a special issue on feminist love studies for *Hypatia*, co-edited with Margaret E. Toye (2017).

Adriana García-Andrade is Professor of Sociology at the Department of Sociology, Universidad Autónoma Metropolitana (UAM), Mexico. She has a Ph.D. in Humanities and specializes in philosophy and sociology of science, sociology of love, and contemporary sociological theories. She is currently vice president for the research committee on Logic and Methodology (RC33) of the International Sociological Association. Her recent publications include reflections on the epistemological conditions of sociological theories, love in the social sciences as a global phenomenon, and love as a sociological problem.

Renata Grossi is an interdisciplinary legal scholar at the Law School, University of Technology, Sydney, Australia. Her research interests are in law and the emotions. She is the author of *Looking for Love in the Legal Discourse of Marriage* (ANU Press, 2014) and co-editor of *The Radicalism of Romantic Love: Critical Perspectives* (Routledge, 2017).

Lena Gunnarsson is a researcher and teacher in Gender Studies at Lund University, and is affiliated with Örebro University, Sweden. She is co-founder and former convener of the Feminist Love Studies Network. Her research interests include feminist theory, social theory, feminist love studies and sexual consent research. Recent publications are 'Hetero-Love in Patriarchy: An Autobiographical Substantiation' (*Hypatia*, 2017), 'The Dominant and Its Constitutive Other: Feminist Theorizations of Love, Power and Gendered Selves' (*Journal of Critical Realism*, 2016), and *The Contradictions of Love* (Routledge, 2014; awarded the Cheryl Frank Memorial Prize).

Anna G. Jónasdóttir is Senior Professor in Gender Studies at Örebro University, Sweden. She has published articles, book chapters, and books in English, Icelandic, Spanish, and Swedish. Her works include *Love Power and Political Interests* (Örebro University, 1991), also published (slightly revised) as *Why Women Are Oppressed* (Temple University, 1994); 'Feminist Questions, Marx's Method, and the Theorization of "Love Power"' (2009); 'What Kind of Power is "Love Power"?' (2011); and 'Love Studies: A (Re)New(ed) Field of Feminist Knowledge Interests' (2014).

Kathleen B. Jones is Professor Emerita of Women's Studies at San Diego State University and Visiting Research Fellow at the University of California–Davis, USA. Her most recent book is a philosophical memoir, *Diving for Pearls: A Thinking Journey with Hannah Arendt* (Thinking Women Books, 2013) and was awarded the Barbara 'Penny' Kanner Book Award by the Western Association of Women Historians (USA).

Olga Sabido-Ramos is Professor of Sociology at Universidad Autónoma Metropolitana, Mexico. She specializes in research on the body, the senses, and affective bonds, and in Georg Simmel's relational sociology. She is the author of *El cuerpo como recurso de sentido en la construcción del extraño* (Séquitur, 2012) and co-editor with Adriana García-Andrade of *Cuerpo y afectividad en la sociedad contemporánea* (UAM-Conacyt, 2014). She has published numerous articles and book chapters theorizing the body, the senses, and embodied love on different analytical levels. She is part of the Editorial Board of *Simmel Studies*.

Justyna Szachowicz Sempruch has a Ph.D. in Comparative Literature from the University of British Columbia and is currently a researcher at the University of Warsaw, Poland. In 2010 she completed transnational research on work–life balance in non/normative family contexts (Toronto, Zurich, Warsaw), funded by the Swiss National Science Foundation. She is the author of two co-edited anthologies, and a monograph, *Fantasies of Gender* (Purdue University Press, 2008). Her current book project, *The Precariousness of Love: The Meanings of Family*, is based on research into the diversity of love bonds in contemporary Europe.

Silvia Stoller is University Docent at the Department of Philosophy, University of Vienna, and also teaches at the Department of Educational Sciences, University of Graz, Austria. Her research areas are phenomenology, feminist philosophy, gender studies, philosophical anthropology, and existential philosophy (on topics such as pain, age, love, laughter, and play). Her most recent book publication, as editor in English language, is *Simone de Beauvoir's Philosophy of Age* (Walter de Gruyter, 2014).

Margaret E. Toye is Associate Professor at the Women and Gender Studies Program and core member of the MA Program in Cultural Analysis and Social Theory at Wilfrid Laurier University, Canada. Her research focuses on feminist theories in relation to poststructuralist ethics, affect, love, consumption, technology, food studies, methodologies, and creative forms of argument. She has published articles in journals including *Feminist Theory, Hypatia, Women's Studies: An Interdisciplinary Journal,* and *Papers on Language and Literature.* With Ann Ferguson she co-edited the special issue of *Hypatia* on 'Feminist Love Studies' (2017).

Preface and acknowledgements

This book is one of the outcomes of the collaborative work between members of the international Feminist Love Studies Network, inaugurated at Örebro University, Sweden in March 2013. The network is connected with the research strand Love and Feminist Theory in the GEXcel International Collegium for Advanced Transdisciplinary Gender Studies. All but one of the core group members of the network contributed to this volume; Eudine Barriteau withdrew from the book project because of the heavy administrative workload entailed by her position as pro vice-chancellor and principal at the University of the West Indies, Barbados. Other research activities arranged by the Feminist Love Studies Network include the guest-editing of two special issues on love, one for *Hypatia: A Journal of Feminist Philosophy* (vol. 32, no. 1, 2017; Ann Ferguson and Margaret E. Toye), the other for the Swedish journal *Tidskrift för genusvetenskap* (vol. 37, no. 2, 2016; Lena Gunnarsson and Anna G. Jónasdóttir); and the conference on 'Love, Sensible Experience, and Feminism', which took place at Universidad Autónoma Metropolitana, Mexico City, on 17–18 September 2015. The conference was co-arranged (through the core group members Adriana García-Andrade and Olga Sabido-Ramos) with the Research Area of Theory and Sociological Thinking at the Department of Sociology, Universidad Autónoma Metropolitana Azcapotzalco.

Along the way this book project benefitted much from the work meeting we had at Örebro University in October 2014, and we thank the Faculty Board of Humanities and Social Sciences, Örebro University, for the grant that made the meeting possible.

We thank the anonymous reviewers for their valuable comments on the initial book proposal. To Emily Briggs and Elena Chiu at Routledge, editor and editorial assistant of the series *Routledge Advances in Feminist Studies and Intersectionality*, now based in Abingdon, UK, we are grateful for their support and patience.

1 The power of love

Towards an interdisciplinary and multi-theoretical feminist love studies

Lena Gunnarsson, Adriana García-Andrade and Anna G. Jónasdóttir

Although love in some form is arguably as old as humankind, many scholars judge that it has never been as socially and existentially decisive as it is in contemporary western societies (Bauman 2003; Beck and Beck-Gernsheim 1995; Ferry 2013; Giddens 1992; Gunnarsson 2014a; Illouz 2012; Jónasdóttir 1994, 2011; Kaufmann 2011; Luhmann 1998; May 2011). The loosening of collective and role-based modes of recognition and existential security has meant that, to an increasing extent, love has become the most significant source of people's 'ontological rootedness' (May 2011) or 'ontological security' (Giddens 1992). For instance, while conceding that it seems to be a universal fact that love is a source of self-enhancement, Eva Illouz argues that 'the sense of self-worth provided by love in modern relationships is of particular and acute importance, precisely because at stake in contemporary individualism is the difficulty to establish one's self-worth and because the pressure for self-differentiation and developing a sense of uniqueness has considerably increased with modernity' (2012: 112; cf. Beck and Beck-Gernsheim 1995; Gunnarsson 2014a; Gunnarsson 1994, 2011; Luhmann 1998). Luc Ferry goes as far as stating that the world is currently going through a 'revolution of love'. When fewer and fewer believe in values like God, the Nation or the Revolution, the only thing in which basically everyone believes is love. Although love, as the new great principle of meaning against which to measure the 'good life', revolves around the private sphere, Ferry states that the revolution of love has repercussions for public and political life as well. For instance, he sees the ecological movement as premised on the historically recent phenomenon of parental love, forming the basis of a concern for the lives of future generations (Ferry 2013). The long-standing feminist insight that the personal is political has now reached into the core of male-stream theorizing.

The increasing social significance of love is a crucial theme also in Anna Jónasdóttir's feminist theorization of contemporary western societies, which is more specifically focused on sexual love, understood as a 'causal power in history'. In line with Illouz and others, she argues that under current social conditions, 'when individuals are forced/free to make and remake themselves under continuously changing circumstances, love as a source of creative/re-creative human power seems to be needed more and more strongly' (Jónasdóttir 2011: 50). She also addresses the historically specific relation between love and the economy (cf. Bryson 2011; Hochschild 2003; Illouz 2007, 2012), tentatively proposing that 'capital is becoming more and more dependent on recreative (as distinct from procreative) love power; and on conditioning people to use and invest their energy [and love power] to serve, directly or indirectly, continued economic growth' (Jónasdóttir 1994: 229).

The growing *de facto* social significance of love is likely to be one crucial factor behind the increasing academic interest in love, forming the new field of what Jónasdóttir terms 'love studies' (Jónasdóttir 2014). While love was long an embarrassing topic for scholars aiming to be taken seriously (Toye 2010) (with literary studies and parts of philosophy as exceptions), it is now commonplace as a male-stream topic of study in many different disciplines, ranging from neuroscience to political science. Given that most people would rate love as one of life's highest values and motivators (Ferguson and Jónasdóttir 2014), as witnessed by its topicality in music, literature and art, this growing academic interest in love is important because it helps bridge the gap between academic and lay inclinations, contributing to a deeper understanding of people's behavior and, consequently, to social life as a whole (Sayer 2011).

As part of the expanding general field of love studies, a revitalized sub-field of feminist love studies has begun to take shape (Ferguson and Jónasdóttir 2014). It has done so only hesitantly though, despite the fact that love is generally thought of as a feminine realm. As Margaret Toye suggests, it is probably precisely *because* of love's association with 'the realm of women, the home, the private, the apolitical, the "not serious"' that, struggling to be taken seriously, feminist theorists feel such a 'nervousness around the topic' (2010: 41). However, since the organization of love under patriarchy is strongly structured by gender, contributing to the subordination of women to men (de Beauvoir 1989; Dempsey 2002; Ferguson 1989, 1991, 2012; Firestone 1970; Gunnarsson 2011, 2014a, 2014b; Illouz 2012; Jackson 2014; Jónasdóttir 1994, 2009, 2011; Langford 1999; Thagaard 1997) and privileging heterosexual love over same-sex love (Butler 1990; Ferguson 1989, 1991; Jackson 2006; Rich 1980), it remains centrally important that feminist theorists take part in shaping the field of love studies.

As part of the generally growing significance of love in late modern societies, love also seems to be becoming an increasingly important arena of gender struggle (Jónasdóttir 2009). As a result of formal gender equality and the relative decline in women's economic dependence on men, we have entered an era in which many middle and upper class women, above all but not exclusively in the West/North, remain bound to men only by the bonds of sexual attraction and love (Giddens 1992; Gunnarsson 2014a; Jónasdóttir 1994 [1991]). The implications of this have not been sufficiently explored by feminist theorists. What are the mechanisms of power internal to love? And what is it that motivates women to continue to attach themselves to men, even when this is not necessitated by economic and other constraints? In other words, what kind(s) of power is the power of love? And what difference does it make in and for feminist theory and politics?

In the feminist work on love that does exist, especially as part of second wave feminism, the dominant way to explain women's choice to attach themselves to men in the name of love, even when this implies subordination and the draining of women's powers, has been by recourse to notions of patriarchal ideology or discourse. With some exceptions (e.g. Leon 1978; Sarachild 1978; Willis 1980), the recurrent theme of second wave feminist discourse on love was to conceive of heterosexual love as a delusion or false consciousness, ensuring that women continue to submit to men (Atkinson 1974; The Feminists 1973; Firestone 1970; see Douglas 1990, Jónasdóttir 2014, and Grossi this volume for overviews). As bell hooks puts forward, this feminist tendency to reduce love to a matter of patriarchal ideology has led to the alienation of most women from feminism. For hooks, to see love itself as the problem was a mistake of second wave feminists. 'We were to do away with love and put in its place a concern with gaining rights and power', she states, highlighting that this inhibited the development of a more complex feminist theorization of love. 'Rather than rethinking love and insisting on its importance and value, feminist discourse on love simply stopped' (2000: 102). Highlighting that the emergence of love studies as a new research field has so far been driven to a large extent by male mainstream theorists, Jónasdóttir echoes hook's plea for more feminist inquiries into love. Since love is 'one of the most vital, and difficult – not the least for women, matters to deal with in practical life and in theory, it should be particularly urgent for feminists to be (pro)active in this area' (Jónasdóttir 2014: 25).

Although ideological notions of compulsory heterosexual love, bound up with norms of femininity and masculinity, are of course immensely important as vehicles reproducing heterosexuality as a dominant system with associated gendered power relations, this book departs from tendencies of *reducing* love to ideology or discourse. A central assumption structuring the book is that although love is a crucial site of (in particular) gendered power asymmetries, it is also a vital source of human enhancement that we cannot, in its basic form, live without. Refraining from tendencies in much work on love to emphasize either love's oppressive or enhancing qualities and implications (see Gunnarsson 2011, 2014a), the book puts the dualities, dynamics, and contradictions of love center stage, in the conviction that love's indisputable *power* can be organized in both mutually enhancing and egalitarian and oppressive and exploitative ways. From a range of different theoretical points of view, it aims to elucidate what makes love such a central value and motivator for people, thereby adding to the understanding of why love can keep people in its grip even when practiced in ways that deplete and oppress. In light of such analyses, ontological as well as historical and empirical, it also offers new perspectives on the conditions and characteristics of non-oppressive, mutually enhancing ways of loving.

The power of love

Taking different routes into the theme of love and its relation to power, the contributions in this volume engage in a collective effort to draw the contours of what we call feminist love studies. What, then, do we mean by 'love'? Reflecting the multifaceted everyday as well as scholarly understandings of love, this book does not endorse a single definition of love. Implicitly or explicitly, the contributions work with and around different notions of love, ranging from understanding it in terms of an emotion, affect, practice, energy, or bond, to an ideology, historical code, and/or methodology. Love is seen as irreducible to sexuality; at the same time, many of the contributors deal with sexual forms of love, acknowledging the practical and ontological links between love and sexuality. An important conceptual backdrop of the research collaboration generally and this book specifically is Jónasdóttir's concept of *love power* (Jónasdóttir 1994, 2009, 2011, this volume). For Jónasdóttir, a social and political theorist based in Sweden, love power refers to that basic human capacity by means of which we can and do empower each other as worthy human existences. Jónasdóttir works with(in) a historical-materialist framework, a mode of thought that assumes the existence of certain basic human powers, coupled with fundamental needs, which in turn provide an ontological foundation for more specific historical accounts of power structures. Jónasdóttir thus operates with a dual notion of power, both in the 'positive' sense of a basic psycho-organic capacity and in the 'negative' sense of oppressive or exploitative power.[1] Rarely made in poststructuralist accounts, such a distinction has begun to be considered in some post-poststructuralist versions of the 'new' feminist materialism, in particular in feminist affect theory (e.g. Brennan 2004). Jónasdóttir's feminist reconstruction of a Marxian historical-materialist perspective takes into account love's dual capacity of power and constraint, highlighting these as two sides of the same coin. Indeed, we can make sense of the human vulnerability resulting from the fact that we need to love and be loved, which can make us prone to accept unequal conditions when this need is not met, only in light of love's constructive power (Gunnarsson 2014a).

 Jónasdóttir thinks of patriarchal love as an exploitative relationship, where men appropriate more of women's loving energies than they give in return. The fact that love is powerful in the constructive sense also means that people are likely to have an interest in exploiting it, providing yet another clue to love's dual empowering/disempowering potential. In Chapter 2 Jónasdóttir continues to elaborate her groundbreaking notion of love power by responding to some typical questions that her theory has provoked. At a time when the historical-materialist perspective is marginalized within feminist theory, a crucial part of the argument operates on the ontological level, elucidating the specific perspective that she takes on power generally and on love power specifically.

Independently of Jónasdóttir but roughly at the same time, US philosopher Ann Ferguson developed her theory of 'sex-affective production' (1989, 1991), which has remarkable similarities to Jónasdóttir's theory of love power. Both applied and expanded basic Marxian categories for the purpose of theorizing gendered power, although where Jónasdóttir talked about men's exploitation of women's love power, Ferguson referred to a similar process in terms of men's exploitation of women's 'sex/affective energy'. In Chapter 3 Ferguson revises her theory somewhat, replacing the notion of sex/affective energy with the twin concepts of 'love energy' and 'sexual energy', and demonstrates how contradictions inherent in current western patriarchy make it impossible for both women and men to meet the sexual and love needs that these structures also produce. Crucial in Jónasdóttir's and Ferguson's work alike is the understanding of power both in terms of a basic, vital human capacity, and in terms of historically constituted power inequalities, where the theorizations of the latter are based in distinct ontologies of the former. As Toye highlights in this volume, by building her account on the notion of 'energy', Ferguson's contribution points towards connections with the new materialist and affective turns that distance themselves from 'old' Marxian materialism and which are explored in both Toye's and Jones' contributions (see below).

When the term 'love' is invoked, people often envision different kinds of sexual couple love. Although heterosexual couple love does constitute a pivotal institution in the work of both Jónasdóttir and Ferguson, neither of them restricts their conceptualization to this specific institution; both work with broad notions of love, opening the concept up for analysis as a continuum differently practiced across social relations. In this volume, Ferguson does center on couple love, proposing that romantic love is inherently alienated and patriarchal. She also suggests that even the feminist ideal of *mutual love* is something that cannot be achieved in our society if conditions such as capitalism and militarism continue to exert and promote contradictory goals among women and men. As in Lena Gunnarsson's chapter, for Ferguson, not only are women losing out, but men are also rendered unable to receive and give more love energy. In Chapter 4, Australian historian and law scholar Renata Grossi reviews the central feminist debate on precisely why and in which sense romantic love is problematic, putting it in conversation with the debate over same-sex marriage as played out in the Australian context. She reviews different strands of feminist critiques of love to interrogate the fact that arguments for same-sex marriage often draw a lot of their force from positive images of romantic love that stand in stark contrast with the traditional feminist discourse on romantic love. Grossi explores to what extent the feminist critique has been based on views of romantic love as *inherently* oppressive and to what extent it has been pictured as precarious only due to its *association* with oppressive orders of power, leaving room for the possibility of equal and liberating forms of romantic love. With some caution, she makes a plea for analytically disconnecting romantic love from its oppressive and heteronormative forms, suggesting that same-sex marriage may open the way for a radicalization of love.

Canadian literary scholar Margaret Toye takes us back in Chapter 5 to more basic ontological discussions about how to think love and power together. She does so by putting feminist love studies in conversation with feminist affect studies, arguing that the present lack of such conversations is the result of a strong Marxian materialist influence in love studies, as contrasted with affect studies' lineage in a poststructuralist paradigm where Toye herself feels at home. Aiming to bridge the gulf between the fields, Toye suggests exploring love in terms of *affective energy*, since energy is a concept that figures in both fields and is often used to conceptualize connections between power, life and love. Whereas the feminist historical-materialist paradigm understands power structures in terms of the exploitation of energy along quite determinate, historically located, gendered lines, the Deleuzian philosophy underpinning much feminist theorizing on affect puts more emphasis on the diffuse character of power. Both, however, dissolve dichotomies between power in the negative, constraining sense and power in the productive, creative sense. Toye discusses the work of Teresa Brennan, which is also touched upon in Jónasdóttir's contribution and comprises a particularly interesting point of potential conversation between the affective and love paradigms. Both affect and love are central conceptual building blocks in Brennan's theory. Despite the fact that she takes a psychoanalytic approach to these themes, her perspective on how feminine and masculine selves are constituted by means of the unequal transmission of living attention converges in intriguing ways with Ferguson's and Jónasdóttir's accounts (see Gunnarsson 2016).

Where Toye embraces the feminist turn to affect, US political theorist Kathleen Jones is warier about its focus on autonomic bodily processes and doubts whether it is compatible with a democratic theory of change. In Chapter 6 she disentangles what consequences the affective ontology would have for analyzing the motivations behind murders followed by suicide – so called dyadic deaths – a phenomenon that can be seen as an extreme expression of the contradictory co-mingling of 'love' with oppression and destruction. By interrogating the affective turn through the lens of the ever-acute problem of male power and violence, Jones raises the question of whether our theories can be useful for understanding the politically pressing issues of oppressive gendered power and how these relate to love.

In Chapter 7 Justyna Szachowicz Sempruch, a Polish scholar of comparative literature and social studies, breaks out of the confines of dyadic love. Taking seriously the rapid growth of non-monogamous communities in Europe, she explores the significance of these forms of bonding in a broader context of neoliberal commodification of self-centrism and the difficulties of maintaining happy love bonds within the traditional nuclear family. Noting that, historically, feminist theorists have tended to avoid investments in the idea of love-as-power, Sempruch's contribution indicates that non-normative, non-monogamous love, involving responsibility and solidarity, is a site where love's positive force could be reclaimed.

Whereas the endemic unhappiness of dyadic love works as a point of departure of Sempruch's contribution, in Chapter 8 Mexican sociologists Adriana García-Andrade and Olga Sabido-Ramos shed new light on what makes couple love so attractive. There are good reasons for focusing on the negative and oppressive aspects of couple love in a general context that tends to obscure them. However, these problematic features are now so taken for granted among feminist scholars that it might be time to get back to basics about love: why do we like and need it so much in the first place? Indeed, it is only in light of the enjoyable things about love that we can make sense of its (potentially destructive) power over us. In contrast to those critiques of couple love which do not take its real benefits seriously, García-Andrade and Sabido-Ramos seek to make sense of the joys of couple love by exploring it in its everyday details. They move the focus away from the theoretical vocabulary of psycho-material powers, affects and energies to foreground the semantic and situational dimensions of love. In addition, they explore the bodily aspects of the loving encounter by incorporating into their framework neuroscientific theories of emotion and affect informing the affect studies considered by Toye and Jones. Besides pointing to gendered asymmetries in love, García-Andrade and Sabido-Ramos raise the issue of power in terms of the way that love, as hegemonically practiced, is a deeply class-structured phenomenon, premised on certain material conditions and cultural and social skills.

Where García-Andrade and Sabido-Ramos base their account of the self–other dyad on classical sociological theory, in Chapter 9 Austrian philosopher Silvia Stoller explores this pivotal relation by drawing on Luce Irigaray's feminist philosophy of sexual difference and thematizing the place of silence in the loving encounter. The previous chapters have been preoccupied mainly with mapping, exploring and explaining love and power as presently configured in our world. In Stoller's contribution more visionary and ethical themes are foregrounded, addressing the question of what precisely are the components of a non-oppressive mode of loving. Implicitly, Stoller's account ties in with the tradition of feminist critiques of romantic love, in the sense that the non-appropriative, non-consuming loving ideal promoted by Irigaray stands in stark contrast with current images of romantic love. Where Ferguson's reciprocal love ideal 'abolishes gender roles in love', in the Irigarayan ideal the acknowledgment of irreducible sexual difference is instead the very ground of non-oppressive love.

Also partly drawing on Irigaray, connecting it with realist and dialectical thought and with Jessica Benjamin's psychoanalytical theory of love and dominance, in the final chapter Swedish gender studies scholar Lena Gunnarsson further explores the potentials and perils at the heart of the self–other relation. She explicitly addresses the issue of the relation between love and dominance, stating that although love is fundamentally at odds with dominance there are also good ontological reasons for why love – or at least 'love' – so often co-mingles with dominance. Gunnarsson puts tensions like these center stage, suggesting that the embrace of such tensions *in theory* is crucial for understanding the relation between love and dominance, and that the harboring *in practice* of tensions at the root of our existence is a condition of non-oppressive and sustainable modes of love. Her contribution is concerned both with exploring the architecture of oppressive modes of love and with envisioning an ethics of love that embodies the opposite of oppression, and a central argument of hers is that the latter cannot happen without insights about the former.

Love as method: differences and synergies

The book has a strongly interdisciplinary and multi-theoretical structure. It is the contributors' conviction that, given the complex and multi-layered character of love and power, they are best addressed from a range of different points of view, which do not necessarily mutually exclude one another despite their radical difference at times. Having come together physically in workshops to discuss the book, the contributors have endeavored to apply what might be referred to as 'love as method'.

Toye elsewhere highlights that love need not be restricted to being the topic of scholarly work; it can also be a way of generating knowledge (Toye in process). This idea is not new and can mean different things. Well known is Evelyn Fox Keller's study of biologist and Nobel Prize winner Barbara McClintock and her scientific method, which included a loving 'feeling for the organism', her 'object' of study (Keller 1983; see also e.g. Jaggar 1989). In a different vein, Rosa Medina-Doménech, Mari Luz Esteban-Galarza and Ana Távora-Rivero foreground the relation between love and epistemological transformation by highlighting how 'research of love can change our deep-rooted emotional understandings and affective consciousness' (2014: 158). For Toye, love as method requires acceptance of the limits of the knowledge possible from one's own particular vantage point. She is inspired by Dawn Rae Davis, who thinks of love as the 'ability of *not* knowing' (2002: 157, emphasis added), where this does not amount to skepticism but to a view of knowledge as generated by its own limits as well as transgressions. The contributors to this book have sought to engage love as method in the sense that we have cultivated an awareness of the partiality of our own outlook as well as a mode of respecting, harboring, and living-through, rather than evading or denying, the tensions created by our disciplinary, theoretical, and personal differences. Our view of tensions as potentially productive has been coupled with acknowledgment of the difficulties they might entail. We have sought to be faithful in practice to the insight that for the constructive potential of tensions to be realized, the strain, even 'impossibility', they encompass needs first to be respected (cf. Gunnarsson this volume).

This method of love can be compared to the idea of 'transversal dialogue' stemming from the activist/political field (Cockburn and Hunter 1999; Yuval-Davis 1999) but also partly applicable to knowledge production involving people who hold different epistemological positions (Lykke 2011). Nira Yuval-Davies states that transversal dialogues are based on the conviction that

> from each positioning the world is seen differently, and thus ... any knowledge based on just one positioning is 'unfinished' – which is not the

same thing as saying it is 'invalid'. In this epistemology, the only way to approach 'the truth' is by a dialogue between people of differential positionings.

(Yuval-Davies 1999: 94–95)

While affirming Yuval-Davies' claim that this reconciliatory idea does not imply that all kinds of different views are compatible, the unfolding of this book has been firmly rooted in a belief that the different disciplinary and theoretical positionings of the contributors constitute a productive asset. We do not underestimate the difficulties, but try to practice an attitude to knowledge production that involves being open to the perspective of the other, premised on the insight that our own perspective always needs to be complemented by those of others and that the multi-dimensional character of reality requires multi-dimensional knowledge. Moreover, in the course of producing this book we have worked with the idea that the most productive way, both in terms of producing relevant and valid knowledge and in terms of building strong bonds, of approaching someone's differing, sometimes opposed, perspective is by trusting that they have good reasons for adopting it. This is not to say that we ought not rigorously criticize perspectives that we find problematic; only that our critique will be more productive and to the point if we respect that there is always a degree of reasonability and intrinsic value behind any piece of knowledge, some ground for the claims made and perspectives taken – otherwise they would not be compelling to the one holding them. We believe that this approach is crucial to support in the face of a general academic climate that tends to foster a culture of attacking, sometimes rather mercilessly, one's scholarly adversaries in order to validate one's own position.

As noted above, and in line with Gunnarsson's argument in this volume, we believe that love as method is premised on the ability to harbor tension, being able to endure conflicts and the irritations that they might imply without letting this end in a lack of rapport. Without idealizing conflicts, we have sought to honor their productively transformative potential not only for solving problems but also for bringing about something new and good. The differences and sometimes conflicts among the contributions in this book operate on a range of different levels. Despite the fact that feminist theory and gender research is in its essence transdisciplinary, meaning its practitioners are likely to be less rigid about disciplinary boundaries than others, the different disciplinary backgrounds of the contributors to this volume do indeed influence the different vantage points. The authors come from philosophy, literature, history, law, political science, sociology, and gender and women's studies, and although much feminist and gender theory has been built on transgressing and synergizing knowledge from diverse disciplines, the different points of reference between, for instance, the social sciences and literature, do narrow the common ground needed for effective communication.

However, and this is a point that Jónasdóttir discusses more generally in her chapter, the fact that the authors are trained in and adhere to different philosophical paradigms marks a more pivotal dividing line than the disciplinary differences. For instance, Ferguson and Stoller are both philosophers, but work within very different paradigms of thought, Ferguson's Marxian meta-theoretical premises being more pivotal than her disciplinary background in philosophy, thus creating a robust platform for precise and in-depth communication with Jónasdóttir's work. Similarly, Stoller's exploration of Irigaray's work resonates in interesting ways with Gunnarsson's, but where Stoller has developed her Irigarayan thinking within a broader phenomenological framework with a poststructuralist twist, Gunnarsson connects Irigaray with a realist tradition of thought rooted in Marxist theory. An intriguing example of the clashing-confusing-synergizing effects of the coming together of scholars adhering to different paradigms was the way that, in various workshops, different authors expressed the feeling that their lines of thinking had very similar aspirations, despite being organized by very different vocabularies and theoretical underpinnings. At the same time, having highlighted the divergence among some of the perspectives drawn on in this book, it should still be clear that different approaches are synergized in the very same analysis in ways that produce new insights about love and power.

This crisscrossing of differences and similarities, oppositions and overlaps between theories is a reflection of the complexity of the very life process of which theories endeavor to make sense. With this book, and its diverse paths into the topics of love, power and their interconnection, we hope to contribute to the developing field of feminist love studies with both complexity and theoretical rigor.

Note

1   Audre Lorde's (1984) notion of 'the erotic as power' differs significantly from Jónasdóttir's concept of love power, but both frameworks are built around a theoretical affirmation of the creative power of love/the erotic (see Barriteau 2014 and Jónasdóttir this volume).

References

Atkinson, Ti-Grace (1974) *Amazon Odyssey*. New York: Links Books.
Barriteau, V. Eudine (2014) 'A (Re)Turn to Love: An Epistemic Conversation between Lorde's "Uses of the Erotic" and Jónasdóttir's "Love Power"', in A. G. Jónasdóttir and A. Ferguson (eds) *Love: A Question for Feminism in the Twenty-First Century*. New York and London: Routledge.
Bauman, Zygmunt (2003) *Liquid Love*. Cambridge: Polity.
de Beauvoir, Simone (1989 [1949]) *The Second Sex*. New York: Vintage.
Beck, Ulrich and Elisabeth Beck-Gernsheim (1995) *The Normal Chaos of Love*. Cambridge: Polity.
Brennan, Teresa (2004) *The Transmission of Affect*. Ithaca, NY: Cornell University Press.
Bryson, Valerie (2011) 'Sexuality: The Contradictions of Love and Work', in A. G. Jónasdóttir, V. Bryson and K. B. Jones (eds) *Sexuality, Gender and Power: Intersectional and Transnational Perspectives*. London and New York: Routledge.

Butler, Judith (1990) *Gender Trouble: Feminism and the Subversion of Identity.* London and New York: Routledge.

Cockburn, Cynthia and Lynette Hunter (1999) 'Introduction: Transversal Politics and Translating Practices', *Soundings* no. 12: 88–93.

Davis, Dawn Rae (2002) '(Love Is) the Ability of Not Knowing: Feminist Experience of the Impossible in Ethical Singularity', *Hypatia* 17(2): 145–161.

Dempsey, Ken (2002) 'Who Gets the Best Deal from Marriage: Women or Men?' *Journal of Sociology* 38(2): 91–110.

Douglas, Carol Anne (1990) *Love and Politics: Radical Feminist and Lesbian Theories.* San Francisco, CA: Ism Press.

The Feminists (1973) 'The Feminists: A Political Organization to Annihilate Sex Roles', in A. Koedt, E. Levine and A. Rapone (eds) *Radical Feminism.* New York: Quadrangle Books.

Ferguson, Ann (1989) *Blood at the Root: Motherhood, Sexuality and Male Dominance.* London: Pandora.

Ferguson, Ann (1991) *Sexual Democracy: Women, Oppression, and Revolution.* Boulder, CO: Westview Press.

Ferguson, Ann (2012) 'Romantic Couple Love, the Affective Economy, and a Socialist-Feminist Vision', in R. Schmitt and A. Anton (eds) *Taking Socialism Seriously.* New York: Lexington Books.

Ferguson, Ann and Anna G. Jónasdóttir (2014) 'Introduction', in A. G. Jónasdóttir and A. Ferguson (eds) *Love: A Question for Feminism in the Twenty-First Century.* London and New York: Routledge.

Ferry, Luc (2013) *On Love: A Philosophy for the Twenty-First Century.* Cambridge: Polity.

Firestone, Shulamith (1970) *The Dialectic of Sex: The Case for Feminist Revolution.* New York: Morrow.

Giddens, Anthony (1992) *The Transformation of Intimacy: Sexuality, Love, and Eroticism in Modern Societies.* Stanford, CA: Stanford University Press.

Gunnarsson, Lena (2011) 'Love: Exploitable Resource or "No-Lose Situation"? Reconciling Jónasdóttir's Feminist View with Bhaskar's Philosophy of Meta-Reality', *Journal of Critical Realism* 10(4): 419–441.

Gunnarsson, Lena (2014a) *The Contradictions of Love: Towards a Feminist-Realist Ontology of Sociosexuality.* London and New York: Routledge.

Gunnarsson, Lena (2014b) 'Loving Him for What He Is: The Microsociology of Power', in A. G. Jónasdóttir and A. Ferguson (eds) *Love: A Question for Feminism in the Twenty-First Century.* London and New York: Routledge.

Gunnarsson, Lena (2016) 'The Dominant and the Constitutive Other: Feminist Theorizations of Love, Power and Gendered Selves', *Journal of Critical Realism* 15(1): 1–20.

Hochschild, Arlie (2003) *The Commercialization of Intimate Life: Notes from Home and Work.* Berkeley: University of California Press.

hooks, bell (2000) *Feminism Is for Everybody: Passionate Politics.* Cambridge, MA: South End Press.

Illouz, Eva (2007) *Cold Intimacies: The Making of Emotional Capitalism.* Cambridge: Polity.

Illouz, Eva (2012) *Why Love Hurts: A Sociological Explanation.* Cambridge: Polity.

Jackson, Stevi (2006) 'Gender, Sexuality and Heterosexuality: The Complexity (and Limits) of Heteronormativity', *Feminist Theory* 7(1): 105–121.

Jackson, Stevi (2014) 'Love, Social Change, and Everyday Heterosexuality', in A. G. Jónasdóttir and A. Ferguson (eds) *Love: A Question for Feminism in the Twenty-First Century.* London and New York: Routledge.

Jaggar, Alison (1989) 'Love and Knowledge: Emotion in Feminist Epistemology', *Inquiry* 32(2): 151–176.

Jónasdóttir, Anna G. (1994 [1991]) *Why Women Are Oppressed*. Philadelphia, PA: Temple University Press.

Jónasdóttir, Anna G. (2009) 'Feminist Questions, Marx's Method and the Theorization of "love power"', in A. G. Jónasdóttir and K. B. Jones (eds) *The Political Interests of Gender Revisited*. Manchester: Manchester University Press.

Jónasdóttir, Anna G. (2011) 'What Kind of Power Is "Love Power"?' in A. G. Jónasdóttir, V. Bryson and K. B. Jones (eds) *Sexuality, Gender and Power: Intersectional and Transnational Perspectives*. London and New York: Routledge.

Jónasdóttir, Anna G. (2014) 'Love Studies: A (Re)New(ed) Field of Knowledge Interests', in A. G. Jónasdóttir and A. Ferguson (eds) *Love: A Question for Feminism in the Twenty-First Century*. London and New York: Routledge.

Kaufmann, Jean-Claude (2011) *The Curious History of Love*. Cambridge: Polity.

Keller, Evelyn Fox (1983) *A Feeling for the Organism: The Life and Work of Barbara McClintock*. New York: W. H. Freeman.

Langford, Wendy (1999) *Revolutions of the Heart: Gender, Power and the Delusions of Love*. London: Routledge.

Leon, Barbara (1978) 'The Male Supremacist Attack on Monogamy', in Redstockings (ed.) *Feminist Revolution*. New York: Random House.

Lorde, Audre (1984) *Sister Outsider: Essays and Speeches*. Trumansburg, NY: Crossing Press.

Luhmann, Niklas (1998) *Love as Passion. The Codification of Intimacy*. Stanford, CA: Stanford University Press.

Lykke, Nina (2011) 'Intersectional Analysis: Black Box or Useful Critical Feminist Thinking Technology?' in H. Lutz, V. M. T. Herrara and L. Supik (eds) *Framing Intersectionality: Debates on a Multi-Faceted Concept in Gender Studies*. Farnham: Ashgate.

May, Simon (2011) *Love: A History*. New Haven, CT: Yale University Press.

Medina-Doménech, Rosa, Mari Luz Esteban-Galarza and Ana Távora-Rivero (2014) 'Moved by Love: How Love Research Can Change Our Deep-Rooted Emotional Understandings and Affective Consciousness', in A. G. Jónasdóttir and A. Ferguson (eds) *Love: A Question for Feminism in the Twenty-First Century*. London and New York: Routledge.

Rich, Adrienne (1980) 'Compulsory Heterosexuality and Lesbian Existence', in *Signs. Journal of Women in Culture and Society*. 5(4): 631–660.

Sarachild, Kathie (1978) 'Going for What We Really Want', in Redstockings (ed.) *Feminist Revolution*. New York: Random House.

Sayer, Andrew (2011) *Why Things Matter to People: Social Science, Values and Ethical Life*. Cambridge: Cambridge University Press.

Thagaard, Tove (1997) 'Gender, Power, and Love: A Study of Interaction Between Spouses', *Acta Sociologica* 40(4): 357–376.

Toye, Margaret E. (2010) 'Towards a Poethics of Love', *Feminist Theory* 11(1): 39–55.

Toye, Margaret E. (in process) *Feminist Poethics of Love and Affect: Feminist Cartographical Methodologies*. Book manuscript.

Willis, Ellen (1980) 'The Family: Love It or Leave It', *New Political Science* 1(4): 49–63.

Yuval-Davis, Nira (1999) 'What Is "Transversal Politics"?' *Soundings* 12: 94–98.

Part I

Questioning love and power

- love as a way of generating knowledge
- navigating personal and academic tensions
- knowledge production among people who hold different epistemological views: "transversal dialogue"

[handwritten top margin: love as a continuum differently practiced across social relations]

2   The difference that love (power) makes[1]

Anna G. Jónasdóttir

[handwritten left margin: – power both as a basic, vital human capacity and as historically constituted power inequalities]

[handwritten right margin: historical materialist perspective: love as power and constraint. love's dual empowering / disempowering potential]

> Reviewing the literature on love I noticed how few writers, male or female, talk about the impact of patriarchy, the way in which male domination of women and children stands in the way of love.
>
> (bell hooks 2001: xxiv)

> [F]or the most part theory will not be a matter just of right answers. It will not be cumulative in any simple sense and it will not be possible for it to be 'completed'.
>
> (Craig Calhoun 1992: 262)

Recently a colleague asked me. 'What would be the difference if you had used "sexuality" rather than "love"; as the central concept in your theory?'[2] An immediate response would be something like this: Love makes all the difference! But, as a matter of fact, sexuality also has a crucial place in my theory. In this chapter I will give a more elaborate answer to this question and clarify how love and sexuality are both distinctive and related in my analysis. The primary focus is on sexual love, and I conceptualize the power of (sexual) love theoretically, both ontologically, as a creative human capacity, and as historically conditioned 'love power'.[3] Sexuality is approached sociologically, not psychologically. It is seen as a web of socio-sexual relationships, a distinctive basic dimension of how people – in using/practicing their capacities to love and be loved – produce and reproduce others, themselves, and their societies. As such, sexuality is interrelated with but not reducible to either the economic, political, or cultural dimensions of the social whole. This conception of love and love power, and sexuality, resulted from *how* I let historical materialism (Marx's method) serve radical feminist questions, emerging in the second Women's Movement in the 1960s and 1970s, aiming to analyze and explain the peculiar form of patriarchy still thriving in contemporary western societies (Jónasdóttir 1994 [1991], 2009, 2011).[4]

In the latter part of the chapter, I give my colleague's question another twist and ask whether my love theory can make any difference to other, more or less (dis)similar love research – or such others' to mine. By this move, however, I want primarily to raise a more general issue concerning the possibility to practice not only interdisciplinary research but also to converse across partly or wholly different traditions of thought or paradigms.[5] These questions are motivated by my active participation in the '(re)new(ed) field of knowledge interests' (Jónasdóttir 2014) in studying love and in promoting 'Love Studies as a feminist field of empirically oriented, theoretically elaborative, and politically relevant scholarship' (Ferguson and Jónasdóttir 2014: 2). My answer will be some very preliminary reflections on the premises for carrying on a mutually enriching conversation between different theories and research traditions in, and beyond, the field of feminist love studies.

The difference that 'love (power) makes' is, briefly, that it offers an elaborated understanding of relational love practices and love power as real bodily-social force, a (re)generative power *sui generis* in history; it offers a novel concept of sexual love, defined as a time-and-space conditioned dialectic of erotic power *and* care; it solves a fundamental problem in the feminist historical-materialist project, i.e. to specify and isolate analytically certain basic mechanisms of (contemporary) patriarchy, semi-independent of capitalism and class systems more generally. This solution rests on my reconstructive reading of Marx's method, which demonstrates: that there is an *open room* in his (and Engels') 'first premises of the materialist method', i.e. in the 'twofold' process of production of life; that this 'room' arguably is built for love as a history-making activity; and that the creative/productive power of this activity – the *care-erotic love power* – is now (in the societies in question here) 'free' to be given and taken, enjoyable *and* exploitable. This reconstruction of historical materialism also implies that my theory adds something new to the feminist question, where to look for *points of intersections between contemporary patriarchy and capitalism*, therefore also where/how social conditions and sources of ongoing changes in both systems should be looked for. Although underdeveloped here, this systemic intersectional perspective would, if developed further, contribute substantially to the ongoing discussions, initiated by (male) anarchist philosophers, about the role of love in how to transform or 'crack' capitalism. As one of the 'few writers' – cf. bell hooks, quoted in the epigraph above – who actually do 'talk about the impact of patriarchy' on love, and *vice versa* of love as a co-constitutive power in the reproduction of patriarchy, *therefore* a potential force in its dismantling, I assume that all visions of the revolutionary powers of love which do not consider the nature of its complex connection with patriarchy are fundamentally flawed.

The rationale of this chapter is twofold: to display the adequacy of historical materialism and critical realism to develop feminist analyses of love, in particular to ask and answer questions about the significance of earthly human love in and for the (re)making of contemporary societies and their political institutions; and, as the adequacy and strength of one research tradition is always relative, and many different perspectives are being employed in this growing field, I want to raise the question of the conditions of possibility for conversing meaningfully between different paradigms dealing with love.

Below, I start with a brief account of my theory and definition(s) of love. Next is a section on how I differentiate between the 'power of love' and 'love power', followed by some points to clarify how I use Marx's method. I then explicate how I theorize sexuality and, after that, why/how love, including the concept of 'love power', is the most essential element in my theory complex. Finally, I discuss the thorny issue of cross-paradigmatic conversations.

My set of theories

My theory of love and love power is an essential part of a broader one, or rather, of a set of theories developed in the 1980s, aiming first and foremost to explain the persistence of men's power over and as compared with women in contemporary western societies. More precisely, three distinct but related theories are sketched in my early works: (i) an alternative feminist historical-materialist social theory (i.e. a general conception of society and history); (ii) a historically (time-and-space) located theory of the formal-legally equal patriarchy in contemporary western societies; and (iii) a historically (time-and-space) located theory of (gendered) interests which establishes a theoretical room for both women's common concerns and their different needs and preferences. In this chapter, theory (iii) will not be considered.

Theory (i) is not a theory in any strong sense but consists of *meta-theoretical guidelines*. It is a meta-theory containing ontological assumptions about the constitutive elements (sociosexual relationships and love processes) that (from my analytically partial perspective) make and remake human societies and history, and methodological principles for how to construct what I call specific theories and concepts aimed to investigate social reality. Ontologically and methodologically my work is guided by realism, which for me includes historical materialism (alias Marx's method), critical realism, and historical institutionalism. The point is to ask historically located (radical) feminist questions and try out the just mentioned meta-theories, or guidelines, to help answer these questions (1994 [1991]: ch. 9; 2009: 60–63).

Theory (ii) is an explanatory theory grounded in, and intertwined with, theory (i). The problem is the persistent, yet changing, well-documented inequality between women and men in the societies in question here. However, I do not ask what or which 'factor' explains the most of women's oppression or subordination; nor do I ask psychological questions about women's submission or men's psychic motives or drives to dominate women. The peculiar fact that needs an explanation here is the persistent power of men (as a group) over and as compared with women (as a group), also in countries and contexts which are world-leading on most parameters of gender equality measurement. In other words: How is men's power position as *men* (i.e. across all other social divisions) reproduced in this kind of formal-legally equal and otherwise *relatively* gender equal society? Explanations considering gender-divided work, paid or unpaid; men's violence against women; or beliefs about women being inferior to men are clearly relevant and obvious but not sufficient. Where, from which non-obvious sources, does men's power as men come from? What kind of power is it? I explain contemporary formally equal patriarchy (a residual, yet crucial part of it) in terms of how love is socially and politically organized and love power exploited (1994 [1991]: chs 5 and 9; 2011). Exploitation of love power does not mean repression, violence, sexual abuse or rape; or '*Why love hurts*' (cf. Illouz 2012). On the contrary, I'm talking about what kind of human powers/energies/capacities are flowing in, transferred and exchanged – given and taken/received – in the sociosexual relations between people (meaning between women and men as well as among women and among men) under *relatively equal and (statistically) 'normal' conditions* (2011: 52–53). What is love, then?

In my theory love is central in at least four analytical contexts, three belonging to theory (i) and one specifically to theory (ii).

- Human love is a theoretically significant biosocial power and practice *sui generis*, necessary for human growth, potentially liberating, yet exploitable by some in others. Based on a developmental analysis of Marx's concept of 'activity' or 'human practice' I define love as both like and unlike labor as human capacities. Both are renewable sources of generativity/creativity, and both are insubstitutable by other social powers, such as rights or money (2009: 73–78; 2011: 54). A fundamental difference between labor and love (as typified human practices) is that the latter is not purposive in the sense of aiming at a predesigned result. Loving (an)other person(s) is not a form of work or labor, not even equal to doing care work or 'love labor' (1994: 73; Lynch 2014). It is the combination of what love is and is not that qualifies love for *companionship*, a unique parity, with human labor as '*practical*, human-sensuous activit[y]' (Marx 1970: 122).

- The above means that love is understood in a process mode, as *relational* practical activity or practices, and 'love power' as a biosocial human capacity, rooted in malleable needs, generated, transferred, and enjoyed/ used in and through the web of socio-sexual relationships. This means that a love relationship is a *three-party relationship* and not simply a dyad, not just a pair, nor a series, of sexual difference/s; a (powerful and empowering) third – love power – is being given and taken/received, thus (re)generating these relationships. This also means that it is the practice or doing aspect of love/loving, and the outcome/effect of loving on the involved parties and their social circumstances, rather than the feeling/ emotion/affect aspect *per se*, that is analytically selected out here. This relational approach includes a novel conception of sexual love; it contains an interplay between two main elements of human power/capacities, an element of erotic/ecstatic power and an element of sociosexual care; and this dialectic makes it both self- and other-oriented, and as such highly significant as a principled possibility for thinking social forms beyond the altruism–egoism dichotomy (1994: 210–11).

- The ontological assumptions (definitions) outlined above lay the ground for my approach to love in the (empirically oriented) theory proper, where I trace a residual explanation of the persistence of men's power as men to time-and-space-specific political conditions of love, and to ongoing, non-obvious exploitation of love power (1994 [1991]: chs 5 and 9; 2011). This is not limited to so-called couple love, but takes place in a society-wide setting. As Lena Gunnarsson puts it in her interpretation of my work: 'Jónasdóttir's view of love transcends narrow notions of romantic, "platonic" and parental love. It includes the broad continuum of practices and attitudes involved in the production of human life, ranging from an approving nod to intense erotic union' (Gunnarsson 2014: 50).
- A fourth analytical context, then, is my argument that love as '*practical, human-sensuous activit[y]*' can take place as an integrated part of the first premises of historical materialism, or the 'materialist method' as Marx and Engels called it (see more on this below in the section 'The difference that love makes').

Love and love power: historically specific concepts

Why do I talk about 'love power' and not just the power of love? The 'power of love', and other similar expressions, is a widely used phrase in poetic as well as prosaic contexts. Just to pick one example, Ethel Spector Person states (1989: 11) that 'love [...] is an extremely powerful force [...] a force capable of changing the lover in profound ways – both good and bad [...] love is a self-transforming and self-transcending experience'. While I think this is true (as probably most people do) the concept of 'love power' launched in my theory of patriarchy is not an odd way of playing with phrases such as 'the power of love'. It is a concept that is, to speak with Craig Calhoun, 'developed in close relationship to specific empirical historical accounts'. It is an abstraction which is 'not free-floating but historically specific and determinate' (Calhoun 1992: 245). Calhoun's discussion is about Marx's concept of labor as an example of a historically specific concept. In my case the 'specific empirical historical accounts' are problems – among them the unequal conditions of sexual love – which women mobilized around and politicized in a new way in the 1960s and 1970s. To be sure, 'love power' as a historically specific theoretical concept, presupposes that Spector Person's and other similar ontological assumptions, like mine, on the powerful nature of love, are valid in some general sense. But my concept formation is not only a philosophical idea about human nature. It also, and in particular, presupposes certain social and political conditions under which people live, work, and love: Both women and men (across practically all other social divisions), in the societies in question here, are formal-legally free to enter love relationships and practice sexual love activities on conditions that are relatively, and in some respects increasingly, equal. Still, the ongoing consequences (whether intended or unintended) of what takes place in sociosexual encounters are unequal gendered conditions of living that cannot be explained solely by either socioeconomic circumstances, patterns of cultural values and norms, or violence. Taking 'love power' to be not only distinguishable in thought but even releasable and transferable as a creative/productive social force, also presupposes a certain form of *structural similarity* (see below), between the historical conditions under which people became free to sell *and* buy human labor power and those under which we later became free to give *and* take/receive our love power. To paraphrase Marx's description of the historical conditions on which the emergence of capital proper rested and labor power became a commodity: *The epoch of formally equal patriarchy is characterized by this; that love power takes in the eyes of Woman herself the form of a gift, a capacity which is hers, and which she is free to give.*[6]

A few points should be underlined here concerning how I use Marx's method in *Capital*. First, when I talk about 'structural similarity' ('between the historical conditions under which people became free to sell *and* buy human labor power and those under which we later became free to give *and* take/receive our love power') it is with emphasis on similarity. I am not talking about the *same* structure, not the *same* social relationships, not the *same* institutionalized power arrangement. Therefore, second, I am not talking about commodification of love, neither literally as Marx does with labor power, nor symbolically as is common (and certainly relevant) in cultural theories of commodity fetishism, when linking a theory of love functionally with the capitalist economy. Exchange of love power, under the conditions in focus here, is *giving-and-receiving*. To be sure, in prostitution sexual 'services' are bought and sold; and whether or not love *can* be involved in such transactions is contested. That issue, I think, is a matter of empirically investigable experience in individual cases (1994: 103–108). Third, and most important perhaps, love power is not *either* exploitable for the benefit of others *or* enjoyable for pleasure, growth, and care of the self, or solidary actions with others. *It is both.* Like labor power, love power is a *renewable* source of bio-social human capacities. If it were not both, the longstanding struggle over access to and control of these sources of energy for human life and means of living would hardly exist. But under the formally fair conditions in focus here, neither love power nor labor power are *depleted*, as if these human sources were gold mines or cash boxes. This latter point brings me to Audre Lorde's 'The uses of the erotic: the erotic as power' and Eudine Barriteau's reading of her as in conversation with me.

Love power and the erotic as power

For Lorde the *erotic*, coming from the Greek word *eros*, means a creative life force, 'the personification of love in all its aspects'. It is a 'resource within each of us [that] offers a well of replenishing and provocative force' (Lorde 2007 [1984]: 53–55). Like my own reading of Lorde, Barriteau's (2014) careful analysis finds that 'Lorde and Jónasdóttir agree men exploit a resource in women, women's power [and that] women's energies [are] being absorbed to serve men in patriarchal societies;' but she thinks we diverge on what it is that men exploit in women. She doubts that Lorde would agree to my exploitation of love power thesis, because 'Lorde's power of the erotic cannot be appropriated, [or] extracted'. Instead, Barriteau underlines Lorde's view that women tend to avoid this power, be afraid of its existence, and that men are able 'to manipulate women's fear of a power within themselves', and I agree. She agrees with most of my analysis of unequal love relationships, with the sharing of women's love power not being equally reciprocated. Yet she concludes:

> Perhaps what is extracted in that unequal love exchange is not what Lorde defines as the power of the erotic, women's love power. Perhaps women still retain that. [...] Perhaps Love Power and the Erotic are two complementary but differing qualities or energies.
>
> (Barriteau 2014: 89–91)

In my reading, however, given that love power *and* the erotic (whether they are similar or different qualities) are renewable human sources of energy, both can be exploited *and* retained; and then the divergence on this point between the two concepts would largely disappear.

Political sexuality; a dimension of society and domain of study

In my theory 'sexuality' is an inclusive historical-sociological concept. Its first meta-theoretical premise is historical-materialist; in that sense sexuality refers to the process of production of life/people/sociosexual existence. This process is seen as a web of socio-sexual relations between – and among – women and men, and by implication as specific activities, love practices, uniquely generated in these relations. This web of relations or relational activities comprises what I call the 'sociosexual system', a 'fundamental part or current in the social existence of individual persons [and] of the weaving together of society as a processual whole' (1994: 101, 12). Sexuality, so understood, is a specific basic dimension of the making and remaking of people and their societies; thus, arguably, a *distinctive domain of study*. Throughout recorded history this subsystem/dimension of societies has been, and still is, structured in varying patriarchal forms. 'Political sexuality' means that this structure is institutionally entangled with the state and the whole complex of other political power arrangements.

In contrast to many feminist conceptualizations of sexuality, mine is neither psychoanalytically nor linguistically framed.[7] This does not mean that all psychoanalytic approaches would necessarily be incompatible with my theory, just that I am not employing psychological or psychoanalytical explanations myself.[8] Also, given that social life is not reduced to language differences, or other forms of symbol worlds, various approaches to analyses of language are certainly compatible with it.[9] It does mean, however, that 'desire', as conceptualized in psychoanalytic theory (Berlant 2012), has no primary *theoretical* status in my work; and 'difference' is not theoretically primary here either.[10] It does mean that the elementary unit of analysis is sociosexual relationships; and *social* relations, in my 'method' (cf. the 'first premises of the materialist method'), is always also about human *activities*, about *'practical, human-sensuous activities'* (Marx 1970: 122); activities in turn, so understood, are always generated/fueled by some human *powers/energies*. In process-oriented thought, like historical materialism, differences (and equalities) in people and their living conditions are outcomes of, thus analytically secondary to, social relationships.

Empirically, in concrete terms, sexuality refers to many, seemingly disparate areas. With Jeffrey Weeks, I would say that 'to understand sexuality we have to understand much more than sex: we have to understand the relationships in which most of it takes place' (Weeks 1986: 28). He includes areas such as 'marriage and the family, illegitimacy and birth control, prostitution and homosexuality, changing patterns of moral, legal and medical regulation, rape and sexual violence, sexual identities and sexual communities, and oppositional cultures'. When we think of sexuality, he continues, we think of a number of things such as 'reproduction [...] relationships [...] erotic activities and of fantasy, of intimacy and warmth, of love and pleasure, [as well as] of sin and danger, violence and disease' (Weeks 2000: 126, 163). As underlined elsewhere (Jónasdóttir et al. 2011) this broad understanding of sexuality connects with works of feminist and pro-feminist historians and historical sociologists about sexuality in history, past and present (Peiss and Simmons 1989). It also connects, in a complementary rather than simply a contrasting manner, with many feminist materialist theories of reproduction, including recent feminist research on social reproduction, underlining the realities of nurturing and the political importance of affective relations, love, care, and solidarity as fields of social action (e.g. Bryson 2011; Ferguson 2011; Lynch 2014).

Methodologically, then, I understand this inclusive notion of sexuality through a four-level framework which has much in common with Derek Layder's methodological principles and 'research map' (Layder 1993). The four, internally linked, levels are: the (micro) level of *self/subjectivity*, the two (meso) levels of *social relations/situated activities* and of (more or less organized) social *settings*, and the (macro) level of societal *contexts* (systems, or 'whole structures', cf. below). Each level has an inbuilt *history/time axis* and room for *power* analyses; and in my work 'power' can mean human powers/capacities (such as love), not only power as dominance or hierarchy. I find this research map useful to show how I explain certain social processes, and outcomes of these processes, in terms of *generating mechanisms*. These are seen as emerging and ongoing in certain relational activities (love practices), occurring in a meso-level setting, *which cuts across the family, working life and all other spheres of society.*

Bringing situated relational activities/practices and transfer of powers into focus as generating mechanisms, means that explanations in terms of either individual selves/subjects or system transformations are secondary in a sense, although both are considered. The societal context, and the self/subject, is the *outcome* of how relational activities are played out in variously formed and changing settings. 'The overall (macro-level) context, in turn, conditions the interactive settings of social life, whereas interactions, transactions and negotiations presuppose concrete individuals using their human capacities' (Jónasdóttir 2011: 47).

The difference that love makes

Why do I focus on sexual love and not just on sexuality? Given the aim of the 'distinctive theoretical project' I'm engaged in (see below) and the 'method' I apply, it has been necessary to identify a distinctive socio-sexual *practical activity* or practice, a practice whose theoretical significance, as a (re)productive, thus causal, power in social life and history, is in a certain essential parity with – but other than – that of work or labor. Sexuality in my perspective is seen as a complex concept equivalent in significance (in its own field) with the concept of economy in the field of classical Marxist theory. As described above, sexuality, and for classical Marxism, economy, refers to the whole set or system of relationships which structure the processes of practical activities mentioned above, namely sexual love and labor respectively.

In a wider context, thus, my work can be seen as a contribution to the ambitious 'distinctive theoretical project' (Jaggar 1983: 118) that marked a third way forward, out of the patriarchy versus capitalism debate between radical feminists and 'abstract socialists' in the early years of contemporary feminist research (Mitchell 1971). In this third way (historical-materialist, or socialist, feminism) a fruitful connection between feminism and Marxism was taken to presuppose the relative independence of each party *and* empirical and theoretical priority of feminist matters. Marxism should be tried out as a 'method of social analysis', thus 'put to the service of feminist questions' (Hartmann 1981: 11). A major issue, of course, was and is which these feminist questions are, as well as what Marxist method is and how it can and should be used for these particular aims.

Heidi Hartmann stated clearly what the distinctiveness of the 'theoretical project' meant. She argued that to explain patriarchy by using Marx's method presupposed that the 'woman question' of Marxism be reformulated to the 'feminist question' and 'directed at the causes of sexual inequality between women and men, of male dominance over women' (Hartmann 1981: 3, 5). Her aim was to specify the basic mechanisms of patriarchy, a task she found difficult because 'the same features, such as the division of labor, often reinforce both patriarchy and capitalism [and] it is hard to isolate the mechanisms of patriarchy. *Nevertheless, this is what we must do.*' Yet, she concludes, that 'most fundamentally' it is 'men's control over women's *labor power*' that is the material base of patriarchy (Hartmann 1981: 29, 15, emphasis added).

As several critics have argued, Hartmann did not succeed in differentiating between the two systems' material foundations and structural characteristics

(Jónasdóttir 1994: 50–51). Ferguson, for instance, was explicit about this difficulty. She concluded, however, that what she called 'sex/affective production', i.e. 'nurturance, social bonding and sex [...] since they must be *produced,* involve *work*' (1989: 94, emphasis added). My argument on this central point is that work (or labor) is not the only *productive* human activity compatible with historical materialism, that love, understood as '*practical* human-sensuous activit[y]' (Marx 1970: 122) is another and the kind needed for a successful basic differentiation between the two systems in question.

The way I ground the argument above – here posed as one main difference that love makes – was not spelled out extensively in my early work (see though the critique of Hartmann in Jónasdóttir 1994: 55). Later, especially in 'Feminist Questions, Marx's Method, and the Theorization of "Love Power"' (2009), my early analyses are more thoroughly and explicitly substantiated. By close reading and a certain reconstruction (renovation) of Marx and Engels's 'First premises of the materialist method', as outlined in *The German Ideology* (1970), and summarized in Engels' preface to *The Origin of the Family, Private Property and the State* (1972), I claim to have justified both my theorization of sexuality and the theoretical status I ascribe to love as a human power and creative activity, semi-autonomous in relation to labor in the making of history. In both these key texts on 'Marx's method' there is a flaw in a crucial aspect of how the 'twofold' process of production is characterized. While being clear that they are talking about two 'kinds of production' (of means of existence and of people/human life itself respectively) and that human *activity* constitutes production and makes history, only one of the two kinds of production is defined according to this fundamental assumption; the other is characterized *institutionally*. In Engels' words (emphasis added):

> The social organization under which the people of a particular historical epoch and a particular country live is determined by both kinds of production: by the stage of development of *labor* on the one hand, and of *family* on the other.
>
> (Engels 1972: 71–72)

Once identified the discrepancy should be obvious, but it has to my knowledge not been observed elsewhere, still less amended, at least not on these materialist premises' own terms.[11] In my 2009 chapter I demonstrate that by removing 'family' (an institutional arrangement, not a specifying activity) a *room opens up*, so to speak, to be filled with a suitable concept, and that love passes the test of being that concept.

To sum up again, the difference that my theorization of love makes is that it offers an elaborated understanding of love practices and love power as real bodily-social force and a causal power *sui generis* in history; it offers a novel concept of sexual love, defined as a time-and-space conditioned dialectic of erotic power *and* a specific form of care; it solves a fundamental problem in the feminist historical-materialist project, i.e. to specify and isolate analytically the basic mechanisms of (contemporary) patriarchy, semi-independent of capitalism and class systems more generally, while staying with *and* essentially renovating a fundamental of historical materialism; which means that it amends a flaw, a conceptual discrepancy, in how Marx and Engels characterized the two 'kinds of production' that they proposed in their meta-theoretical 'first premises'. If sexuality alone *without love* was central to my theory these contributions would not have come about.

The difference that love makes does not end here though. If love counts as a transformative human power in a certain parity with labor, it has important implications; both for a (much-needed) feminist rapprochement with earlier dual-system and multi-system theories, *and* for feminist assessments of the growing use of *love terms* in non-feminist analyses of contemporary capitalism.

Love and systemic 'interpenetration'

The challenge for the 'project' of feminist historical materialism was and is not only to differentiate between contemporary patriarchy and contemporary class society/capitalism, as if dealing with totally separate or closed systems (all system concepts are *not* implying closure!). Essential as it is, the differentiation and distinctiveness of each should be understood in a way which also implies ideas about theoretically significant *points of intersection* between the two systems, in Hartmann's words: 'their interpenetration' (Hartmann 1981: 12). Thus, the theoretical challenge here has at least two aspects: the question of different bases *and* the question of systemic intersections. While Hartmann did not succeed in dealing satisfactorily with the first question, she did develop an important answer to the second one. For her, patriarchy and capitalism overlap most importantly in the process of hierarchical distribution of women and men (and other concrete categories of people) into the primarily 'empty places' of the capitalist system's occupational structure. I think Hartmann is partly right, but hers is not a final answer to the question of how contemporary patriarchy and capitalism intersect. In my work the intersectional aspect is much less developed than the basic differentiation aspect. I have considered it though, but my focus is not on the distribution of concrete people in the class structure of capitalism. It is on the seemingly growing importance assigned to love *for capital*, for economic growth in the value production itself, on how struggles over access to love power, consequently, occur in both kinds of relations of production (the sociosexual production of life/people and the socioeconomic production of means of life) and how such struggles affect both systems reciprocally but open-endedly. In addition to Hartmann's explanation of the gender hierarchy within the class structure, I think we must attempt to understand how contemporary patriarchy and capitalism are *internally related* in and through the unique productive forces of each, love power and labor power. Then, we must investigate how people, in their various groupings and social circumstances, are involved in, i.e. active in and affected by, the making and the outcome of the twofold *and* confluent, love process and labor process (Jónasdóttir 2009: 69–79).

My reconstructive move into historical materialism implies that love is assigned a certain parity with (but not displacing) labor as a basic transformative activity in history; and I dare think that the growing academic interest in studying love indicates that my proposing love for a *relatively* central role in the 'given process of history' is valid (1994: 102, 244–245 note 14; 2009: 64–65). Precisely therefore I find the turn to love and affect in many non-feminist analyses of contemporary capitalism so interesting, *and* in need of various feminist readings. Recently, for instance, *affect* in the general sense of the 'power to act' is seen as having displaced labor and labor power because of a 'radical innovation in the historical process' (Negri 1999: 85). Moreover – in this philosophically radicalized way of thinking (global, postmodern) political economy as a process of struggle over affect-value 'in biopolitical society' – a political concept of *love* is claimed as '[w]hat is missing' (Hardt and Negri 2009: 179, 316). This approach to a political/economic notion of love, as well as the rest of Hardt and Negri's 'grand narrative of globalization' (Steger 2006: 380) has engaged many feminist theorists, both critically and by developing Hardt and Negri's theories in constructive analyses.[12] Hardt and Negri's work, including their use of 'love', is informed by Gilles Deleuze's total philosophy of the world (social *and* natural) as flows of affective energy, and of a micropolitics of desire. In Deleuze's philosophy capitalism is described as an 'axiomatic of flows', and, as Paul Patton puts it, the philosophical method followed 'is one that eschews argument in favor of the deployment of new vocabularies that enable new forms of description' (2012: 63). This philosophy, and the branch of affect theory derived from it, has become influential in many academic quarters, especially after the decline of poststructuralism's exclusive focus on language and the symbolic, and the turn towards 'new materialism'. It is grounded in Spinoza's materialist monism (Deleuze 1988 [1981]), which becomes the ontological first premise, as it were, of this version of affect theory. Among feminist scholars affect theory is both being embraced as very fruitful and also fundamentally criticized (cf. Toye and Jones this volume).[13]

Obviously now, love (in one sense or another) is taken seriously as a productive power in many intellectual quarters. For instance, by many leftist radicals, who couple love terms with the longstanding issue about the relativity of labor as the central activity in economic production and the revolutionary remaking of societies, love is thought to make a vital political difference. But the 'impact of patriarchy' (to quote hooks in the epigraph again) or other oppressive social divisions, on how love is, or should be, deployed for changes of global capitalism is ignored. To keep that question alive and open for attention presupposes active feminist research interests in such questions.

The question of cross-paradigmatic conversation

Love studies is a broad, theoretically heterogeneous, and expanding inter-disciplinary field (Jónasdóttir 2014; Jónasdóttir and Ferguson 2014). Inter-disciplinarity usually means that different aspects of the same problem are addressed in different disciplines, and often are complementary. In feminist love studies, therefore, we want to promote cross-disciplinary questions and conversations aimed at mutual learning and deeper knowledge. However, as practically all other fields of knowledge, interdisciplinary *and* disciplinary, feminist love studies is also *multi-paradigmatic*. Theoretical as well as empirical research is guided by various, often fundamentally different, meta-theories, and to communicate across different paradigmatic boundaries is another thing and much more difficult than *ditto* across disciplines but within the same research tradition or paradigm.[14] Why?

In *The Structure of Scientific Revolutions* the historian of science Thomas Kuhn (1962) famously launched the idea of 'incommensurability' between different paradigms (or successive theories); and he explains what he means by this key notion aimed to characterize the 'revolutionary' discontinuity he had charted in his historiography:

> Though most of the same signs are used before and after a revolution – e. g. force, mass, element [...] In the transition from one theory to the next words change their meanings or conditions of applicability in subtle ways [and successive] theories are thus, we say, incommensurable.
>
> (Kuhn 1974: 266–267)

Similarly, Michel Foucault in his *Archaeology of Knowledge* presents his approach to the 'history of the systems of thought', built around the 'use of concepts of discontinuity, rupture, threshold, limit, series, and transforma-tion', as dealing 'not only with questions of procedure, but with theoretical problems' (1972 [1969]: 21). He is concerned with those discursive formations and non-discursive practices and domains that 'constrain the material content of what is said and thought' (Gutting 2005: 36).

For Kuhn the discontinuity between incommensurable paradigms did not mean – as many of his critics thought – that a paradigm was necessarily completely *incomprehensible* at the theoretical level to all but those who worked within it. Neither does it mean that different paradigms are *incom-parable* even if their theories are largely *incompatible*. Kuhn also agrees with his critics that scholars who 'hold different theories do communicate and sometimes change each others' views'. More important, though, he writes, 'critics often slide from the observed existence of such communication, which I have underscored myself, to the conclusion that it can present no essential problems' (Kuhn 1974: 267). Also for Foucault, his archaeology is a 'com-parative analysis', but it is 'not intended to reduce the diversity of discourses'. It does not have a 'unifying, but a diversifying, effect', and discontinuity and diversity in the history of systems of thought also sometimes take the form of an 'almost entirely new descriptive vocabulary' (Foucault 1972 [1969]: 157, 159–160, 162, 170).

Foucault's concrete study objects were discourses of, for instance, economics and medicine from previous centuries, but also contemporary French philosophy and related theoretical approaches frequently emphasize discontinuity and ruptures with existing modes of thought. Thus, post-structuralism 'set out to make a "radical break" [with all 'essentialist paradigms']' and dissolve all unitary thinking into differences (Jónasdóttir and Jones 2009: 25). But the paraded example of an 'almost entirely new descriptive vocabulary', and the claim, to speak with Jameson (2010: 182), 'to have confronted omnivorously the immense field of everything that was thought and published' would be Gilles Deleuze's philosophy. So, what may lead to communicative troubles between Deleuzians and others is not only the odd Deleuzian vocabulary. Some other aspects of Deleuze's philosophy of affect seem more problematic, such as its grandiose generality. Most troublesome, though, for what is in question here (the possibility of mutually useful communication), is the style of writing, the deliberate use of irony and manipulative 'games and snares' instead of argument when confronting adversaries (Foucault 1977: xiv; Patton 2012). To learn something new from that kind of work seems to be an all-or-nothing business.

Would then, for instance, Toye's call (in this volume) for committed dialogue between feminist love studies and (Deleuze-inspired) feminist affect theory be doomed to failure? Is a historical-materialistically framed theory of love and love power like mine incommensurable with approaches to love grounded in other paradigms, such as affect theory, or sexual difference theory? Are these theories so fundamentally different in their discursive forms and content that only constraining what can be said and thought would come out of a conversation? It depends! (In)commensurability can mean either (in)comparability or (in)compatibility. Fundamentally different theories can often be compared but not be compatible or complementary. I believe we can learn from comparing incompatible theories and concepts, but we should not underestimate the difficulties. These are practical and also political in a sense. It is time-consuming to read and grasp many different traditions of thought. More serious, though, is that communication across paradigms has typically been more conflictual than peaceful, more about 'Wars of Positions' (Brennan 2006) than a shared will to learn. It is no overstatement to say that the history of knowledge production is a history of often fierce struggles, and the history of feminist scholarship is no exception. However, most paradigms consist of several, internally different, branches, and a branch-wise overlapping between different paradigms is quite common. Thus, as Ferguson (1989) and Toye (this volume) show, all feminist theorists who are informed somehow by Deleuze need not and do not 'take all of him', or copy his rhetorical style. What does all this suggest to the more general question about the possibility for serious cross-paradigmatic conversations, for instance about love?

One answer might be that 'transversal dialogues' should guide this kind of difficult conversation (see Chapter 1 of this volume). Another possible answer could be to practice 'love as method', but what that means is far from clear. It can easily be taken as just another example of the current overuse of love talk in commercial as well as everyday language, or as a mistaken extension of the growing academic interest in studying love as a subject of research. Moreover, love as method can be seen as a contradiction in terms; it is not self-evident that love can or should be seen as a means to some end beyond its lived practice.[15] However, many different modes of thinking exist which see love as a method, *or* a way leading somehow to reliable knowledge (Ferguson and Jónasdóttir 2014: 3–5; Chapter 1 and Toye this volume). Obviously, the question what love as method means, or could mean, in feminist and other research communities, would need a chapter of its own. However, apart from the answer that such a 'chapter' would bring, there are of course well-tried forms of debate and dialogue between different paradigms, and also testimonies of constructive outcomes. Nancy Fraser, for instance, states: 'I often don't know what I really think about something until I've encountered others who (it turns out) think differently' (Fraser and Naples 2004: 1119). I assume many people have experienced similar developmental insights from transversal reflections, in face-to-face conversations or when reading other people's texts.

To exemplify my own experience let me share with you some very preliminary outcomes of my reading of two feminist theorists, Teresa Brennan's theory of affect and Luce Irigaray's philosophy of sexual difference. In both, love is also crucial. Both work in the psychoanalytical tradition, which Brennan combines with sociological and social-psychological readings whereas Irigaray is firmly anchored in sameness–difference thought and phenomenology. I see clearly both similarities and divergences between their theories and mine, but reading these two generates different kinds of insight. In Irigaray I see mainly a parallel running argument, comparable but less compatible than Brennan's with my mode of thought. Reading Brennan (on the transmission of affect and the historically shifting attention to affects/emotions and cognitions in philosophy and science) stimulates me, for instance, to revisit two underdeveloped arguments in my early work, for further elaboration and an attempt to make them more useful for empirical research on love relationships. One is the assumption, which my exploitation thesis presupposes is valid (although it took me a long time to dare come out with it in the 1980s), that human powers/energies actually are being transferred/transmitted between people (a 'net transfer of powers') (1994: 80–81, 252 note 1).[16] The other is my argument that the concept of *attitude*, in its classic social-psychological definition, should not be disregarded, as it usually has been, by historical materialists. Brennan echoes both ideas, and makes much of them, especially in her last book *The Transmission of Affect* (2004). The classic concept of attitude is three-dimensional, containing distinctive and dynamically intra-related components, emotions, cognitive reasoning, and inclination to act. It links the experiential, sociocultural, and the bodily-material without reducing people to stimulus-response machines:

> With a materialist concept of attitudes referring to the social as well as the physical being, a mental and neural state of readiness in embodied human beings, organized through social experience, possibilities are opened for operating with more all-round conceptual tools with regard to relations in which we are continuously involved but which we are unaccustomed to 'seeing' scientifically.
>
> (Jónasdóttir 1994: 56–57; see also 251 note 15)

Although Brennan does not elaborate 'attitude' explicitly as a theoretical concept, I read her discussion in *Transmission* (chs 1 and 3) on the conceptual history of its components as being in tune with my view of the classic concept as fruitful and highly relevant today. Furthermore, other feminist affect theorists have recently taken up the long overlooked socio-psychological analyses of tensions and 'dissonances' in the self/subject attitudinal complex between its emotive, cognitive and agency/practice components, although usually, unlike Brennan, without references to the socio-psychological forerunners.

Irigaray's philosophy is constructed around 'sexual difference', a notion she also claims is the 'most universal question we can address', and the central idea of our historical epoch (Irigaray 1996: 47). With time, she has turned her attention increasingly to love, and more loving encounters between women and men, which also means a full recognition of their difference, is her proposal for a 'possible felicity in history'. For her love project she went 'back to Hegel, and his conception of love as labor' after having found 'Marx's *oeuvre*' inadequate 'as regards alienation in sexual difference' (Irigaray 1996: 13). Her theory, however, has no concept of a specific creative power which corresponds to 'love power' in mine, and seemingly there is no theoretical room in it for that kind of enminded bodily power. What she does have is a vision of a new language and a critical use of Hegel's master-slave model of recognition. In her philosophical tradition difference as such is seen as *productive* (cf. 'fecundity of sexual difference [and of] words' [1996: 8–9])). In historical materialism mere difference does not produce anything, only social relations entail productivity. Irigaray often uses the word 'fecundity' when talking about love and sexual relations, but without specifying it theoretically. When I read sentences like 'We know nothing of that dimension Hegel called the labor of love', or 'We still know nothing of the fecundity between a woman and a man, women and men' (i.e. other than the 'natural act' of having children) (1996: 29, 143), I cannot but think that she is looking for something like my concept of sociosexual love power, but has not found it. Immodestly, I think that Hegel's *oeuvre* may be adequate to solve the problem of 'the negative' and 'alienation in sexual difference', as Irigaray puts it. But I doubt that it can, not even as complemented by her 'discussion [...] with Heidegger' (2002: x), help her discover very much that is theoretically viable about the 'positive access' power (1996: 13) engendered in love relationships, i.e. the 'fecundity' she thinks we 'know nothing' about, but on which her philosophical vision of how loving encounters between differences will make 'felicity in history' possible depends.

Therefore, I'm tempted to end my reflections, open-endedly and somewhat unconventionally, by redirecting the first main question of this chapter and put it, reversed, to Irigaray: *What difference would it make if you put love rather than sexual difference at the center of your theory?* And how would you do that given the traditions of thought you are employing?

Notes

1 A first version of this chapter was presented at the conference 'Love, Sensible Experience and Feminism', September 17–18, 2015, at Universidad Autónoma Metropolitana, Mexico City. A second version was a key note at 'Product, Production, Productivity: A Women's Studies Symposium', December 10–11, 2015, at Nanyang Technological University, Singapore.

2 Ann Ferguson put this question to me in one of our many conversations when we were working on our co-edited book, *Love* (2014). Her theory of sexuality and love is similar to mine in many ways and different in others, and I will comment on this briefly in connection with my answering her question, which stimulated me to write this chapter. For her account of meeting me/my work, see Ferguson and Toye (2017: 7).

3 For the sake of style, and unless otherwise stated, I use 'love' and 'sexual love' interchangeably throughout this chapter; and 'love power' refers to the latter. The focus on sexual love, as distinguished from other modalities, even parental and other forms of kinship love, is empirically and theoretically justified. It depends on my delimitation of the central research question and mode of answering it. This does not mean, though, that I ascribe any general theoretical privilege to sexual love, or that the kind of care-erotic power that I assign specifically to sexual love (2011: 53–57) is the one and only important power of love. However, I think that the significance of sexual love for social and political theory would need much more feminist analyses.

4 My 1994 book is a slightly revised version of the 1991 volume, which was my dissertation in political science. For page references I refer to the former.

5 Throughout I use 'research tradition', 'paradigm' and 'meta-theory' interchangeably (cf. Jónasdóttir 1994: 215, 263–264 note 1).

6 Marx (1967: 170) describes analytically the historical conditions under which capital and labor power emerged.

7 My approach to sexuality also differs fundamentally from Catharine MacKinnon's 'dominance approach' (Jónasdóttir 1994: 97–98, 242 notes 5–6). See also Gunnarsson (2013: part I).

8 Here Ferguson's theory and mine diverge. For her a psychological theory of human agency and the self, that 'includes a psychology of human domination', is needed to explain contemporary male domination. It must be able, she states, to explain the 'irrationality of the oppressed groups' submission to social domination'. For this aim she aligns with feminist and other radical re-readings (Deleuze) of Freudian thought on sexual desire and the formation of subjects/selves. We both think that sexuality is a field of bodily social and political power relations, that can be theorized as semi-autonomous systems of production; that it is 'in part through these systems that different forms of male dominance [are] reproduced'; and that

an 'adequate feminist theory of male domination must be [...] historically specifiable'. But my deliberately delimited research questions do not ask for psychological explanation (rational *or* irrational) of why individual people act as they do in sociosexual relational encounters, or about the 'internal effects of domination and oppression on the selves of both dominators and oppressed' (Ferguson 1989: 31, 32, 77–78; Jónasdóttir 1994: 20–23). This divergence does not make our respective theories incompatible, but rather complementary, I think. So would also, for instance, aspects of Gunnarsson's microsociological (2014) and psychoanalytically informed (this volume) analyses of sexual love relations be compatible with mine.

9   Interestingly, Michael Gratzke (2017: 8) attempts to 'build a bridge between a deconstructionist and a materialist-feminist approach' to studying love, and a leading light for that building work is a definition of love given by Ferguson and myself (2014). Whether I find his 'bridge' tenable enough to walk on must wait for a more careful reading of his article.

10 Herein lies a main divergence between my historical-materialist relational theory of love and (re)production and Luce Irigaray's Hegel-informed sexual difference philosophy of love and recognition (Irigaray 1996: 11–16). On the relevance and limits of different 'differences', see Jónasdóttir (1994 [1991]: ch. 8).

11 A 'mode of desire', seen as articulating with but analytically distinct from the 'modes of production', has been used to analyze and explain patriarchy (cf. Witz 2000: 4), thus linking historical materialism with one or another version of the psychoanalytic discourse. This may be more or less fruitful but differs fundamentally from my intervention into historical materialism.

12 See Hawkesworth (2006), Wilkinson (2017), and many chapters in Jónasdóttir and Ferguson (2014), as well as numerous references in these works.

13 Also, in a recent Deleuze-inspired argument/appeal directed to 'us' to unite and 'crack capitalism' Holloway (2010) combines economistic capital-logic theses with anarchistic political ideas of 'autonomist Marxism'. He uses 'love' loosely, I would say, to strengthen his argument about the mono-causal power of capitalism, under which he subsumes all other social divisions and power structures (gender as well as race/ethnic relations). The reductionism in his work has been effectively criticized by Cynthia Cockburn (2012) among others.

14 This does not mean that interdisciplinary collaboration is just easy. The whole field of contemporary feminist research once grew out of interdisciplinary collaboration and challenging both disciplinary principles and strict boundaries between academic and extra-mural knowledge interests, and this was and is not always easy; neither so for non-feminist scholars. As Norbert Elias noted, 'despite the ease with which the word 'interdisciplinarity' rolls off our tongues, in practice the establishment of closer cooperation, or simply of better communication, between different professional groups of scientific specialists encounters some basic difficulties which are easily overlooked' (2003: 117–118).

15 For instance, the criterion by which I distinguish love as non-result-oriented practice from labor as a purposive action makes me hesitate to think about love in terms of method.

16 Brennan's analysis and mine do not focus on the same social relationships. For me it is the assumption about the occurrence as such of transfer/transmission that is interesting.

References

Barriteau, Eudine (2014) 'A (Re)Turn to Love: An Epistemic Conversation between Lorde's "Uses of the Erotic" and Jónasdóttir's "Love Power"', in A. G. Jónasdóttir and A. Ferguson (eds) *Love: A Question for Feminism in the Twenty-First Century.* New York and London: Routledge.

Berlant, Lauren (2012) *Desire/Love.* New York: Punctum Books.

Brennan, Teresa (2004) *The Transmission of Affect.* Ithaca, NY and London: Cornell University Press.

Brennan, Timothy (2006) *Wars of Position. The Cultural Politics of Left and Right.* New York: Columbia University Press.

Bryson, Valerie (2011) 'Sexuality: The Contradictions of Love and Work', in A. G. Jónasdóttir, V. Bryson and K. B. Jones (eds) *Sexuality, Gender and Power: Intersectional and Transnational Perspectives.* London and New York: Routledge.

Calhoun, Craig (1992) 'Culture, History, and the Problem of Specificity in Social Theory', in S. Seidman and D. G. Wagner (eds) *Postmodernism and Social Theory.* Cambridge, MA and Oxford: Blackwell.

Cockburn, Cynthia (2012) 'Who Are "We"?, Asks One of Us', *Journal of Classical Sociology* 12(2): 205–219.

Deleuze, Gilles (1988 [1981]) *Spinoza. Practical Philosophy.* San Francisco, CA: City Lights Books.

Elias, Norbert (2003) 'Sociology and Psychiatry', in S. Foulkes and P. G. Stewart (eds) *Psychiatry in a Changing Society.* London: Routledge.

Engels, Friedrich (1972) *The Origin of the Family, Private Property and the State.* London: Lawrence & Wishart.

Ferguson, Ann (1989) *Blood at the Root: Motherhood, Sexuality and Male Dominance.* London: Pandora/Unwin Hyman.

Ferguson, Ann (2011) 'How Is Global Gender Solidarity Possible?' in A. G. Jónasdóttir, V. Bryson and K. B. Jones (eds) *Sexuality, Gender and Power. Intersectional and Transnational Perspectives.* London and New York: Routledge.

Ferguson, Ann and Anna G. Jónasdóttir (2014) 'Introduction', in A. G. Jónasdóttir and A. Ferguson (eds) *Love: A Question for Feminism in the Twenty-First Century.* New York and London: Routledge.

Ferguson, Ann and Margaret E. Toye (2017) 'Feminist Love Studies: Editors' Introduction', *Hypatia* 32(1): 5–18.

Foucault, Michel (1972 [1969]) *The Archaeology of Knowledge.* New York: Vintage.

Foucault, Michel (1977) 'Preface', in G. Deleuze and F. Guattari, *Anti-Oedipus: Capitalism and Schizophrenia.* London: Penguin Books.

Fraser, Nancy and Nancy A. Naples (2004) 'To Interpret the World or to Change It: An Interview with Nancy Fraser', *Signs* 29(4): 1103–1124.

Gratzke, Michael (2017) 'Love Is What People Say It Is: Performativity and Narrativity in Critical Love Studies', *Journal of Popular Romance Studies.* www.jprstudies.org (accessed 20 June 2017).

Gunnarsson, Lena (2013) *On the Ontology of Love, Sexuality and Power. Towards a Feminist-Realist Depth Approach.* Örebro Studies in Gender Research 2. Örebro, Sweden: Örebro University.

Gunnarsson, Lena (2014) *The Contradictions of Love. Towards a Feminist-Realist Ontology of Sociosexuality.* London and New York: Routledge.

Gutting, Gary (2005) *Foucault. A Very Short Introduction.* Oxford: Oxford University Press.

Hardt, Michael and Antonio Negri (2009) *Commonwealth.* Cambridge, MA: The Belknap Press of Harvard University Press.

Hartmann, Heidi (1981) 'The Unhappy Marriage of Marxism and Feminism: Towards a More Progressive Union', in L. Sargent (ed.) *Women and Revolution: The Unhappy Marriage of Marxism and Feminism. A Debate on Class and Patriarchy.* London: Pluto Press.

Hawkesworth, Mary (2006) 'The Gendered Ontology of Multitude', *Political Theory* 34(3): 357–364.

Holloway, John (2010) *Crack Capitalism.* London and New York: Pluto Press.

hooks, bell (2001) *All about Love. New Visions.* New York: Perennial.

Illouz, Eva (2012) *Why Love Hurts.* Cambridge: Polity Press.

Irigaray, Luce (1996) *I Love To You. Sketch of a Possible Felicity in History.* New York and London: Routledge.

Irigaray, Luce (2002) *The Way of Love.* London and New York: Continuum.

Jaggar, Alison (1983) *Feminist Politics and Human Nature.* Totowa, NJ: Rowman & Allanheld.

Jameson, Fredric (2010) *Valences of the Dialectic.* London: Verso.

Jónasdóttir, Anna G. (1991) *Love Power and Political Interests. Towards a Theory of Patriarchy in Contemporary Western Societies.* Örebro Studies in Gender Research 7. Örebro, Sweden: Örebro University.

Jónasdóttir, Anna G. (1994) *Why Women Are Oppressed.* Philadelphia, PA: Temple University Press.

Jónasdóttir, Anna G. (2009) 'Feminist Questions, Marx's Method, and the Theorization of "Love Power"', in A. G. Jónasdóttir and K. B. Jones (eds) *The Political Interests of Gender Revisited.* Manchester: Manchester University Press.

Jónasdóttir, Anna G. (2011) 'What Kind of Power Is "Love Power"?' in A. G. Jónasdóttir, V. Bryson and K. B. Jones (eds) *Sexuality, Gender and Power: Intersectional and Transnational Perspectives.* London and New York: Routledge.

Jónasdóttir, Anna G. (2014) 'Love Studies: A (Re) New(ed) Field of Knowledge Interests', in A. G. Jónasdóttir and A. Ferguson (eds) *Love: A Question for Feminism in the Twenty-First Century.* New York and London: Routledge.

Jónasdóttir, Anna G. and Ferguson, Ann (eds) (2014) *Love: A Question for Feminism in the Twenty-First Century.* New York and London: Routledge.

Jónasdóttir, Anna G. and Kathleen B. Jones (2009) 'Out of Epistemology: Feminist Theory in the 1980s and Beyond', in A. G. Jónasdóttir and K. B. Jones (eds) *The Political Interests of Gender Revisited.* Manchester: Manchester University Press.

Jónasdóttir, Anna G., Valerie Bryson and Kathleen B. Jones (2011) 'Introduction', in A. G. Jónasdóttir, V. Bryson and K. B. Jones (eds) *Sexuality, Gender and Power: Intersectional and Transnational Perspectives.* London and New York: Routledge.

Kuhn, Thomas (1962) *The Structure of Scientific Revolutions.* Chicago, IL and London: University of Chicago Press.

Kuhn, Thomas (1974) 'Reflections on My Critics', in I. Lakatos and A. Musgrave (eds) *Criticism and the Growth of Knowledge.* London and New York: Cambridge University Press.

Layder, Derek (1993) *New Strategies in Social Research.* Cambridge: Polity Press.

Lorde, Audre (2007 [1984]) *Sister Outsider.* Berkeley, CA: Crossing Press.

Lynch, Kathleen (2014) 'Why Love, Care, and Solidarity Are Political Matters: Affective Equality and Fraser's Model of Social Justice', in A. G. Jónasdóttir and A. Ferguson (eds) *Love: A Question for Feminism in the Twenty-First Century.* New York and London: Routledge.

Marx, Karl (1967) *Capital I. A Critique of Political Economy*. New York: International Publishers.

Marx, Karl (1970) 'Theses on Feuerbach', in K. Marx and F. Engels, *The German Ideology: Part One. With Selections from Parts Two and Three and Supplementary Texts*. Edited with an introduction by C. J. Arthur. New York: International Publishers.

Mitchell, Juliet (1971) *Women's Estate*. Harmondsworth: Penguin.

Negri, Antonio (1999) 'Value and Affect', *Boundary 2* 26(2): 77–88.

Patton, Paul (2012) *Deleuzian Concepts*. Stanford, CA: Stanford University Press.

Peiss, Kathy and Christina Simmons, with Robert A. Padgug (eds) (1989) *Passion and Power. Sexuality in History*. Philadelphia, PA: Temple University Press.

Spector Person, Ethel (1989) *Love and Fateful Encounters. The Power of Romantic Passion*. London: Bloomsbury.

Steger, Manfred B. (2006) 'Review Essay: Imperial Globalism, Democracy, and the "Political Turn"', *Political Theory* 34(3): 372–382.

Weeks, Jeffrey (1986) *Sexuality*. Chichester: Ellis Horwood; and London and New York: Tavistock.

Weeks, Jeffrey (2000) *Making Sexual History*. Cambridge: Polity Press.

Wilkinson, Eleanor (2017) 'On Love as an (Im)Properly Political Concept', *Environment and Planning D: Society and Space* 35(1): 57–71.

Witz, Anne (2000) 'Whose Body Matters? Feminist Sociology and the Corporeal Turn in Sociology and Feminism', *Body and Society* 6(2): 1–24.

3 Alienation in love

Is mutual love the solution?

Ann Ferguson

Western feminism currently finds itself in a debate as to how gender, love and sexuality are connected with male dominance and heteronormativity in contemporary western culture. In this chapter I develop a theory of the affective economy in order to understand the relation between ideology and practices of contemporary heterosexual love and male domination in the US (cf. Ferguson 1989, 1991). I historically situate couple love, often identified as romantic love, as an ideal and a relation characterized by social practices. The romantic love ideal is part of the social imaginary (Castoriadis 1987) of most advanced capitalist countries. Often confused with this ideal of *romantic love* (cf. Solomon 1988) is that of *mutual love* (hooks 2000a). Although these love ideals are at odds in important ways with each other, under present conditions in US society, most of those acting according to both ideals find themselves involved in forms of alienated love that perpetuate male dominance and heteronormativity. Other non-democratic institutions, such as militarism, misogyny, white supremacy, and capitalism are added factors that support alienation in love.

The ideal of mutual love has been developing recently around the world, but especially in advanced capitalist countries, due to the emphasis on individual freedom, equality, and mutuality characteristic of capitalist ideology. Using ideas from feminist theorists de Beauvoir, Jónasdóttir, Gunnarsson, Digby, Illouz, and hooks, I will describe the present conflict in love ideals in advanced capitalist societies, and argue that this has created a historically specific problem of alienation in love, not only for heterosexual couples, but also for many LGBTQ love partners. While I still agree with my earlier work (which coincides with the analysis of Anna Jónasdóttir [1994, 2011]) that a key mechanism for perpetuating male domination in the US and similar countries is men's exploitation of women's love, this chapter makes a somewhat different point: that both men and women in such countries are *alienated* in heterosexual couple love. The existence of alienation in love, particularly under contemporary conditions where achieving personal love is so central to many people's life goals, provides one explanation for the rise of male feminists and LGBTQ activists who want to challenge the existing structures of masculinity and heteronormativity to eliminate such alienation.

However, achieving unalienated mutual love, whether in couples or in poly-amorous relationships, will require a sustained challenge to other forms of social domination besides male domination.

The history of love

Various sociologists of the twentieth and twenty-first century have argued that the ongoing depersonalization of capitalist bureaucratic orders has created a search for meaning that has led to an increasing emphasis on the value of personal love, whether as couple or parental love. This search for love and affection shows up in many indicators, such as increasing rates of divorce, romantic comedies both as movies and as TV serials, love advice columns, dating websites, and various online support groups for people in various categories – singles, couples, divorced, widows, LGBTQ etc. (cf. Illouz 1997, 2012).

While in the nineteenth and early twentieth century the old mantra seemed true (at least for middle- and upper-class women) – women for love and men for work and sexuality – it is not so clear that there is such a strong gender difference today as in these earlier periods on the centrality of love for a happy life. Does the increasing gender overlap in finding meaning both in love and in sexual practices indicate that gender equality is occurring in issues of love and sexuality in popular culture?

Niklas Luhmann gives a theory which could support the view that changes in love as an institution of intimacy have made it increasingly important for both men and women in our contemporary western societies. In his books on love (1986, 2010) he argues that the transition from traditional societies to modern society involves the transition from traditional stratifications of class, caste and ethnicity to more individualist modern systems of economy, politics, science, intimacy, law, and art. In advanced capitalist societies family and personal love relations are involved in a relatively autonomous system of meaning that involves a culture of intimacy with its own symbolic codes and system of communication of love as passion. The practice of love based on this concept of love creates a shared world of meanings for those involved: 'Being in love means to internalize another person's subjectively systematized view of the world' (Luhmann 1986: 26).

In my view Luhmann has something right and something wrong. He is right to see that there is a distinctive historical institution of romantic love that connects to modernity and capitalist individualism. But Luhmann's functionalist thinking about communication lacks a critical theoretical approach which focuses on how the conflictual tendencies within both the cultural production of gender and modern romantic love are exacerbated by contradictions in other institutions that support male dominance, such as the military, the economy, the heterosexual family, and marriage.[1]

As opposed to platonic and courtly love ideals thought only possible for the elite, the philosopher Irving Singer (1984, 1987) argues that love is a relation that meets a human material need for love that even ordinary men and women can achieve. He argues that Christianity introduced a democratic spirit into the notion of love in the institution of marriage, but held that love could only be ideal if it transcended mere passion and achieved something of the transcendental by a marriage sanctified by God and the Church. When romantic love developed as a more democratic idea in the eighteenth and nineteenth century with the developing bourgeois class, it was initially seen as a dangerous passion that interfered with the calm sentiments necessary for a stable marriage (cf. Wollstonecraft 1988 [1792]). But eventually, although still mired in strong gendered virtues, romantic love became the ideal that allowed ordinary people to adopt the goal of self-realization in couple love. Couple love is thought to allow each to engage in personal growth, become morally better, and to meet both their sexual and emotional needs for affection and care. Thus, in general, romantic love replaces the ideal of a transcendent love attained through a religious connection to God.

But Singer's history of the philosophy of love only presents the *ideologies* that justify understandings and practices of love and sexuality for ruling classes in different economic modes of production, e.g. slavery, feudalism and capitalism. What he leaves at the level of ideology I tie to material love and affective caring *practices* that accompany these modes of production. Such practices are part of the 'affective economy', as I will explain below.

I disagree with Singer (1984, 1987) and Anthony Giddens (1992), who assume that women have today achieved gender equality with men, and hence that a democratic romantic or confluent love is an unproblematic ideal. There is an ideology/reality gap between our ideals of love and our practices of love in advanced capitalist societies that is based on the continuing political, social and economic inequality of men and women – that is, the continuation of male domination.

Our contemporary love ideology does not distinguish between the ideal of *romantic love* and *mutual* or *reciprocal love*. [2] Romantic love is still mired in its patriarchal past. It still contains aspects of the gendered virtues reflective of a patriarchal militarist society as it has been modified by the possessive individualism characteristic of capitalist society. In contemporary US and western advanced capitalist societies the practices of romantic love promote exploitative, alienated love relations, whether it is between men and women or LGBTQ couples, or even in polyamorous relations. Mutual love, on the other hand, is an ideal and practice that abolishes gender roles in love, and expects love partners to develop the skills to work reciprocally on all the tasks that preserving and developing love requires. As bell hooks (2000a) argues, what she calls 'mutual love' involves caring, honest, and reflective communication, caretaker work for the other(s), sharing domestic and paid work, and democratic decision-making within the couple or between the partners. Our present social order contains both the ideals and practices of romantic and mutual love, but as I hope to show, most of us are thwarted in the full achievement of mutual love because of structural constraints that leave both men and women alienated in love.

A materialist-feminist ontology

In 1989 I argued in *Blood at the Root* for what I called a 'social energy' theory of sexuality. Contrasting my position with that of Freud, who posits sexuality or libido as an instinctual drive for reproduction, I argued that sexuality is both a bodily and a social energy to unite with others. Unlike Freud, who saw the essence of libido as being a drive for orgiastic pleasure that when not aim-inhibited, also normally leads to heterosexual reproduction, I still would argue, in a vein similar to Deleuze and Guattari (1977) that bodily desires to unite with others always involve an ongoing bodily energy, a physical pleasure in connection with others that does not have to be taught, since it is part of the ontology of humans as living social animals. But whether this bodily desire is channeled into what we define as explicitly sexual forms, to pursue reproduction in heterosexual intercourse, or to be a form of affection, as in Platonic love or friendships, or into parental love, or group solidarity, is due to the historical form that exists in a particular society of what I called 'sex/affective production', and what Deleuze and Guattari call 'desiring production'.

While in the 1980s I theorized a social 'sex/affective energy', today I think it is more helpful to name the two strands of this energy separately, as a 'love energy' and as a 'sexual energy'. In this way we can be more alert to the historical ways that these different energies have been socially combined or opposed to each other. *Love energy* includes the energy which connects people as work mates, as kin, as friends, as parent and child, in compassion, and as those united to promote a cause (solidarity love), as well as religious love felt by people for their god. *Sexual energy* connects people who desire sexual satisfaction for pleasure, which may (but need not) involve reproductive aims. Sexual love between couples or a group of individuals combines love energy with sexual energy. In the case of a reproductive unit (whether a couple or a polyamorous relationship) there are several love energies involved: those that connect adult couples (or more), and those that connect them and the children in a family/kin relationship.

Love and sexual energies are harnessed together in our contemporary 'affective economy' not only to reproduce children, but to meet ongoing human needs for affection/love and sexual satisfaction.

Materialist feminist views on alienation and love

What is meant by saying that a love relationship, such as that based on romantic love, is alienated? I shall defend a historical rather than an ontological view of alienation, but to do this I first need to explain my understanding of what I call the 'affective economy'. The affective economy (Ferguson 2012, 2014, 2017) is unlike the material economy that Marx analyzed, although in practice both are always intertwined. There is a joint dependence between the material economy, that is the social relations and practices humans engage in to produce and exchange the material goods necessary for bodily health, and the affective economy, that is, the social relations and practices engaged in to meet affective needs such as love and sexuality and to care for children.

Working from an analogue of Marx's argument for capitalist labor exploitation, Jónasdóttir argues that in patriarchal societies most heterosexual love relations involve the exploitation of women by men (1994, 2011). In my earlier books (Ferguson 1989, 1991) I also argue that what I call the 'sex-affective energy' that people get in sexual and caring relations is unequally exchanged in patriarchal societies, and this can be seen as an exploitative relationship, although not exactly analogous to Marx's concept of exploitation. I agree with Eva Illouz (1997, 2012) and others that personal love is one of the important ways that both men and women receive self-esteem and social status in contemporary western societies. So if the norms and practices of a romantic love relation in a patriarchal society create a situation where the masculine gendered partner in the relationship is receiving more self-esteem and social status than they give to the feminine gendered one, then that lack of reciprocal exchange can be said to be exploitative. This can also be true in queer couple relationships and polyamorous ones where there are gender roles involved (cf. Easton and Hardy 2009; Schneebaum 2014).

Alienation as a historical concept

But if in heterosexual love relationships most men are exploiting women, how can men as well be said to be alienated in love? Most feminist theorists who discuss alienation as a problem for feminism start from modernist ideals of individual freedom, equality and democracy that came out of the Enlightenment revolutions of the seventeenth and eighteenth centuries in Western Europe. For example Simone de Beauvoir (1989 [1949]) and Sandra Bartky (1990) assume that women are oppressed because we find ourselves in a system of universal patriarchal alienation which denies us individual autonomy, since we lack full subject status; that is, we see ourselves and are seen only as sex or maternal objects for men rather than full agents. On this view of alienation, it is women not men who are alienated, since men are afforded individual autonomy and full subject status in patriarchal societies, even if they may be further oppressed by their class, race, ethnicity or sexuality in relation to others with more powerful positions.

Starting from Marx's theory of alienation gives us a more historical approach, since it ties alienation not to a universal human condition but to historical features of capitalism that both create the values of modernism – freedom, particularly the freedom of self-development, democracy, and social equality – yet thwart their achievement.

Marx characterizes these modernist ideals well in his discussion of alienation in the *Economic and Philosophic Manuscripts* of 1844. He assumes values of individual freedom and self-development when he critiques the system of capitalist wage labor for alienating, that is, separating, a person *from them-selves* (that is, from the possibility of fully developing a sense of self[3]). Marx thought such a potential was part of the distinctive 'species-being' of humans (cf. Ollman 1971). Capitalist wage labor also separates a person *from others* (whom one must 'objectify' or see as objects, since they must be seen as competitors not cooperators), *from the process of one's labor* (since out of one's control: not democratically controlled by the producers) and *from one's product of labor* (which is owned by others).[4] We can note that the ideal human life that Marx thought communism would exemplify is thoroughly based on the acceptance of a type of individualism not characteristic of pre-modern societies – that is, the emphasis on individual autonomy or freedom in all aspects of life.

Materialist feminist theorists have attempted to expand Marx's approach to cover the alienated love relations between men and women characteristic of capitalist societies. The more Marxist-feminist of these explain gender alienation as an extension of the economic alienation caused by the capitalist mode of production. For example, Ann Foreman (1977) sees feminine alienation as due to the development of the public–private split in capitalist production. Since men are alienated from themselves in wage work they see the private world of the home as the place where they can be 'themselves'; but unfortunately these selves think of themselves as sovereigns, objectify their wives/lovers as their property, and think of them as less socially valuable than themselves. The gendered division of labor where women are expected to do unpaid housework makes invisible and devalues their socially necessary caring labor, and hence themselves.

While I agree with Foreman's critique of the alienating tendencies of capitalism, I think her analysis is somewhat simplistic because it does not theorize affective economies of exchanging love, care and sexuality with patriarchal forms that precede capitalism. Hence, I argue that we need at least a socialist-feminist dual systems theory of the connection between patriarchy and capitalism (cf. Hartmann 1981; Jónasdóttir 1994), as well as to analyze the further system of institutional racism/white supremacism developed on a world scale by European imperialism and its related system of racial slavery (Ferguson 1991).

Lena Gunnarsson (2014) appropriates the work of Bhaskar (2002), arguing that women's alienation in love can be explained in terms of the dialectic between two levels of reality. In economic and sociosexual reality, social domination operates through institutions that force the oppressed (workers, people of color, and women) into exploitative labor and love practices that alienate them. In the deeper level of what Bhaskar calls metaReality, love is the ground of human life. Hence, on this level there are no exploitative exchanges of love since everyone is bound together in love. But since the economic and sociosexual level is also real, both men and women are constrained into alienating practices of love.

These practices, though they are to men's power advantage and allow them surplus love energy through their ability to control women, nonetheless

alienate them from their dependence on women's love in the deeper metaReality. Gunnarsson defends this type of ontology for a feminist vision. Such an
ontology recommends a feminist practice such as that of bell hooks (2000a,
2000b) that advocates that feminists not only empower ourselves through love
but also to empower men to reconstruct their masculinity so that it is a
'feminist masculinity', hence no longer exploits women's love.

Although I agree with the vision, I reject this type of metaphysical explanation for sexual and love alienation in our society as well as any theory
which posits that we have a deeper 'authentic' self which exists but is repressed on the visible social level. A more plausible hypothesis is a historical one
based on a simpler ontology, that human nature involves malleable human
needs, with changeable objects, for love/affection/intimacy/bonding and
(sexual) pleasure. Selves, based on more or less conscious projects for achieving these needs and the other material needs for physical survival, also change
and develop through time (cf. Ferguson 1991). Thus, if we wish to argue that
women are more alienated than men in a given social formation, we can posit
that both men and women have certain erotic and emotional/love/intimacy
needs as humans but because our gendered selves are historically constructed
so as to channel meeting these needs in certain ways in patriarchal contexts,
heterosexual men are less frustrated than heterosexual women in meeting
both their needs for personal love, and those for self-respect, connected to social
status, and peer love. I will discuss this further below, as well as the claim that
men as well as women are alienated in love in our capitalist patriarchal
system, even though women are more alienated.

A historical view of sexual and love alienation

Theorizing different historical modes of affective economy, I define an affective economy as *alienated* if (1) there are contradictory values built into the
social construction of its sexual symbolic codes (or norms); (2) gendered
sexual roles require an either/or choice of sexual and love values which an
alternative social construction of sexuality and love (one which is historically
possible to achieve) would make unnecessary; and (3) social structures in the
present social formation make it impossible to achieve all the aims and
objects of sexuality and love as socially constructed.[5] This characterization of
love and sexual alienation provides a motivation to demand social change to
those who understand the bind we are put in by our current contradictory
value system.

Just as capitalism is a system with conflicting tendencies, some of which
undermine its own ability to reproduce itself, so public patriarchal affective
economies in the contemporary west produce sexual and love desires that they
cannot satisfy, thus undermining their own ability to reproduce themselves.

I have argued (Ferguson 1989, 1991) that in patriarchal forms of affective
economy, children learn gender identities based on symbolic norms of masculinity and femininity. These symbolic gendered norms also inform the sex-

love codes or principles that inform our practices of romantic love, and our inability to achieve all of them is one of the grounds for love and sexual alienation in contemporary western societies today.

Here are the principles I think are operative in western capitalist patriarchal sexual/love codes today:

1   *The principle of romantic love:* A voluntary love partnership, that is, a love between equals, is an important human value, and provides a central meaning in one's life.
2   *The principle of sexual equality and freedom:* Everyone of whatever gender has an equal right to sexual pleasures and the right to consensual interactions.
3   *The natural complement gender principle:* Since men and women are naturally different, they ought to engage in complementary gender roles in sexuality, love and parenting.
4   *The male-in-charge/female submission principle:* The masculine gender role is to initiate, while the feminine role is to submit.
5   *The male performance/female responsiveness principle:* Men generate sexual desire while women generate responsiveness.

The first two beliefs, the right to consent and equality in love and sex, develop from market principles of capitalist production. They stem from what MacPherson (2011) calls the ideology of 'possessive individualism', that is, the view that individuals have natural rights to promote their own happiness through controlling their own bodies (seen as their personal property) and to use inherent or acquired skills (their human capital) to amass property to meet their needs. They thus have the right to enter into voluntary contracts to meet their needs with others equally thought to be possessive individuals, i.e. peers able to choose means to develop their own happiness, in this case, consensual relationships to achieve love and sexual pleasure. Singer (1987) and others (e.g. Solomon 1988) point out that this aspect of romantic love, which Robert Solomon calls 'affective individualism' (1988), was originally at odds with the priority given in early capitalism to arranged marriages in the bourgeois class to ensure the consolidation of property and inheritance without conflicts about the legitimacy of heirs.

Dating from the seventeenth and eighteenth century, feminist critics of romantic love such as Mary Astell and Mary Wollstonecraft, and including second wave feminists Simone de Beauvoir (1989 [1949]) and Shulamith Firestone (1972), have argued that romantic heterosexual love is deeply flawed as a feminist ideal and practice because the first two principles cannot be achieved in a capitalist patriarchal system which rests on a gender division of labor in the economy, society, family and personal life that gives men power over women. These feminists conclude that true consent and equality are only rarely possible in heteronormative sexual love relationships.

Although contemporary US and European societies have equalized men and women's economic and social rights so that men are not automatically assumed to have the right to dominate women in family and personal life, it is still true that the last three principles in romantic love are present in the cultural programming of society, as evidenced in cultural media such as movies and TV images of gendered romantic and sexual relations which generally stereotype women as naturally dependent on men and as having complementary traits – nurturance and empathy rather than authority and rationality, submissiveness rather than authority (Douglas 2010). Clearly there are now some opposing images of some men and women, and even of lesbian and gay couples, that point toward a new ideal of mutual love, but romantic love as generally practiced and portrayed is still on a continuum, slightly modified, of the earlier gender ideology of the family patriarchal societies typical of pre-capitalism and early capitalism.

Principle 3, the Natural Complement principle, is a constant through different male-dominant affective economies. It has been used to justify the distinction between public spheres, where men hold political and economic power, and the private sphere of the family where women are expected to concentrate their energies. It has also justified a gender division of labor, whether in the public or the private sphere, since men and women are seen to have different capacities and skills such that it is more efficient for the social order that they be trained to do different work.[6] Principles 3, 4, and 5 are explicitly challenged by the new mutual love ideal developing in feminist and LGBTQ contexts, since strong gender roles are seen to inhibit partner equality, whether in heterosexual or queer couples, including polyamorous relationships (Sempruch this volume).

The Natural Complement principle of romantic love may be under attack more recently in the US because of cultural changes that challenge the gendered ideal of romantic love, particularly the view that women, not men, are those who self-reflectively express their own emotions and also help their (male) partners to understand (his) repressed feelings. Andrew Cherlin (2014) argues that standards of masculinity are changing in the US, not only in the educated classes of dual wage-earning professionals, but also in young, working-class, non-college educated young men. His interviews with this cohort suggest that, in part due to the lack of secure, skilled employment, hence male breadwinner jobs, the younger generation of the American working class is changing its standard of successful masculinity from that of the disciplined self who is a provider, and for whom authority in the couple rests in the male, to a more feminized standard of masculinity connected to the ideal of the expressive self – one who is able to discuss and process anger, pain, and relationship and addiction problems with therapeutic approaches.

A somewhat different take on the contemporary ideology of heterosexual love is given by Tom Digby (2014). He argues that patriarchal heterosexuality, what he calls 'heterosexualism', is *transactional*. That is, it is seen as a bargaining situation in which each partner relies on the needs of the other for their services, and in a situation of male dominance this sets up the 'battle of the sexes', where men try to continue to dominate in order to achieve the gender ideal of masculinity of militarist warrior cultures like ours. In such cultures, men must have the virtues of warriors – tough, unemotional, and in command (both protectors and providers), and women try to attain a complementary femininity – maternal, emotionally nurturant, and submissive. But since women now have more material resources to be educated and economically independent, they have the economic possibility to leave an unsatisfactory love relationship; and consequently they can try to use their emotional power over men to gain more power indirectly.

Digby describes heterosexualist love relations as characterized by gender dualism and gender complementarity as well as male dominance, much as my principles 3, 4, and 5 above suggest. Digby's view of this alienating type of heterosexual love is clearly influenced by de Beauvoir, who in her groundbreaking work *The Second Sex* (1989 [1949]) argues that because of male dominance, men and women seek different things in love, with women seeking to attain value through merging with a man in a love relation, while men seek women as possessions, as a complement to their other life projects that give them value. To quote de Beauvoir, speaking of male lovers:

> even on their knees before a mistress, what they still want is to take possession of her; at the very heart of their lives they remain sovereign subjects; the beloved woman is only one value among others. [...] For woman, on the contrary, to love is to relinquish everything for the benefit of a master.
>
> (1989 [1949]: 642)

De Beauvoir makes clear, however, that this is not a natural or inevitable difference between the sexes, but is based on the social situation of male dominance in which women (and men) find themselves. Indeed, she later distinguishes between what she calls 'idolatrous love' by women of men and 'authentic love' and argues that the latter is possible.

My own and bell hooks' ideal of mutual love and de Beauvoir's authentic love overlap. For de Beauvoir, in authentic love each partner is conceived by self and other as a free subject with independent value, and experiences the love bond as enhancing (not losing) each self in the bond with the other (de Beauvoir 1989 [1949]: 667). For hooks,

> Through giving to each other we learn how to experience mutuality. To heal the gender war rooted in struggles for power, women and men choose to make mutuality the basis of their bond, ensuring that each person's growth matters and is nurtured. [...] The mutual practice of giving and receiving is an everyday ritual when we know true love.
>
> (hooks 2000a: 164)

I suggest a more nuanced historical understanding of capitalist patriarchal love and sexuality culture than offered by de Beauvoir, hooks or Digby.

Actually, the possessive individualism of capitalist patriarchy and its related affective individualism have created a contradictory situation for many men and women regarding their norms and practices for love and sexuality. Principles 1 and 2 of romantic love, based on consent and equality of the partners, promote gender mutuality in love as an ideal and provide more complicated possibilities for gendered masculinity and femininity depending on economic class and racial and ethnic positioning. But principles 3, 4, and 5 continue to promote gender inequality in heterosexual love practices, and hence promote male dominance.

Digby is correct to assume that the US and indeed most advanced capitalist societies are militarist. But this in itself does not require that all American men adopt the masculinity of warriors. In the US we now have a mostly male warrior class which is a voluntary, not required, option for men. Other career possibilities like doctors, academics, other professional and manual work, provide less patriarchal options for defining masculinity. The warrior class now includes some women, who, though they don't have an easy time in the still-male-dominated army, instantiate, along with female professional athletes, an alternative notion of femininity not based primarily on the nurturant, dependent, maternal role. More women are in careers and jobs which allow them to be economically independent of men if necessary. This is true even though their gender-coded work tends to give them less pay than men in comparable jobs, and hence an incentive to seek love partnerships that will allow for joint incomes to make ends meet. Being required to be in the capitalist paid work force has tended to promote possessive individualism in women as well as men. But in their roles as mothers and emotional providers in the family and caring-affective service providers in gender-typed wage work, they find themselves with conflicting values – trying to reconcile mutual love with the one-sided emotional nurturance expected from feminine-defined persons.

Digby argues that mutuality, where men learn the skills of emotional nurturing and women of being economic providers, provides a base for a 'strong' heterosexual love, in contrast to the reigning heterosexualist model that leads to gender inequality and violence against women (and against men, especially gay and trans men who don't achieve warrior masculinity). I agree with Digby's important distinction here between mutual love (his strong heterosexual love) and romantic love (what he calls the heterosexualist model), and his critique of the 'transactionalist' logic of this latter model is excellent.

But what Digby doesn't do so well (because he over-generalizes about militarist societies and their warrior-mother gendered norms) is to make it clear how this new ideal of mutual love arises because of changing conditions in gender roles caused by advanced capitalism, as well as by people's struggle to challenge the alienation caused by the contradictory and unachievable model of romantic love.

The dialectic of love (intimacy) vs. sexuality (pleasure): romantic vs. mutual love

Two conflicting dialectics of sexuality, the dialectic of pleasure and the dialectic of love/intimacy, are at work in contemporary western society. These two dialectics involve the changing relations of women and men in love and sexual practices (including marriage), as well as parenting practices. Together they demonstrate the way we are alienated by our affective economy, since it subjects us to conflicting codes of love and sexuality.

Our contemporary meanings for sexual pleasure and emotional intimacy/ love have a history tied to the development of the public–private split engendered by capitalist production. Pre-capitalist society organized sexuality to emphasize neither the possibilities of sexual pleasure nor emotional intimacy but primarily to regulate biological reproduction so as to strengthen the extended kinship networks through which economic production was organized.

The father patriarchies characteristic of early capitalist states involved an emerging nuclearization of the family which had two important effects in developing the modern structure of public/private spheres. On the one hand, acknowledging men as patriarchal heads of household allowed the emerging capitalist state to undermine the extended kin ties of the aristocracy which challenged its hegemony. On the other hand, the creation of the private domestic sphere for bourgeois women and children set the stage for the eroticization and intimatization of nuclear family relations – the sentimental family (cf. Nicholson 1986; Seidman 1991; Shorter 1975; Stone 1977).

The transition from father to husband family patriarchies in the first two phases of western European and American capitalist development carried with it three important shifts in the affective economy: (1) the emphasis on the maternal affectionate bond; (2) the development of the concept of romantic love as a base for marriage; and (3) with the help of the bourgeois sexology of the late nineteenth and early twentieth centuries, a developing emphasis on sexual pleasure between husbands and wives as an important goal of marriage (Ferguson 1989).

Contemporary public patriarchy continues the emphases of husband patriarchy, with some important changes. Husband patriarchy had a clear gender double standard for intimacy and sexual pleasure. Mothers but not fathers were expected to be emotionally intimate with children, wives but not husbands were expected to be emotionally nurturant to their mates, and the sexual pleasure relevant in marriage was generally assumed to be the man's not the woman's.

In today's US, however, there is now increasing support for elimination of the gender double standard; that is, that women and children have rights to emotional nurturance by men, and women have rights to reciprocal sexual pleasure from men as well as other women partners.[7] Studies of the effects of the twentieth-century norm of companionate marriage (Ehrenreich et al. 1986; Seidman 1991) suggest not only that many men value love and intimacy more highly than casual sexual pleasure but also that women are increasingly demanding physical satisfaction in their relations with men. But this egalitarian tendency is countered by the continuing gender dualism of our society which teaches girls but not boys to value and develop skills for producing emotional intimacy and teaches boys to treat egoistic sexual performance as a mark of successful masculinity.

The dialectic of pleasure developed in advanced capitalism is based on a sexual consumerism that assumes both women and men are sexual consumers and, thus, sexual subjects, which in turn suggests that sexual partners should be equal negotiators of sexual pleasure for themselves. But there are still strong suggestions in cultural norms that a man is considered more 'sexy' if he is in charge of the sexual practices: otherwise he is in danger of being considered an unattractive 'wimp' and too feminine for most heterosexual women's tastes.

A close examination of the material and symbolic possibilities for women in the US today reveals a set of structures with contradictory implications. For one thing, the increased possibility of divorce and availability of birth control have made possible the separation of sexuality from reproduction. This empowers women, not merely to have less fear of unwanted pregnancies, but also to value the pleasurable aspects of sex and to demand more reciprocity as sexual subjects – including the possibility of lesbian sexuality. The growth of lesbian feminism in the 1970s and 1980s is a result both of the influence of the sexual revolution on women and of the idea of 'women-loving women' (cf. Rich 1980) as a feminist option to patriarchal (heteronormative) constructions of sexuality. The growth of queer feminism in the twenty-first century, where gender identity is not tied to sexual preference or to gender dualism, makes gender-powered roles in love more negotiable since partners do not automatically accept the symbolic norms of masculinity and femininity outlined above that connect to patriarchal heteronormativity. But a conservative effect of the recent gay politics around achieving legal same sex marriage may involve a homonormativity that pressures lesbian and gay couples to act more like heterosexual couples, thus reinforcing gender dualist romantic love practices (cf. Grossi this volume).

For heterosexual women, although the interest in sex for pleasure has led many to sexual consumerism (one night stands, college hook-ups, internet dates for sex, etc.), it has also relatively empowered women in the sense that women as sexual consumers can objectify men. Eva Illouz (2012) talks about the increasing importance of the erotic capital that some women have in the otherwise male-dominated sexual and marriage markets of the twenty-first century. This means that, increasingly, women can use men for pleasure in a way that only men were able to do with women in the past. Though aspects of women's sexual practices remain alienated (see for example Bartky 1990 on the effects of the disciplinary regimes of diet and beauty on women), women still have greater sexual negotiating power than they used to.

The mass media have supported both genders' sexual consumerism by creating contradictory sexual images. Thus, radical feminists are mistaken to pick out merely violent pornography and passive housewife examples of the mass media presentations of femininity, since it also presents strong feminist images in rock stars like Tina Turner and movies such as *Alien*, TV shows like *Sex and the City* with a number of powerful sexually active women characters, and androgynous role models like Michael Jackson and Lady Gaga.[8] Indeed the New Right's attempts to censor pornography can been seen as an attempt to challenge the newer images of sexually autonomous and demanding women by reverting to the Victorian image of asexual women.

As the legitimacy of pleasure increases as a goal for both sexes, feminism, lesbian, gay, and queer liberation challenge the natural complement, male-in-control, and male performance principles, thus creating a dialectic of pleasure. These conflicting tendencies are handled in the mass media by a division of the images of sexual fantasy into two separate areas: (1) gendered interests: harlequin romances for 'good women' and hard pornography for men (Snitow 1983) and (2) images that are not gender divided, and include some erotica for mixed audiences of men and 'bad' women, feminists, LGBTQ people, and other deviants.[9] In such a category we could include sexual fantasies such as vampire and superhero novels, comics, advertisements, and movies that mix weak and strong woman images (cf. Douglas 2010). We could also see the development of 'gonzo' porn, explicitly violent and humiliating images of women in sex scenes, as being made for that audience of men who feel threatened by the growth of economic and social power for women that may threaten their sense of entitled masculinity (cf. Digby 2014).

The other dialectic, that of love intimacy, is created by the continuing gender division of labor in parenting which organizes more of women's affective emotional energy, across race and economic class divisions, into mothering and nurturing priorities than into orgiastic sexual pleasure. The fact that an overwhelming number of children of divorced parents live with their mothers reinforces the prioritization by women of love and affective emotional intimacy over that of genital sexual pleasure (Modleski 1982). Even lesbians tend to prioritize love and intimacy over auto-erotic pleasure in their affective relations, in part because of gender priorities that most mothers, whether heterosexual or not, have learned from their mothers, and consciously or unconsciously may communicate to their children.

Gender dualism as an ongoing structural feature

There are both material and symbolic supports for the gender dualism of contemporary sexual and love normative codes. Materially, heterosexual sex is still dangerous for women in the sense that it involves greater risks: pregnancy, single mother poverty, and reproductive diseases. Furthermore, the wage labor inequalities of men and women tend to make an economic connection to a man more important for a woman than the reverse and are an incentive for women to learn how to meet men's emotional needs, while men are usually not taught such skills.

And skills they are, as Gunnarsson convincingly argues (2014) when she analyzes the asymmetrical role-taking theory of women's learned ability to 'pivot the center' to see the situation from men's perspective, when most men do not do this. This structural difference in gender skills in love is what creates exploitation in love practices, since most women do not get their emotional/love needs satisfied in a reciprocal way from men in heterosexual love relationships.

In addition, more women than men fail to get their sexual needs satisfied in a reciprocal way in the sexual practices of heterosexual love. The sexual symbolic code of gender dualism teaches boys and girls different gender messages about the legitimacy of searching for orgiastic bodily pleasures. Boys are generally encouraged to think it manly to be assertive, in order to achieve their own bodily pleasure. This normative assumption of male performance is coupled with the assumption of male seduction: men are more masculine to the degree that they can influence women to acquiesce to genital intercourse which results in orgiastic pleasure for the man but not necessarily for the woman. This requirement for a successfully masculine man to 'be a stud' out for his own pleasure may not even be true of many men, but the fear of losing status and peer homosocial love from other men leads many men to continue to engage in patriarchal sexual practices.

On the other hand, the dialectic of pleasure brought about by the sexual revolution has encouraged many men to promote orgiastic pleasure for their women partners. Most women in advanced capitalist societies know that most men today want to think they are good lovers by giving their partners orgasms. But since this is a secondary goal to the male orgasm, women often fake orgasms because their partners are inept in helping them to achieve them, and women want the men to have the satisfaction of thinking themselves good lovers.

Though premarital sex and living together without marriage are increasingly tolerated across class and race/ethnic differences, there is still the assumption that marriage is the ultimate requirement for a woman, but not a man, to have achieved social success. This disadvantages women in heterosexual sexual and love relations with men. Further, in the twenty-first century, the ease and legitimacy of divorce and the cultural imperative to seek for love in personal relationships have created many 'blended families', that is, women and men in second and third partnerships with their children from previous partnerships. Such a situation creates inequalities more for the mother or stepmother than the stepfather, since she is the one expected to harmonize the conflicting needs and jealousies of the children with each other and with the other partner (cf. Ferguson 1991 on the 'sex/affective triangle').

Conclusion

I have argued that in the contemporary separation of the search for love (coded as emotional intimacy) from the search for sexual pleasure, women still lose out by not achieving either in any lasting way. Men, who tend to prioritize sexual pleasure as an attribute of manhood but who also are marked by the contemporary desire for romantic love, also lose out by being alienated from the kind of ongoing emotional intimacy that would allow them success in achieving lasting couple love. Many men haven't learned emotional intimacy skills, and end up seeking intimacy/love through sex. This strategy, not shared by most women for reasons given above, keeps these men from achieving the emotional equality and shared self they crave in one relationship, so they end up in one uncommitted relationship after another (cf. Illouz 2012). Thus, as I have argued above, most men as well as women are in a state of love and sexual alienation in western societies today.

I have also argued that women are more alienated than men in our contemporary affective economy because ongoing gender norms and social structures of capitalist patriarchy make it more likely that heterosexual women will receive less pleasure and emotional nurturance from their male partners than they give; and further that women who are 'primary' mothers (that is, do more caring mother-work than their partners), are more likely to have to forego sexual pleasure and emotional intimacy goals with adult partners because of their mothering role than are fathers or non-primary mothers in lesbian or trans relationships (cf. Schneebaum 2014).

But men who insist on dominating their love relationships also lose something. They fail to receive as much love as they could be getting if they were providing reciprocal love to their partners: more love energy would be generated for both of them, including the men's satisfaction in having provided the intrinsic value of love. This is an argument that men who harm women by withholding reciprocal love receive harm themselves. Such a line of thought provides the possibility of the emergence of feminist men's movements to challenge the patriarchal social construction of masculinity (cf. Ferguson 2017).

bell hooks argues that feminist women should support the goal of feminist masculinity: that is, the rejection by men of patriarchal masculinity and the rebuilding by them of a feminist masculine identity, or 'feminist masculinity' (hooks 2000a, 2000b). hooks claims that both men and women need to learn how to love in a mutual way. For Gunnarsson (2014) and hooks, this is both a spiritual and a material practice involving trust, commitment, and giving (hooks 2000a: 164). Like these authors, I have argued that there is an emerging ideal of mutual love. But this ideal is not fully achievable in the existing hierarchical society in the US, still so divided by race, class, and gender, and so prone to use of physical force (militarism) to resolve political conflicts.

Nonetheless, if we theorize heteronormative love exploitation as one of the ways male domination is perpetuated, and analyze the harm that the historical alienation in love and sexual relations causes both men and women, we can see a way to challenge both. We need not only to work toward mutual love in our personal love relations but also to espouse a collective feminist love ethic (what I call a solidarity ethic). I am not able to develop this claim here, but have done so in other works (Ferguson 2012, 2014, 2017). We will require solidarity love in order to fight against social injustice in all its forms and the patriarchal superiority/inferiority logic that supports it (hooks 2000a: 97; Lorde 1984).

Notes

1 One might argue that the function of marriage has changed in the US since the Supreme Court decision in June 2015 making it legal for same sex partners to marry. Now the institution in the US, some claim, is more about a committed love relationship and less about property relations and parental rights to control of children, so how can it be oppressive to women in heterosexual marriages? What this claim ignores is that marriage as practiced is part of a traditional gendered culture in which most heterosexual married women do the bulk of unpaid housework and childcare. In a system where most women still make less money in paid work than their male husbands, marriage remains an institution that supports male domination by making it more difficult for women to leave an abusive or unequal situation because of the economic repercussions on them and any children (cf. Ferguson 2007).

2 Thanks to Anna Jónasdóttir for reminding me of this distinction.

3 Richard Schmitt's *Alienation and Freedom* (2003) provides an excellent discussion of the modern theory of alienation as it was developed by Rousseau, Kierkegaard, Marx, and Nietzsche. His examples are persuasive, showing how even people who see themselves as happy can be seen to be alienated if they lack the ability to be self-reflective. But the persuasiveness of his examples, I would argue, show not a universal truth about self-reflexivity and human nature, but how deep within our modern approach to the world is the goal of self-development.

4 Bertell Ollman (1971) has persuasively interpreted Marx's views on alienation to stem from an essentialist vision of the distinctive human species-potential for a fully free, rational social life that is only achievable in communism.

5 My approach here is consistent with that taken by Rosemary Hennessy (2000) in her claim that advanced capitalist societies have created what she calls 'outlawed needs', including those for love of others and a shared common.

6 However, the last two principles are somewhat different from their analogues in family patriarchies, which involve the male seducer/female resister model. These earlier patriarchal principles still operate in many subcultures in advanced capitalist patriarchies today as well as in non-western societies, and in these contexts and societies create an explicit conflict between men and women.

7 Compare the differences in lesbian culture in the US today, where both partners expect reciprocal sexual pleasure, to the earlier 1930s–1960s butch–femme lesbian codes, in which the 'stone butch' was expected to bring her femme partner to orgasm but not have orgiastic sex herself (cf. Kennedy and Davis 1993).

8 Of course these images are more complicated: Rosi Braidotti (2002) points out that the movie *Alien* contrasts the positive strong mother image of the Sigourney Weaver character with the monster mother of the alien spider. Tina Turner underwent years of abuse from her former husband Ike Turner. Bonnie Mann points out that the new popular vampire novels and movies at once show women as active subjects pursuing sex, but still in mortal danger from the results of their sexual attractions to vampire men (Mann 2009).

9 It should also be pointed out that racism is alive and well in the way pornographic images are categorized on the internet, with images of more assertive Black and Latin and more passive white women in heterosexual porn, which caters to masculine tastes developed in a racialized sexist system of erotic imaginations.

References

Bartky, Sandra Lee (1990) *Femininity and Domination: Studies in the Phenomenology of Oppression*. New York: Routledge.

Bhaskar, Roy (2002) *Meta-Reality. The Philosophy of Meta-Reality: Creativity, Love and Freedom*. London: Sage.

Braidotti, Rosi (2002) *Metamorphoses: Towards a Materialist Theory of Becoming*. Cambridge: Polity Press.

Castoriadis, Cornelius (1987) *The Imaginary Institution of Society*. Cambridge, MA: MIT Press.

Cherlin, Andrew J. (2014) *Labor's Love Lost: The Rise and Fall of the Working-Class Family in America*. New York: Russell Sage Foundation.

de Beauvoir, Simone (1989 [1949]) *The Second Sex*, trans. H. M. Parshley. New York: Vintage.

Deleuze, Gilles and Felix Guattari (1977) *Anti-Oedipus*. New York: Viking.

Digby, Tom (2014) *Love and War: How Militarism Shapes Sexuality and Romance*. New York: Columbia University Press.

Douglas, Susan (2010) *Enlightened Sexism*. New York: Times Books.

Easton, Dossie and Janet W. Hardy (2009) *The Ethical Slut: A Practical Guide to Polyamory, Open Relationships and Other Adventures*. Berkeley, CA: Celestial Arts.

Ehrenreich, Barbara, Elizabeth Hess and Gloria Jacobs (1986) *Re-Making Love: The Feminization of Sex*. New York: Doubleday.

Ferguson, Ann (1989) *Blood at the Root: Motherhood, Sexuality and Male Dominance*. London: Pandora/Unwin & Hyman.

Ferguson, Ann (1991) *Sexual Democracy: Women, Oppression, and Revolution*. Boulder, CO: Westview Press.

Ferguson, Ann (2007) 'Gay Marriage: An American and Feminist Dilemma', *Hypatia* 22(1): 39–57.

Ferguson, Ann (2012) 'Romantic Couple Love, the Affective Economy, and a Socialist-Feminist Vision', in A. Anton and R. Schmitt (eds) *Taking Socialism Seriously*. New York: Lexington Books.

Ferguson, Ann (2014) 'Feminist Love Politics: Romance, Care, and Solidarity', in A. G. Jónasdóttir and A. Ferguson (eds) *Love: A Question for Feminism in the Twenty-First Century*. New York: Routledge.

Ferguson, Ann (2017) 'Love as a Political Force', in R. Grossi and D. West (eds) *The Radicalism of Romantic Love*. London: Routledge.

Firestone, Shulamith (1972) *The Dialectic of Sex*. New York: Wm. Morrow

Foreman, Ann (1977) *Femininity and Alienation: Women and the Family in Marxism and Psychoanalysis*. London: Pluto Press.

Giddens, Anthony (1992) *The Transformation of Intimacy: Sexuality, Love, and Eroticism in Modern Societies*. Stanford, CA: Stanford University Press.

Gunnarsson, Lena (2014) *The Contradictions of Love: Towards a Feminist-Realist Ontology of Sociosexuality*. London and New York: Routledge.

Hartmann, Heidi (1981) 'The Unhappy Marriage of Marxism and Feminism', in L. Sargent (ed.) *Women and Revolution*. Boston, MA: South End Press.

Hennessy, Rosemary (2000) *Profit and Pleasure: Sexual Identities in Late Capitalism*. New York: Routledge.

hooks, bell (2000a) *All about Love*. New York: Harper Perennial.

hooks, bell (2000b) *Feminism Is for Everybody: Passionate Politics.* Boston, MA: South End Press.

Illouz, Eva (1997) *Consuming the Romantic Utopia: Love and the Cultural Contradictions of Capitalism.* Berkeley: University of California Press.

Illouz, Eva (2012) *Why Love Hurts.* Cambridge: Polity.

Jónasdóttir, Anna G. (1994) *Why Women Are Oppressed.* Philadelphia, PA: Temple University Press.

Jónasdóttir, Anna G. (2011) 'What Kind of Power Is "Love Power"?' in A. G. Jónasdóttir, V. Bryson and K. B. Jones (eds) *Sexuality, Gender and Power: Intersectional and Transnational Perspectives.* New York: Routledge.

Kennedy, Elizabeth Lapórsky and Madeline Davis (1993) *Boots of Leather, Slippers of Gold: A History of a Lesbian Community.* New York: Routledge.

Lorde, Audre (1984) *Sister Outsider.* Trumansburg, NY: Crossing Press.

Luhmann, Niklas (1986) *Love as Passion: The Codification of Intimacy.* Cambridge, MA: Harvard University Press.

Luhmann, Niklas (2010) *Love: A Sketch.* Cambridge: Polity.

MacPherson, C. B. (2011) *The Political Theory of Possessive Individualism.* New York: Oxford University.

Mann, Bonnie (2009) 'Vampire Love: The Second Sex Negotiates the 21st Century', in R. Housel and J. Wisnewski (eds) *Twilight and Philosophy: Vampires, Vegetarians, and the Pursuit of Immortality.* London: Blackwell.

Modleski, Tania (1982) *Loving with a Vengeance: Mass-Produced Fantasies for Women.* New York: Methuen.

Nicholson, Linda (1986) *Gender and History.* New York: Columbia University.

Ollman, Bertell (1971) *Alienation: Marx's Conception of Man in Capitalist Society.* Cambridge: Cambridge University Press.

Rich, Adrienne (1980) 'Compulsory Heterosexuality and Lesbian Existence', *Signs* 5 (4): 631–660.

Seidman, Steven (1991) *Romantic Longings: Love in America 1830–1980.* New York: Routledge.

Schneebaum, Alyssa (2014) 'All in the Family: Patriarchy, Capitalism and Love', in A. G. Jónasdóttir and A. Ferguson (eds) *Love: A Question for Feminism in the Twenty-First Century.* New York: Routledge.

Schmitt, Richard (2003). *Alienation and Freedom.* Boulder, CO: Westview Press.

Shorter, Edward (1975) *The Making of the Modern Family.* New York: Basic Books.

Singer, Irving (1984) *The Nature of Love,* vol 1. Chicago, IL: University of Chicago Press.

Singer, Irving (1987) *The Nature of Love,* vol. 3. Chicago, IL: University of Chicago Press.

Snitow, Ann Barr (1983) 'Mass Market Romance: Pornography for Women Is Different', in A. Snitow, C. Stansell and S. Thompson (eds) *Powers of Desire: The Politics of Sexuality.* New York: Monthly Review Press.

Solomon, Robert C. (1988) *About Love: Reinventing Romance for Our Times.* New York: Simon & Schuster.

Stone, Lawrence (1977) *The Family, Sex and Marriage in England 1500–1800.* London: Weidenfeld and Nicolson.

Wollstonecraft, Mary (1988 [1792]) *A Vindication of the Rights of Woman.* Edited by C. H. Poston. 2nd edn. New York: Norton.

4 What has happened to the feminist critique of romantic love in the same-sex marriage debate?

Renata Grossi

> Hoping to escape suffering it is to suffering that they run. In the desire for happiness, out of delusion, they destroy their own happiness, like an enemy.
>
> (Śāntideva, seventh century)[1]

The same-sex marriage debate in Australia has centralized romantic love and attributed to it the power to demolish conservative readings of marriage. The debate has largely been seen as a battle for the meaning of marriage between procreation and romantic love.[2] In this battle love's power is great. It becomes the destroyer of traditional and long entrenched barriers as it opens the institution up to same-sex couples. This battle expresses a particular view of romantic love as radical and subversive and ignores critiques of romantic love that categorize it as the opposite. That romantic love is capable of such power finds expression among others, in the ideas of philosopher Robert Solomon (1994, 1998) and social theorist Anthony Giddens (1992). However, feminists have long argued that romantic love is oppressive and patriarchal. Their critique resonates with that of queer theory which reinforced the feminist critique by arguing that romantic love is heteronormative.

This essay will begin with a brief overview of the legislative history of the battle for same-sex marriage in Australia. This history will document the centralization of romantic love in the struggle. The discussion will then turn to an overview and general discussion of the feminist positions in relation to romantic love. This discussion will show that while romantic love is regarded as a problem for many feminists (especially when considered alongside marriage and sex), many also welcome the radical nature of romantic love and are therefore not willing to remove it altogether from the modern imagination and way of life. When both sides of the feminist critique are taken together, what emerges is that feminists want to see some redefinition around romantic love and the institutions it is practiced in. In this project the same-sex marriage debate may be of assistance. Like romantic love, the same-sex marriage debate can be read both as a radical, and a conservative project, and neither readings are inevitable. This essay makes a pitch for keeping both in the radical sphere.

The battle for same-sex marriage in Australia[3]

The battle for the legal recognition of same-sex marriage in Australia began in 2004 with the Liberal Federal Government, led by well-known conservative John Howard, introducing into parliament the Marriage Legislation Amendment Bill 2004. In the second reading speech the attorney-general explained that the Bill was needed to reinforce the 'fundamental institution' of marriage (Ruddock 2004). To achieve this aim the Bill provided a definition of marriage as a voluntary union between a man and a woman, prevented Australian courts from recognizing same-sex marriages that had occurred in other countries, and third, prevented same-sex couples from adopting children from overseas. This Bill can be seen as a comprehensive attempt to keep both marriage and family as heterosexual institutions and can be seen as the beginning of the same-sex marriage debate in Australian legislative history.

The most significant part of this battle has taken place in the small jurisdiction of the Australian Capital Territory (ACT). The narrative of this project shows just how contentious the issue has become in Australia. In March 2006 the Labor government, led by Jon Stanhope, introduced the Civil Union Bill. In introducing the Bill to Parliament the then chief minister said that '[a] civil union will be treated in the same way as marriage under territory law. A civil union is not a marriage but, will, so far as the law of the ACT is concerned, be treated in the same way' (Stanhope 2006).

This Bill was quickly met with opposition. An alternative Bill, the Registration of Relationships Bill 2006, was tabled by the opposition that created a scheme of registration significantly distinguishable from marriage. A petition lead by the Australian Christian Lobby was also tabled in Parliament arguing that the Civil Union Bill 'creates a marriage like relationship which so mimics marriage as to confuse and diminish it' (Stephaniak 2006). The Liberal Federal Government quickly opposed it by arguing that the Bill was incompatible with federal law and contravened the idea of marriage as an institution between one man and one woman. Nevertheless, the Civil Union Bill became the Civil Union Act (2006) (ACT) but it never became effective. On 13 June 2006, the governor-general Michael Jeffry on the advice of the Federal Government disallowed the Civil Union Act (2006).[4]

The ACT Government persevered. On 12 December 2006 it presented the Civil Partnership Bill 2006. This new Bill made a number of changes aimed at removing any similarity between the new relationship it sought to create and marriage. But the changes were not enough. The new Bill was still not considered acceptable to the Federal Government and the federal attorney-general announced that his government would not rule out using the governor-general's disallowance power to override the Act once again (Ruddock 2007). The ACT government left the Bill on the books, but waited till after the next federal election, in the hope of a change of government, to determine its next move. This change of government did come but alas was not met with a change of position. In November 2007, the Rudd Labor Government was elected and the ACT announced it would revive the earlier legislation (Alexander 2007). However, negotiations between the ACT Government and the Federal Government came to a conclusion in May 2008 with a clear understanding that the Federal Government would not allow the ACT to pass legislation which in any way mimicked marriage. The ACT had no choice but to scrap all previous plans, and to introduce legislation which instead introduced a relationship registration model which other jurisdictions had successfully introduced (Peake 2008).

On 11 November 2009 the ACT legislature once again opened up the issue by passing the Civil Partnerships Amendment Bill 2009. This Bill introduced by the ACT Greens and supported by the ACT Labor Party, introduced the right of parties to declare their relationship before a civil partnership notary, and thus introduced a ceremony that had been attempted by past versions of the legislation.[5] The first 'partnership' under the new law took place on 25 November 2009. This law remained untouched until 2013 when the ACT, sensing a change in the mood, made one more attempt to introduce a model of recognition for same-sex couples which came as close to marriage as possible. The Marriage Equality (Same Sex) Act 2013 was passed by the legislative assembly in October 2013, but it was short lived. The Act was successfully challenged in the High Court on the constitutional ground of inconsistency with a federal law (section 109). Same sex marriage finally became legal in the whole of Australia after a protracted public campaign leading to a controversial plebiscite in December 2017.

Marriage equals romantic love

There are many arguments made in the debate in favor of the legal recognition of same-sex marriage. A group of these are about material benefits and protections. For example, the right of same-sex couples to represent each other and be recognized as family for medical and financial reasons is not an automatic right in the same way that it is for married couples. Opponents of same-sex marriage are quick to point out the many legislative reforms that have corrected many of the discrepancies that have existed in the past, but the fact remains that a certain level of connectedness leading to practical entitlements is automatically assumed upon marriage that is denied to the 'non-married'.[6]

A second group of arguments is made around the requirement of status and equality. That is, that there is no excuse in a modern world-view entrenched in anti-discrimination and human rights practices and policies to deny people in same-sex relationships access to the institution of marriage. As Tamara Metz puts it, while the institution of marriage is problematic,

> so long as the state defines, confers, and uses marital status as a vehicle for protecting and supporting associations of intimate caregivers [...] it must offer the status to same-sex intimate caregiving couples. A commitment to equal treatment before the law demands it. Period.
>
> (Metz 2010: 120)

Another set of arguments which have become more prominent as time has gone by, has been to do with the meaning of marriage and the centrality of romantic love to the institution. The argument has been that marriage is about romantic love more than it is about anything else (predominantly pro-creation) and there is no reason therefore to exclude same-sex couples from the institution. Romantic love has become a platform in the intellectual, legislative and political debate.

Romantic love had been raised in the federal parliamentary debates around the changing of the Marriage Act (Bevis 2004), but it became more central in debates about the ACT's Civil Unions Bill. Andrew Barr, Member of Legislative Assembly, said that the Civil Union Bill was about 'supporting loving, caring relationships regardless of the sexuality of those involved. [...] Saying no to civil unions is to say [...] that some loving, committed long-term relationships are; for some inexplicable reason, of lesser value' (Barr 2006). Jon Stanhope said that '[t]hose of us who enjoy rich and enduring marriages might ask ourselves how we would feel if we were to be suddenly and rudely informed that our love was a lesser love' (Stanhope 2006). In the Senate (around the disallowance debate), Senator Kerry Nettle said that the debate over same-sex marriage is 'about love. It is about who can love each other and who can have their relationship recognized' (Nettle 2006). Senator Bob Brown also thought it was a debate about love: 'What is it about these gentlemen that they cannot recognize thousands of Australia's loving relationships' (Brown 2006). Similarly, Senator Christine Milne argued that: 'it is about recognizing love and commitment – and isn't that the very definition of the marital ideal, of what marriage, of what civil union is fundamentally about; love and commitment?' (Milne 2006). And, finally, Senator Adam Bandt said:

> It is the power of love which has brought us to this moment in the debate over marriage equality, and it is the power of love which will force this parliament and this country to face the reality of what marriage and love means in the twenty-first century.
>
> (Bandt 2010)

That same-sex marriage is about the recognition of same-sex romantic love, is also evident in the way the struggle is being conceived by activists. For example, in Australia and in Britain the rights group that campaigns for same-sex relationship recognition is called 'Equal Love'. Recently the mayor of the New South Wales town of Byron Bay has moved a motion to recognize gay marriage and establish in the town a 'Love Park' as a symbol of recognition and acceptance of gay and lesbian relationships. That it is a love park rather than a 'tolerance', 'acceptance', 'inclusion', 'justice', 'equality', or 'human rights' park is telling. The same-sex marriage debate is very much about making romantic love visible outside of heterosexual relationships; it is firmly about breaking down the disassociation that exists between same-sex couples and romantic love, because romantic love, as much as marriage, carries with it the badges of legitimacy and respectability. But to attribute such power to romantic love requires some discussion.

Against marriage

Within the debate much has been said about marriage, what it is and what it should be. For those conservative (predominantly Christian) arguments against same-sex marriage it has been about wanting to retain heterosexuality as the corner-stone of marriage and of family. However there has also been a considerable opposition to same-sex marriage within the 'queer' community itself. These arguments are to do with a need to reject the institution of marriage because of its connection with conservative religious and heteronormative norms.

Judith Butler, for example, views agitating for marriage as problematic for a group of people who have identified themselves as part of a radical sexual culture. She says: '[f]or a progressive sexual movement, even one that may want to produce marriage as an option for non-heterosexuals, the proposition that marriage should become the only way to sanction or legitimate sexuality is unacceptably conservative' (Butler 2002: 21). Similarly, Michael Warner argues that agitating for same-sex marriage replicates and privileges heterosexuality and further works to stigmatize other relationships. Hugh Ryan in a recent opinion piece warned that the agitation for same-sex marriage has the potential to make marriage the only option for relationship recognition and the effect of that would not be to queer marriage but rather to straighten queers (Ryan 2014). The answer for many in the queer community is to fight for the recognition of the actual relationships that exist and not for the heterosexual ideal of marriage (Slavin 2009). The fact is that the issue of same-sex marriage has created a dilemma for many in the LGBTQI[7] community of how to reconcile their opposition to marriage as a fundamentally conservative institution with a desire to support a campaign for recognition of LGBTQI relationships, and equality (cf. Ferguson 2007).

This radical critique of same-sex marriage has resonance with the rich history of the feminist critique of marriage (cf. Ackelsberg 2010; Jeffreys 2004; Wise and Stanley 2004). Feminists have fought against marriage because it has historically rendered women powerless and subjected them to the harshest abuses of patriarchal power. Even after significant legal reforms, married women can find themselves locked into oppressive and disadvantageous relationships, and this is largely ignored in the debate (Wise and Stanley 2004: 339). For many feminists marriage as an institution has no redeeming features. As Sheila Jeffreys says:

> I do not think marriage can be saved and made into a neutral and egalitarian institution that would be open to either heterosexuals or lesbians and gay men. Marriage exists to form the cement for the hetero-patriarchy. The demolition of male dominance requires that marriage should, as the foundation stone, be withdrawn.
>
> (2004: 330)

The call for marriage to be abolished altogether and that alternatives to regulating intimacy and care should be legislated for has therefore gained a substantial momentum (cf. Brake 2012; Fineman 1995). It is regrettable that this argument against marriage has not received more traction in the debate, and that the progressive argument against same-sex marriage has been sidelined by the conservative one. But it is not the only argument that has been ignored. What is also regrettable is the lack of evidence in the debate of the equally rich feminist critique of romantic love itself.

Against romantic love

Romantic love, from the very beginning, was considered a dangerous idea. Its connection with liberty and freedom, its disconnection from family, class, social and religious duty, make it an obvious target of criticism. Its association, no matter how misconceived, with free love and sexual freedom, made it a threat to traditional family structures and to life-long monogamous marriage. This point has some weight. It is a fact that the association of romantic love with marriage has been shown to make the institution of marriage a less stable and more fickle one (Wilcox and Dew 2010) characterized by high divorce rates, loneliness, poverty and social instability. As Solomon puts it:

> Most of the world looks upon our romantic fantasies as a source of social chaos and irresponsibility [...]. Our emphasis on romance encourages vanity instead of camaraderie, seclusion instead of community, whimsicality instead of responsibility, emotional excitement instead of social stability. The result seems to be a culture that is fragmented, frustrated and lonely just as much as (and because) it is romantic.
>
> (1994: 54)[8]

Ulrich Beck and Elizabeth Beck-Gernsheim, echoing some of the feminist's arguments we will see shortly, claim that modern romantic love can turn into a destructive force. The meaning of romantic love, they suggest, is always open for negotiation and always at risk. Romantic love can end on one person's say-so at any time; there is no right of appeal. Romantic love is the opposite of instrumental and rational behavior, it makes its own rules without any reference to moral or legal obligations (Beck and Beck-Gernsheim 1995: 194). They argue that:

> For individuals who have to invent their own social settings, romantic love becomes the central pivot giving meaning to their lives. In this world where no one demands obedience or respect for old habits, romantic love is exclusively in the first person singular, and so are truth, morality, salvation, transcendence and authenticity. [...] Growing out of itself and its own subjective views, it easily turns totalitarian; rejecting any outside

authority, and agreeing to take over responsibility, to compromise and be fair only for emotional reasons.

(1995: 171)

The feminist critique

The most sustained critique of romantic love (not just marriage and not just sex) comes from feminism. The feminist critique of romantic love is varied. Some of it cannot be disconnected from critiques of the institutions in which it is practiced, but this must not obscure those critiques that focus on the internal structures and ideologies of romantic love itself. The complexity of this critique is discussed in the other chapters of this book. Here, however, I am limiting the discussion to a general philosophical, sociological and political overview, which is only enough to enable me to make my analysis of its interaction with the same-sex marriage debate.

Shulamith Firestone described romantic love as the pivot of oppression for women. She described it as a holocaust, a hell and a sacrifice (Firestone 1970). In this she echoed Simone de Beauvoir, who argued that given the unequal position of men and women, romantic love becomes 'a curse that lies heavily upon a woman confined in the feminine universe, woman mutilated, insufficient unto herself. The innumerable martyrs to romantic love bear witness against the injustice of a fate that offers a sterile hell as ultimate salvation' (1953: 669). These views have been reiterated by later feminists. As Carol Smart puts it, feminists have identified romantic love as an aspect of 'patriarchy's ideological armament through which women became hooked into dependent relationships with men, enter into an unfavorable legal contract (namely marriage) and ultimately end up with care of the children' (2007: 60). Here Smart points to one of the central underpinnings of the feminist critiques. Romantic love is not itself oppressive but it becomes so via marriage, procreation and family. In turn, romantic love ties women to the private sphere and also reduces them to being guardians of sentiments and privacy. It is true that this embodies some power but it is a hidden power that not only creates inequality but also masks it (Pulcini 2000: 41–42).

Romantic love must also be understood within the wider context of economics and of care. Ann Ferguson (2010, 2014, this volume) has analyzed romantic love as part of capitalism's affective economy. The affective economy is where romantic love and care are exchanged and where women (as well as other groups arranged by race, ethnicity and nationality) are exploited. This exploitation is possible because work that occurs in this economy is undervalued economically, and therefore confers less status on the workers in it. At the heart of this undervaluing is the reflection of social domination that exists at large (according to gender, race, ethnicity and nationalism) as well as the fundamental fact that the values which derive from the affective economy are in conflict with the values of capitalism itself (the affective economy values goodness over profit and self-interest). Men in general, are the winners from this because they get all of the benefits from the affective economy as well as all of the benefits and status that capitalism confers on labor which occurs in the economic market place.

Anna Jónasdóttir (1994, this volume) says we must analyze people's love power, in a way analogous to the analysis of a worker's labor power. When we do, this analysis reveals that men are able to exploit women's love power in exactly the same way that a capitalist exploits labor. Jónasdóttir defines love power as people's erotic and caring functions and abilities. This love power is essential in understanding modern gender relations because increasingly, as economic, social and cultural ties between people become less dominant, love power remains the bond which keeps people together. Unfortunately, however, it is a site of exploitation. This is so because women do not control the 'conditions' and the 'products' of love (1994: 224).

Eva Illouz in her latest book, *Why Love Hurts* (2012), adds to this insight when she examines the problems of romantic love as they occur in our social structures. The problems and miseries of romantic love, she argues, stem from the 'institutional arrangements' around it. Love is played out in 'the market-place of unequal competing actors' where some people, mostly men, are able to 'command a greater capacity to define the terms in which they are loved by others' (2012: 6). Control is exercised by the ways in which choice, freedom, autonomy, and commitment are differently played out between men and women. Within all of these structures, Illouz argues, there is a mismatch of goals and expectations, and 'a set of conundrums' (2012: 241–244). For example in relation to commitment men are less likely to want marriage and a family because these are no longer sites of control and domination; men now measure success not according to a successful commitment, but rather, success on the sexual market. As such, men wish to remain uncommitted for as long as possible. Women on the other hand, see the sexual market as a marriage market and are in it for a shorter period of time because of career goals, and because of the prevalence of the categories of sexiness and beauty closely tied to age.

In these above critiques, love's problems are embedded in the political, economic and social context in which it is practiced – thus we should understand the ideas and practices of love as interacting with the ideas of capitalism, the affective economy, the philosophy and practices of caring, love power, the division between the private and the public, the institution of marriage, the markets of sexual intercourse and marriage, patriarchy, gender stereotypes, and traditional family structures. To some extent this could look like letting romantic love itself off the hook. However, some feminists' critiques have focused on romantic love's internal ideology itself and have found it to be problematic.

While acknowledging the power of patriarchy and the division of spheres as problematic, Marilyn Friedman considers the central problem of romantic love to stem from its long association with the idea of merger.[9] Friedman argues that the features of merger experienced within romantic love are that: the needs and interests of each person become entwined or pooled together;

couples feel each other's highs and lows; there is mutual consideration and awareness; couples care for and protect each other; couples can communicate with each other efficiently; couples make joint decisions and long term plans; there is a division of labor; couples desire to be seen as good by each other, and want to be valued by their partners in a way that they value themselves (1998: 167–168). Friedman does not necessarily see these features as negative in themselves, but they can represent a significant reduction in personal autonomy, and this is more dangerous for women than for men for a number of reasons (Illouz's point also). First, she argues that romantic love, when seen in a social context, 'is guided by norms and stereotypes. Foremost among these are gender norms and ideals of heterosexual love'. One such ideal, for example, is that women should marry 'up'; that a woman should marry someone who is 'taller, stronger, older, richer, smarter and higher up on the social scale' (Friedman 1998: 173) than she is. The result of this is that women will always be seen as bringing less to the relationship than the men, and it is this, Friedman claims, which makes the romantic merger of identities riskier for women than for men (1998: 178). But even overall she argues that the concept of merger is risky. She argues:

> Lovers may be very different from each other in their resources, capacities, and commitments they bring to their love. These differences can create imbalances of power, authority, and status within a romantic relationship. When two lovers become one, the one they become may very well be more than the other. Or the merger might take place within one lover alone, so to speak

> (Friedman 1998: 169)

Wendy Langford sees love's ideology as inherently unethical. Romantic love is not the great ideal that it is claimed to be. She argues that while the idea that romantic love has spread principles of justice and fairness widely is an attractive and optimistic view, it is empirically unsustainable, and conceptually misguided. In fact she, along with others (cf. Jamieson 1993), is a very strong critic of romantic love as the embodiment of freedom and democracy (Anthony Giddens' thesis). Langford says that while our society has come to 'venerate deliverance' through romantic love, with promises of 'liberty, equality and togetherness', in fact romantic love is a 'process by which restrictions, inequality and dissatisfaction are merely obscured' (1999: 21). She argues that the rhetoric that romantic love takes us higher and allows us to develop is wrong. She says that '[l]ove does not merely fail to give us what we desire but in so doing compounds painful feelings of dissatisfaction and low self-esteem'. Its effects are not positive, not even neutral, they are largely negative (1999: 50). While love promises happiness and freedom from social constraint, it in fact delivers the opposite (1999: 4). Echoing some of what Friedman argues, the problem is, according to Langford, that the success of romantic love depends upon a particular abstract individual type and model of rational behavior that is seldom found in reality. The individual required is 'self-aware and operates on the basis of reason'. Not only is this individual rarely found in society at large, she is rarely found among women, and even more rarely found in the context of love (1999: 152).

Echoing this, Mary Evans argues that 'accumulated evidence of the last centuries suggest that people in the West have suffered more in their personal lives from "love" than any other single ideology'. Evans links romantic love with rape and violence against women, claiming that those 'cultures which condone romance are also beset with the misreadings' of it (1998: 273).[10]

These critiques above identify a number of internal problems: the idea of merging and of romantic love's lack of ethics. Taken together with the external factors identified earlier in this chapter, romantic love appears only fit for the scrap heap of history. But this would be to ignore another side to the feminist view of romantic love, because alongside this critique exists an equally strong defense of it. This defense dismisses romance as a site of women's oppression and complicity in patriarchal structures and instead sees romantic love as a site of resistance, transformation and agency. Lynne Pearce and Jackie Stacey (1995), like Janice Radway (1991) before them, argue that romantic love is able to liberate women from patriarchy because of its 'narrativity'. They argue that an engagement with the narrative of romance enables women to facilitate the 'rescripting of other areas of life'. Clare Langhamer has also shown how in everyday courtship behavior, young women in twentieth-century Britain have been able to act as 'architects of their own lives and as active agents of social change' (2007: 196).

The idea that romantic love is capable of achieving these progressive goals is recognized even among some of its strongest critics. For example, despite her critique, Illouz remains committed to romantic love as a central idea of modernity, she champions its egalitarian optimism and its ability to subvert patriarchy. We must not forget she says, that the dominance of romantic love has directly correlated with a decline in men's power over women, and with an increase in equality between men and women (2012: 5). Furthermore, she argues that it is capable of delivering its promises when it is practiced within the ideas of equality, freedom, self-satisfaction and when it embodies gender-blind display of care and autonomy (2012: 239). This point is also made by Jónasdóttir, who says that love power can be an agent for change that is positive and liberating (1994: 221–223; 2011; 2014). Langford says it is neither possible nor desirable to return to a time when personal relationships were not seen within the paradigm of romantic love. 'No remedy', she argues, 'is to be found in a reactive return to the regulation of romantic love along traditional lines. Justice and humanity cannot thrive through the imposition of a repressive moral order and the institutionalization of oppressive practices' (1999: 151). More than this, some feminist scholarship has specifically attempted to reconcile the negative and positive aspects of romantic love within a feminist framework (Gunnarsson 2011, 2014, this volume).

Many feminists do not want to do away with romantic love as a central idea in society but they do want to see some modifications in its ideology. In general terms, looking at the feminist critiques, we can say that romantic love should be clearly distinguished from marriage and from sexual intercourse. These ruptures will disconnect romantic love from patriarchy, procreation, family and domesticity. In this goal feminists may draw some lessons from queer theory, whose call to broaden the idea of romantic love promises fulfilment of some of this agenda. Queer theorists have argued that romantic love is steeped in heterosexual scripts and always relegates 'other' romantic love to either sex or friendship. However, just as there are positive feminist readings of romantic love, so too are there positive queer readings of romantic love. For example, Lauren Berlant argues that romantic love is ultimately a site of optimism, change and transformation: 'love approximates a space to which people can return, becoming as different as they can be from themselves without being traumatically shattered; it is a scene of optimism for change, for transformational environment' (2000: 448). Paul Johnson claims that 'whilst romantic love may create the hell of mutual alienation it also retains its primacy as an anti-alienating potential because it offers a way of expressing forms of pleasurable subjective transformation' (2005: 83). To be able to achieve this, however, romantic love must be seen as connected to rather than disconnected from agency, as being connected to but not subordinate to desire, and importantly, to be seen as something that exists outside of the heterosexual scripts. Berlant says that when queer thought enters the discourse of romantic love it must not teach 'that we are all alike and compelled to repeat our alikeness intelligibly, but by teaching some of what we've learned about love, under the surface, across the lines, around the scenes, informally' (2000: 448). Queering romantic love, for Berlant, is achieved when it lives up to its promises of existing outside of established institutions, when it challenges all rules connected with it which presume to establish principles for living (2000: 448). In other words such queering is achieved when love lives up to its radical rhetoric and delivers what it promises, that is, intimate relationships that are free of oppressive and traditional forms, and which reject established rules and barriers.

But broadening the sites of romantic love is not enough. Illouz, for example, argues that 'ethics is urgently demanded back into sexual and emotional relations' (2012: 247). More precisely she argues that romantic love must be compatible with commitment and with duties to others, and it must be built around the social experience of women as well as men. Illouz here is particularly focusing on romantic love as experienced through the market of sexual encounters where, as discussed earlier, she sees a great inequality between men and women. She says: 'When detached from ethical conduct, sexuality as we have known it for the last thirty years has become an arena of raw struggle that has left many men and especially women bitter and exhausted' (2012: 247).[11]

When considering the feminists' critique of romantic love in its entirety we can see that it is more complex than initially stated. Feminists have been critical of romantic love particularly when seen in the context of marriage and sexual 'markets', but empirically as well as theoretically feminists are not willing to 'check out' of romantic love (Illouz 2012: 246) and want instead to reorganize it or redefine it. In this project the same-sex marriage debate may be useful.

Feminism, romantic love, and same-sex marriage

In determining the significance and impact of romantic love on the same-sex marriage debate we need to acknowledge the feminist critique of romantic love and its two sides. On the one hand feminists have trashed romantic love. They have associated it with, and possibly have overstated its connections with marriage, sexual exploitation, patriarchy, heterosexuality, procreation, and the exploitation of women's labor and sexuality. When considering romantic love through this lens then its use in the same-sex marriage debate understandably sets off alarm bells. Using this conception of romantic love in the debate erases any radical/subversive element that same-sex marriage might bring to the institution of marriage. This is further strengthened by the fact that marriage, leaving aside whether it is heterosexual or same-sex, is an institution with conservative and oppressive meanings rusted on to it.

However, if we take the other reading of romantic love that feminists have identified, namely the reading that centralizes equality, autonomy and the realization of self-satisfaction, the reading that has the potential to subvert patriarchy by being an avenue through which women rescript their lives, then its use in the same-sex marriage debate is neither surprising nor problematic. This view of romantic love supports and even reinforces the radical nature of same-sex marriage and in turn the radical impact it can have on the institution of marriage.

Above I have asked what romantic love does for the meaning of same-sex marriage. It is also helpful to reverse the question and ask what the same-sex marriage debate does for the meaning of romantic love. Again we must acknowledge that same-sex marriage can be understood in different ways. Linking back to the earlier discussion on the opposition to same-sex marriage within queer and feminist ideas, same-sex marriage can be seen as an unwelcome shifting of a radical sexual culture towards traditional and conservative ideas. If this is what the legal recognition of same-sex marriage constitutes, then romantic love's radical and subversive nature is diminished if not lost altogether.

However, the same-sex marriage debate, as it has been argued by the parliamentarians who support it and by the activists who are fighting for it, represents a shattering of traditional marriage, a rupturing away of it from the traditions which have dominated it for centuries. This reading of same-sex marriage relies upon, champions, and entrenches romantic love as a radical and subversive force. If we see both romantic love and same-sex marriage in their radical guise then the project of radical romantic love is kept alive.

Feminists (and queer theorists) are right to say that accepting marriage into their political frameworks can be read as a watering down of the radical nature of their romantic love, but equally it can be argued that it will have the opposite effect. The recognition that romantic love can be played out in different kinds of relationships based on new scripts, is central to the break-down of patriarchy and the heteronormativity of romantic love and central to a positive reading of romantic love.

Recognition of same-sex marriage does not have to be a recognition of the oppressive and heteronormative romantic love that feminists and queer theorists have warned us against, but rather it can be the recognition of the radical and optimistic romantic love that can break down barriers of culture, religion, class and sexuality – an approach that values a romantic love that creates equality. On this reading, same-sex marriage will expand romantic love beyond the narrow heterosexual model that it now is, and progress us along the road to making romantic love even more radical than we now think it is.

It might be that this is too much of an optimistic view and one that ignores real concerns that have been expressed around the negative impact of the use of romantic love in the debate. Eleanor Wilkinson, for example, has questioned whether the same-sex marriage campaign is anything more than a 'narrow personal politics which fails to move beyond an individual's right to love' (2010a: 50). And even further than this she correctly points out that romantic love has been employed by conservative and neoliberal agendas to hinder rather than foster transformative change (2014: 241).[12] Historically too we have examples to make us wary. As Jyl Josephson points out, anyone who argues that same-sex marriage will deliver equality to LGBTQI people is 'inattentive to history' – one need only to consider women and gender roles to see that the institution is not that easily transformed (2010: 130). And Katherine Franke's comparison of the campaign for gay marriage with the campaign for the right to marry for African-Americans following their emancipation as slaves leads her to worry that it might have some of the same outcomes. She documents how the right to marry once granted became a weapon to 'civilize' African Americans and get them to adopt the domestic patterns of elite white Americans. She argues that, in that period, a right to marry collapsed into an obligation to do so, a negation of other relationships they once enjoyed, and a punitive approach to those who broke the rules and duties of marriage (Franke 2012). This point is also made by Slavin (2009) and Ryan (2014). Furthermore, as Ferguson (2007) points out, marriage alone cannot supply the equality many want from it, if all other sites of inequality and exploitation remain unchallenged and unchanged, particularly if women's labor in the market and affective economy continues to be exploited. These are real concerns that I share and that should be voiced loud and clear in the hope that they will steer our thinking of romantic love away from conservative agendas and toward the more radical ones.

Conclusion

While the same-sex marriage debate has included some of the feminist critiques of marriage, it has largely ignored the feminist critique of romantic love itself. It is important to foreground this critique. Romantic love has been used as the argumentative tool in the fight for the legal recognition for same-sex marriage. In fact, arguments in support of material benefits and protections, human rights and justice, and status and equality, have become less prominent as the debate has narrowed around the issue of the meaning of marriage, and whether it is, or should be, about procreation or about romantic love. When proponents of same-sex marriage argue that it is about romantic love, the idea of romantic love which informs them is the radical, subversive romantic love, the one that can break down barriers of class, social standing, race, religion, ethnicity, and ultimately sex and sexuality.

Feminists have disputed this view of romantic love and have highlighted romantic love's oppressive and conservative potential. This strong critique must, however, be read in the light of the fact that few feminists wish to do away with romantic love completely. My discussion of the feminist critique of romantic love has shown a more nuanced critique than is often presented. Feminists are both critical and idealist when it comes to romantic love. This dual position is also evident in the queer critique of romantic love. When considered in the contexts of patriarchy, the public and private divide, and the institutions of marriage and family, romantic love is seen as reinforcing women's disadvantage. Furthermore, romantic love's association with nature, merger, and unification enhance its discriminatory potential (see Grossi 2012). Romantic love as practiced is also seen as lacking in ethics and therefore unable to deliver its promise of an egalitarian society. But romantic love is also associated with an ability to subvert patriarchy, with a re-scripting of lives, and with an ability to create real autonomy, freedom and equality. Accepting this more complex reading of romantic love has interesting consequences for its association with the fight for the legal recognition of same-sex marriage. The same-sex marriage debate has equally complex readings. It can either be seen as a co-opting of what has been a radical sexual culture into its traditional net, or alternatively as a radicalization of a traditional institution. While there is room for pessimism, (romantic love has been used as a tool in conservative social discourses), the way that romantic love has been employed in the debate reflects the radical and subversive reading of it, and this should be lauded and applauded.

Notes

1 Here after Langford (1999: v).
2 In this article I am discussing romantic love only. At times, for stylistic reasons, I use the term love by itself but I am always only discussing romantic love.
3 The same-sex marriage debate has been a central issue in many countries for a number of decades. Same-sex marriage is currently (January 2018) legal in 25 countries. Many other countries recognize civil unions only. To review the way in which the debate has been carried out in many jurisdictions, see Sáez (2015).
4 This is possible under Australia's constitutional arrangement that allows the federal government to disallow legislation passed in its two territories, the Australian Capital Territory and the Northern Territory.

5 The bill also facilitates the creation of civil partnership notaries and the recognition of civil partnerships made in other jurisdictions. It avoids the issue of mimicking marriage by being for the exclusive use of same-sex couples.
6 See for example Millbank (2006), who argues against same-sex marriage from a feminist and queer perspective on the grounds that equality can be achieved without it.
7 Lesbian, gay, bi-sexual, transsexual, queer, and intersex.
8 Even more than this, romantic love, along with romanticism in general, is seen as containing within it a deathly streak because it portrays true love as something that must be not only indifferent to, but even welcoming to death. A preoccupation with death was, indeed a recurrent feature of romantic thought (West 2005: 112).
9 Aristophanes' myth in Plato's symposium and followed by courtly and romantic love make the idea of unification between two bodies and souls central to its understandings and workings.
10 Another similar and strong polemic against love can be found in Kipnis (2003).
11 In this project it may be, as Simon May (2011) hints, that some answer lays in a more Aristotelian concept of love, one that links love to mutual goodness and flourishing. While Aristotle's focus is on friendship love, there is no reason why some of his principles cannot be encompassed in an erotic love context.
12 See also Wilkinson's (2010b) concerns over Negri's ideas of love as a political concept.

References

Ackelsberg, Martha (2010) 'Whatever Happened to Feminist Critiques of Marriage?' *Politics and Gender*, 6: 119–120.

Alderson, Kevin and Kathleen Lahey (2004) *Same-Sex Marriage: The Personal and the Political*. Canada: Insomniac Press.

Alexander, Cathy (2007) 'Corbell to Revive Gay Union Act', *Canberra Times*, 30 November.

Australian Capital Territory, Parliamentary Debates Legislative Assembly, 28 March 2006, 655–659 (Jon Stanhope). Available: www.hansard.act.gov.au/start.htm (accessed 12 May 2008).

Australian Capital Territory, Parliamentary Debates Legislative Assembly, 11 May 2006, 1596–1651 (Andrew Barr). www.hansard.act.gov.au/start.htm (accessed 12 May 2008).

Australian Capital Territory, Parliamentary Debates Legislative Assembly, 12 December 2006, 3953–3956 (Bill Stephaniak). Available: www.hansard.act.gov.au/start.htm (accessed 12 May 2008).

Bandt, Adam (2010) '"Power of Love" Driving Gay Marriage Debate,' *ABC News*, 16 November. Available: www.abc.net.au/news/stories/2010/11/15/3067122.htm (accessed 18 November 2010).

Beck, Ulrich and Elizabeth Beck-Gernsheim (1995) *The Normal Chaos of Love*, trans. M. Ritter and J. Wiebel. Cambridge: Polity Press.

Berlant, Lauren (2000) 'Love (a Queer Feeling)', in T. Dean and C. Lane (eds) *Psychoanalysis and Homosexuality*. Chicago, IL: Chicago University Press.

Bernstein, Anita (2006) 'Questioning Marriage', in A. Bernstein (ed.) *Marriage Proposals: Questioning a Legal Status*. New York: New York University Press.

Brake, Elizabeth (2012) *Minimizing Marriage: Marriage Morality and the Law*. New York: Oxford University Press.

Butler, Judith (2002) 'Is Kinship Always Already Heterosexual?' *Differences*, 13(1): 14–44.

Commonwealth, Parliamentary Debates House of Representatives, 27 May 2004 (Arch Bevis). Available: http://parlinfoweb.aph.gov.au/piweb/view_document.aspx? ID=2259205 (accessed 13 May 2008).

Commonwealth, Parliamentary Debates House of Representatives, 27 May 2004 (Phillip Ruddock). Available: http://parlinfoweb.aph.gov.au/piweb/view_document. aspx?ID=2259205 (accessed 14 April 2008).

Commonwealth, Parliamentary Debates Senate, 17 June 2004 (Guy Barnett). Available: http://parlinfoweb.aph.gov.au/piweb/view_document.aspx?ID=2014889 (accessed 15 May 2008).

Commonwealth, Parliamentary Debates Senate, 15 June2006 (Bob Brown). Available: http://parlinfoweb.aph.gov.au/piweb/view_document.aspx?ID=2345425 (accessed 13 May 2008).

Commonwealth, Parliamentary Debates Senate, 15 June2006 (Christine Milne). Available: http://parlinfoweb.aph.gov.au/piweb/view_document.aspx?ID=2345449 (accessed 13 May 2008).

Commonwealth, Parliamentary Debates Senate, 15 June2006 (Kerry Nettle). Available: http://parlinfoweb.aph.gov.au/piweb/view_document.aspx?ID=2345413 (accessed 13 May 2008).

de Beauvoir, Simone (1953) *The Second Sex*, trans. H. M. Parshley. New York: Alfred A. Knopf.

Evans, Mary (1998) 'Falling in Love Is Falling for Make Believe: Ideologies of Romance in Post-Enlightenment Culture', *Theory, Culture and Society*, 15: 265–276.

Evans, Mary (2003) *Love: An Unromantic Discussion*. Cambridge: Polity Press.

Ferguson, Ann (2007) 'Gay Marriage: An American Feminist Dilemma', *Hypatia*, 22: 39–57.

Ferguson, Ann (2010) 'Love, Caring Labour and Community: Issues for Solidarity and Radical Change', in S. Strid and A. G. Jónasdóttir (eds) *GEXcel Work in Progress Report, vol. VIII*. Linköping and Örebro, Sweden: GEXcel.

Ferguson, Ann (2014a) 'Love Solidarity and a Politics of Love', in S. Strid and A. G. Jónasdóttir (eds) *GEXcel Work in Progress Report, vol. IX*. Linköping and Örebro, Sweden: GEXcel.

Ferguson, Ann (2014b) 'Feminist Love Politics: Romance, Care, and Solidarity', in A. G. Jónasdóttir and A. Ferguson (eds) *Love: A Question for Feminism in the Twenty-first Century*. New York: Routledge.

Fineman, Martha Albertson (1995) *The Neutered Mother, the Sexual Family, and other Twentieth Century Tragedies*. New York: Routledge.

Firestone, Shulamith (1970) *The Dialectic of Sex: The Case for Feminist Revolution*. New York: Bantam Books.

Franke, Katherine (2012) 'The Curious Relationship of Marriage and Freedom', in M. Garrison and E. Scott (eds) *Marriage at the Crossroads*. Cambridge: Cambridge University Press.

Friedman, Marilyn (1998) 'Romantic Love and Personal Autonomy', in P. French and H. K. Wettstein (eds) *Midwest Studies in Philosophy, XXII (1998): The Philosophy of Emotion*. Notre Dame, IN: University of Notre Dame Press.

Friedman, Marilyn (2003) *Autonomy, Gender, Politics*. New York: Oxford University Press.

Giddens, Anthony (1992) *The Transformation of Intimacy: Sexuality Love and Eroticism in Modern Societies*. Cambridge: Polity Press.

Graycar, Regina and Jenny Millbank (2007) 'From Functional Family to Spinster Sisters: Australia's Distinctive Path to Relationship Recognition', *Journal of Law and Policy*, 24: 160–161.

Grossi, Renata (2012) 'The Meaning of Love in the Debate for Legal Recognition of Same-Sex Marriage in Australia', *International Journal of Law in Context*, 8: 487–505.

Gunnarsson, Lena (2011) 'Love – Exploitable Resource or "No-Lose Situation"? Reconciling Jónasdóttir's Feminist View with Bhaskar's Philosophy of Meta-Reality', *Journal of Critical Realism*, 10(4): 419–441.

Gunnarsson, Lena (2014) *The Contradictions of Love: Towards a Feminist-Realist Ontology of Sociosexuality*. London and New York: Routledge.

Illouz, Eva (2012) *Why Love Hurts: A Sociological Explanation*. Cambridge: Polity.

Jamieson, Lynn (1993) 'Intimacy Transformed? A Critical Look at the Pure Relationship', *Sociology*, 33: 477–494.

Jeffreys, Sheila (2004) 'The Need to Abolish Marriage', *Feminism and Psychology*, 14 (2): 327–331.

Johnson, Paul (2005) *Love, Heterosexuality and Society*. London: Routledge.

Jónasdóttir, Anna G. (1994) *Why Women Are Oppressed*. Philadelphia, PA: Temple University Press.

Jónasdóttir, Anna G. (2011) 'What Kind of Power Is "Love Power"?' in A. G. Jónasdóttir, V. Bryson, and K. B. Jones (eds) *Sexuality, Gender and Power: Intersectional and Transnational Perspectives*. New York: Routledge.

Jónasdóttir, Anna G. (2014) 'Love Studies: A (Re)New(ed) Field of Knowledge Interests', in A. G. Jónasdóttir and A. Ferguson (eds) *Love: A Question for Feminism in the Twenty-first Century*. New York: Routledge.

Josephson, Jyl (2010) 'Romantic Weddings, Diverse Families', *Politics and Gender* 6 (1): 128–133.

Kipnis, Laura (2003) *Against Love: A Polemic*. New York: Pantheon Books.

Langford, Wendy (1999) *Revolutions of the Heart: Gender, Power and the Delusions of Love*. London: Routledge.

Langhamer, Clare (2007) 'Love and Courtship in Mid-twentieth-century England', *The Historical Journal*, 50(1): 173–196.

May, Simon (2011) *Love: A History*. London: Yale University Press.

Metz, Tamara (2010) 'Demands of Care and Dilemmas of Freedom: What We Really Ought to Be Worried About', *Politics and Gender*, 6(1): 121–122.

Millbank, Jenni (2006) 'Recognition of Lesbian and Gay Families in Australian Law – Part One: Couples', *Federal Law Review*, 34: 1–44.

Peake, Ross (2008) 'Angry Corbell Abandons Gay Plan', *Canberra Times*, 5 May.

Pearce, Lynne, and Jackie Stacey (eds) (1995) *Romance Revisited*. London: Lawrence & Wishart.

Pulcini, Elena (2000) 'Modernity Love and Hidden Inequality', trans L. Fraser, in Y. Kravaritou, P. Fitzpatrick, E. Pulcini, J. L. Schroeder, N. Lacey, T. Pitch, M. Virgilio and L. Ferrajoli (eds) *Love and Law in Europe: Complex Interrelations*. EUI Working Paper 2000/2, European University Institute.

Radway, Janice (1991) *Reading the Romance: Women, Patriarchy and Popular Literature*. Chapel Hill: University of North Carolina Press.

Ruddock, Phillip (2007) 'LP MP Attorney General: "ACT Civil Partnerships Bill Does Not Remove Concerns"', press release, 6 February.

Ryan, Hugh (2014) 'We Didn't Queer the Institution of Marriage. It Straightened Us', *Guardian*, 29 June. Available: www.theguardian.com/commentisfree/2014/jun/29/same-sex-marriage-straightened (accessed 30 June 2014).

Sáez, Macarena (ed.) (2015) *Same-Sex Couples: Comparative Insights on Marriage and Cohabitation*. Dordrecht: Springer.

Slavin, Sean (2009) '"Instinctively, I'm Not Just a Sexual Beast:" The Complexity of Intimacy Among Australian Gay Men', *Sexualities*, 12(1): 79–96.

Smart, Carol (2007) *Personal Life*. Cambridge: Polity Press.

Solomon, Robert C. (1994) *About Love: Reinventing Romance for Our Times*. Lanham, MD: Rowman & Littlefield.

Solomon, Robert C. (1998) 'Love and Feminism', in R. Baker, K. J. Winniger and F. A. Elliston (eds) *Philosophy and Sex*. 3rd edn. New York: Prometheus Books.

West, David (2005) *Reason and Sexuality in Western Thought*. Cambridge: Polity Press.

Wilkinson, Eleanor (2010a) 'Equalise Love! Intimate Citizenship Beyond Marriage', in S. Strid and A. G. Jónasdóttir (eds) *GEXcel Work in Progress Report, vol. VIII*. Linköping and Örebro, Sweden: GEXcel.

Wilkinson, Eleanor (2010b) 'Revolutionize Love? A Queer-Feminist Critique of Love as a Political Concept', in S. Strid and A. G. Jónasdóttir (eds) *GEXcel Work in Progress Report, vol. IX*. Linköping and Örebro, Sweden: GEXcel.

Wilkinson, Eleanor (2014) 'A Feminist Critique of Love as a Political Concept', in A. G. Jónasdóttir and A. Ferguson (eds) *Love: A Question for Feminism in the Twenty-First Century*. New York: Routledge.

Wilcox, W. B. and Jeffrey Dew (2010) 'Is Love a Flimsy Foundation? Soulmate Versus Institutional Models of Marriage', *Social Science Research*, 39: 687–699.

Wise, Sue and Liz Stanley (2004) 'Beyond Marriage: "The Less Said about Love and Life-Long Continuance Together the Better"', *Feminism and Psychology*, 14(2): 332–343.

Part II

Love and affect

5 Love as affective energy

Where feminist love studies meets feminist affect theory

Margaret E. Toye

'Feminist love studies' and 'feminist affect theory' describe two distinct, emerging interdisciplinary bodies of feminist research that have largely developed along parallel trajectories. As in any case where discrete fields of study are proclaimed, disagreements as to their exact boundaries as well as questions about the need to identify autonomous fields in the first place are central components of the conversation. I employ these terms in this chapter not to exclude nor to police definitions, but rather to highlight significant contemporary dialogues within feminist theory about these subjects in order to foreground their importance and to examine how they are (and are not) being discussed. My main argument is that in certain corners of feminist theory, significant intensive conversations are reconsidering the topic of love, while in other corners, largely separate concentrated discussions are rethinking affect and emotion in general terms as well as in terms of specific affects and emotions. Some of these latter studies include discussions of 'love', but it has not received the attention other discrete emotions have, and not, I contend, in enough of a reconsidered way. It is my observation that these two sets of conversations – a feminist rethinking of love, and a feminist rethinking of affect and emotion[1] – have mostly developed independently of one another. One of my aims in this chapter, as a researcher with feet in both worlds, is, therefore, to argue that a more committed dialogue between these two 'fields' is timely; the resulting conversations promise exciting and new theories of the phenomenon called love that would be beneficial to scholars in both areas, and feminist theory generally.[2]

This chapter is organized in two sections. The first provides brief overviews of both feminist love studies and feminist affect theory as recent separate studies that have emerged; it contemplates what disciplinary or discursive obstacles might be preventing alliances between them; and it offers some possible points for future dialogue. The second section focuses on one point of intersection in particular: love conceived as an 'affective energy'. Because 'affective energy' is a concept that some theorists in both fields share, I suggest that it could offer a possible basis for a productive dialogue between these two fields; by examining the contributions of three theorists in and across these fields, I lay the groundwork for such a dialogue.

Feminist love studies meets feminist affect theory

Feminist love studies

'Feminist love studies' is a new term that overlaps with, and distinguishes itself from, the previously newly claimed area of 'love studies'. This volume, together with the special issue of *Hypatia*, 'Feminist Love Studies' (Ferguson and Toye 2017), are the first publications to claim the term 'feminist love studies' as a recognizable area of thought, and in so doing join the earlier volume *Love: A Question for Feminism in the Twenty-first Century* (Jónas-dóttir and Ferguson 2014b) and the conference and conference proceedings (Strid and Jónasdóttir 2011) from which it emerged, which did not explicitly use this term but foregrounded love studies from feminist perspectives. In *Love*, Jónasdóttir and Ferguson call for the recognition of 'love studies' and its importance for feminism. Love studies, as they explain, is a 'new, expanding field of academic scholarship' that has been growing since the 1990s and which is observable across many disciplines and fields.[3] Love is increasingly being considered a serious area of study on its own terms, and while it continues to examine negative aspects of love, it is significant for its focus on its productive, or positive, possibilities (2014a: 2). The editors' dual aim is 'to interject a stronger feminist presence into studies on love' and provide 'an intervention into the direction of feminist theory as well' (1).

As the preface of our volume indicates, the founding members of our network – Anna Jónasdóttir, Ann Ferguson, Kathy Jones, Lena Gunnarsson, Silvia Stoller, Adriana García-Andrade, Renata Grossi, Eudine Barriteau and myself – felt that coining the more specific area of 'feminist love studies' was timely. On the one hand, a distinctly *'feminist* love studies' questions the continual tendency within both traditional examinations of love and this new turn to contemporary 'love studies' to build on and take as the norm patriarchal and heterosexist assumptions; *feminist* love studies stresses the importance of developing other models, while also illuminating the importance of feminist contributors within past and present examinations. On the other hand, a distinct 'feminist *love* studies' calls the feminist community's attention to the growing area of 'love studies', including its focus on the productive aspects of love, which differs from feminist theory's tendency to focus on criticizing patriarchal concepts of love; it also allows for the retrospective claiming of the considerable historical feminist work in this area that is often not known and serves as a rallying point for more feminists to engage in these dialogues.

All identity projects, which include establishing discrete areas of study, involve the drawing of borders and boundaries that both include and, inevitably, exclude; further, all creation stories engage in what Clare Hemmings calls 'feminist storytelling' (2011) and are anything but neutral. According to one of the central tenets of feminist methodology, it is important to be self-reflexive about our storytelling and our practices of drawing borders and boundaries. One of the stories that the Feminist Love Studies Network tells about 'feminist love studies' is that it situates itself as an interdisciplinary endeavor (see Jónasdóttir and Ferguson 2014a and Chapter 1 in this volume) and that it names both the work of those of us who are explicitly naming ourselves as the Feminist Love Studies Network and work that has been exploring similar questions alongside of us. Approaches include but are not limited to: philosophy – both analytic and continental – sociology, literary studies, political science, social justice studies, women's and gender studies, and various interdisciplinary studies, informed by phenomenology, poststructuralism, critical realism, critical race studies, postcolonial studies, as well as many other perspectives. From the beginning, our network has attempted to be as open as possible to a wide range of approaches and to be aware of our limits as we want to create opportunities for a range of contributions while being aware of what we might be excluding. There are a few observations regarding the kinds of love that tend to be privileged, the historical figures featured, and disciplinary/theoretical perspectives that dominate that are worth noting at this point.

In spite of the network's stated desire to consider many different kinds of love, 'romantic love', especially 'couple love', and more specifically, 'heterosexual couple love' remains the main focus of feminist love studies' examinations of love; the subject and object of love are also presumed to be human. Feminist work such as Christian Klesse's on polyamory (2014) (see also Sempruch, this volume), Kathy Rudy's on loving animals (2011), and Kelly Oliver's on love of the earth (2015), as well as studies that focus on feminist theories of friendship, compassion and other kinds of love, will be important for feminist love studies to consider as it develops. Further, while our network is very much aware that critical race and postcolonial studies need to be more central to its investigations, many of our historical stories continue to foreground figures like Simone de Beauvoir and Shulamith Firestone for their criticism of patriarchal love, and Luce Irigaray, and increasingly Hannah Arendt, for their important work on rethinking love. However, scholars including Eudine Barriteau (2012) and Dawn Rae Davis (2002) point to the important historical work of black feminists, including Audre Lorde, bell hooks and Chela Sandoval, who were critically and creatively thinking about love well before the more general 'turn to love', as they also develop and foreground contemporary scholarship on feminist love studies rooted in critical race and postcolonial questions.

My own contributions/limitations are informed by my background in feminist poststructuralist theory and literary studies; my work on feminist love studies has concentrated on a theory/methodology that I have termed a 'poethics of love' (2010). This theory/method describes a writing method employed by some feminist poststructuralist theorists and feminist postmodern creative writers when they take up the subject love, and a reading strategy that I suggest we employ in relation to these texts, as it can help us to understand the theoretical complexity of these writers' contributions, which examine love as a phenomenon that needs to be addressed simultaneously as political, ethical, aesthetic, and embodied.

From these disciplinary and theoretical perspectives, two more aspects within feminist love studies, as it has so far emerged, seem significant. First, across the many disciplines and schools, there has been a predominance of socialist and materialist feminist voices among its contributors. This situation is not surprising, given that Marxist discourses have tended to approach love as an opiate of the (especially feminine) masses (Toye 2010) and, therefore, it makes sense that a strong call for a change in critical attitude should come from this same place, especially from sociologists and others who are rooted in a tradition of Marxist critique; the work of Anna Jónasdóttir (1994), whose early theories of 'love power' as theorized in response to Marx's theory of production therefore plays such a significant role in this turn. Second, there is both a relative absence of, as well as a sometimes opposition to,[4] feminist poststructuralist, postmodernist and/or posthumanist feminist approaches. I want to argue for the importance of what the latter approaches bring to feminist love studies, consider briefly why the stories told from these perspectives might conflict with the predominant socialist/materialist approach, and suggest ways of creating places where more dialogue between them might occur.

A main difference seems to come down to an issue of aesthetics. Feminist 'post' approaches stress the importance of foregrounding the aesthetic dimension of love, including taking the performative and creative nature of language into account. Moreover, as I foregrounded in the neologism 'a poethics of love', feminist poststructuralism highlights how aesthetic aspects are always intertwined with politics, ethics, and embodiment. Feminist poststructuralism is, after all, not just rooted in the post-Lacanian French psychoanalysis and the post-Saussurian linguistics of Derrida, but, importantly, also in the post-Marxist theories of Michel Foucault, Louis Althusser, Jacques Derrida and Gilles Deleuze. Their theories of language are not about mere postmodern play; their aesthetics are connected to their theories of power and social change – these poststructuralist theorists were involved in social movements and their ethical, political, and aesthetic theories developed in relationship to their involvement with them. Contributions by feminists who have been rethinking love informed by feminist poststructuralist theory, such as Luce Irigaray, Julia Kristeva, Hélène Cixous, Gayatri Spivak, and others, therefore need to be included as foundational work in feminist love studies. These thinkers all rethink love from feminist perspectives, and their positions within materialist thinking as well as poststructuralism can be directly related to this work. It is thus my belief that feminist debates about the relationship between the body and discourse can be located *within* rather than *outside* of feminist materialism and that feminist materialism needs to take the aesthetic into account in general but also, crucially, within their theories of love, as it goes forward.

Rather than setting up an oppositional relationship between feminist Marxist/socialist/materialist approaches to love and feminist poststructuralist/

postmodernist/posthumanist ones, I am suggesting an emphasis on their common theoretical lens of materialist analyses with a recognition of their difference aesthetics. These emphases will be important as we move into an examination of feminist affect studies, where similar possible barriers to conversation could arise as feminist poststructuralist attention to the aesthetic becomes intensified in the work of many feminist affect theorists who, arguably, extend the former's attention to performative language and embodied discourse, just as they increase attention to the aesthetic category of 'sensation'. That some of those who are being claimed as feminist affect theorists overlap with those feminist theorists who are being identified as 'neo' or 'new materialists' is also significant. Not all are identified with both areas[5] and the differences amongst these three groups is a topic for another paper; however, the significance of materialism to all three groups is worthwhile to underline. My focused argument in this chapter is to begin a discussion around how the discourse of 'energy' could provide a common ground between feminist love studies and feminist affect studies, but there is a larger connected discussion that could be pursued with regard to how materialist concepts of energy as labor and love as labor are connected, which is a topic to which materialist feminists of all kinds could contribute.

Feminist affect studies

What Patricia Clough (2007) has dubbed 'the affective turn' describes an increasing interest in the humanities and social sciences since the late 1990s, as well as in other fields such as psychology, business, neurology, biology, cognitive and computer science, in the study of emotion and/or affect in new, reconsidered ways. Michael Hardt (2007) considers the affective turn to be both a consolidation and extension of the most productive current research trends, namely research on the body, especially by feminist theorists, and the exploration of emotions by queer theorists. The pervasive interest in theories of the body and trauma in relationship to war, terrorism and especially 9/11 are an important additional precursor to note. There are many definitions of affect, emotion, and their relationship to one another, including to the connected concepts of feeling and sensation. One of affect theory's key emphases is something that feminist theory has done for some time, namely to question western thinking's binary opposition of reason/emotion, mind/body, and male/female which it links together. While emotion has always been studied, and different disciplines all have different traditional approaches to emotion, Clough and others working within 'affect studies' argue that in the last couple of decades many disciplines are making emotion more central to their research and also asking new questions about it.

A discrete body of work that can be labeled as specifically 'feminist affect studies' has emerged, which I often qualify as 'feminist/queer affect studies' given that so many of its central theorists are rooted in queer theory. Three excellent reviews of the literature which help to define this area include

Kristyn Gorton (2007), who lists Sara Ahmed, Lauren Berlant, Teresa Brennan, Ann Cvetkovich, Sianne Ngai, Elspeth Probyn, Denise Riley, and Eve Kosofsky Sedgwick as key names; Carolyn Pedwell and Anne Whitehead (Pedwell and Whitehead 2012), who add Judith Butler, Ranjana Khanna, and Clare Hemmings to this list; and Naomi Greyser (2012), who repeats the focus on Ahmed, Ngai and Hemmings, but adds Deborah Gould and, instead of Sedgwick, focuses on Robyn Wiegman.

According to these reviews of the literature, feminist affect theory is highly self-reflexive; while many of the above writers are asking new questions about emotion, they simultaneously question the rhetorical appeals to this 'new' turn as a way to flatten out and ignore previous work, and they also consider what Ngai refers to as the 'ugly' side of feminism. These reviews are careful to highlight the ways in which this work continues long-standing work in feminist theory on women's emotions and affective labor and that while new possibilities for affect and revolution are being considered by these thinkers, they constantly caution how affect is continually used to reproduce hierarchies and question how much affect can be harnessed by a particular political aim, including by feminism. For example, while the increasing intimacy in the public sphere calls for new theories of the personal as the political, and more attention is being paid to 'everyday' feelings, these thinkers are careful to question the extent to which personal affect can have a revolutionary effect on global structures. Earlier work on transnational capital, biopolitics, and legacies of colonialism are being extended by an analysis of how power often circulates through affective relations. On the one hand, these thinkers consider the possibilities for feminism in theorizing the connection among bodies, change, solidarity, and affect, as well as on rethinking method; on the other, they foreground how feelings are often used to manage populations and question what kind of basis a focus on affect can provide scientific inquiry. These descriptions suggest that feminist affect theory shares many crucial similarities with feminist love studies, in terms of a high degree of self-reflexivity, and a sense of embedding any new claims in an important history of previous examinations.

'Schools of affect'

Critical affect studies tend to be divided into two main branches: the Silvan Tomkins/Eve Sedgwick school and the Gilles Deleuze/Brian Massumi approach (Hemmings 2005).[6] The first approach focuses on affect/emotion in terms of discrete and nameable affects/emotions (e.g. shame, happiness, anger, fear, envy), while the second tends to stress how affect escapes language and any kind of 'capture'. Using the work of writers who study 'discrete affects or emotions' would seem to be an obvious choice for love studies scholars, as love has obviously been studied for thousands of years as a discrete emotion. Hemmings, Ahmed, and Ngai, as mentioned above, are all examples of feminist theorists drawing on this tradition, as an important alterative to psychoanalysis. In my view, this approach also has affinities with the long-standing feminist method of consciousness-raising and is aligned with many feminist cultural studies approaches rooted in Marxist/Althusserian analysis of ideology. It also nicely expands upon the influential school of feminist thought informed by Foucauldian discourse analyses of power/knowledge, such as those of Judith Butler. Due to space restrictions, I will not spend time detailing this school here, but note that at present, for various reasons, this approach has not produced a concentrated feminist analysis of love,[7] although I think that it both *could* and *should* if it overcame pervasive preconceptions about this emotion.

Instead, I want to highlight the possible usefulness of the second approach. Massumi, identified as the figure who ushered in this second approach to affect, takes his inspiration from the theories of Gilles Deleuze, who offers a different critique of psychoanalysis to that of Tomkins.[8] Most of those figures identified by Gorton, Pedwell and Whitehead, and Greyser as engaging in feminist affect theory most easily fit into the first approach, but it is not as easy to identify feminists who would be aligned with the second. Jane Bennett, Erin Manning, and some of the contributors to the Gregg and Seigworth (2010) collection could be associated with this school, although many of these theorists are *informed by* feminist theories but not necessarily explicitly producing distinct 'feminist theories of affect'. A major thinker of affect informed by feminist theory, who works within this Massumi/Deleuzian tradition, is Patricia Clough and so I will draw largely on her work for articulating this school of thought.

One important way in which this Deleuzian school of thought is described is in terms of the ways it differentiates affect from emotion, namely, affect is that which is left when conscious states, including emotion, are subtracted: 'Affect constitutes a nonlinear complexity out of which the narration of conscious states such as emotion are subtracted, but always with a "never-to-be-conscious autonomic remainder"' (Clough 2007: 2). It is not just about the human body but also relates to that which is beyond this body's organic and psychological states, including technological bodies: 'The affective turn, therefore, expresses a new configuration of bodies, technology, and matter' (2). Clough explains:

> affectivity as a substrate of potential bodily responses, often autonomic responses, in excess of consciousness. For these scholars, affect refers generally to bodily capacities to affect and be affected or the augmentation or diminution of a body's capacity to act, to engage, and to connect, such that autoaffection is linked to the self-feeling of being alive – that is aliveness or vitality.

> (2007: 1–2)

However, this approach, because of the implications for ontological theories of subjectivity and political theories of agency, is not well-received by some feminists (see, for example, Kathleen Jones in this volume). Many of these concerns about these theories of affect are similar to the concerns that some feminists have raised around Deleuzian and feminist new materialist approaches more generally.[9]

Indeed, the question about the borders and boundaries of discrete areas of study starts to trouble this splitting of approaches to affect into these schools of thought, when it would seem that other Deleuzian feminists such as Rosi Braidotti (2006), Elizabeth Grosz (1994, 2008), and other new materialist feminists like Karen Barad (2007) and others (Coole and Frost 2010) are theorizing ontology, ethics and politics – including around concepts of labor, energy, production, creativity, matter, and zoë – in more similar ways than with feminists associated with the Tomkins/Sedgwick school. Further, whereas I indicated that a genealogy of feminist analysis of this first school could be traced through feminist Althusserian and Foucauldian analyses, it is worthwhile noting how many feminists currently working in relation to Deleuze's theories are also Irigarayan scholars and have offered comparisons of Deleuze's and Irigaray's work (e.g. Braidotti 2006; Grosz 1994; Lorraine 1999). What both Deleuze and Irigaray seem to offer these thinkers is a radical alternative aesthetic, that is, a way of thinking our way out of a phallogocentric capitalist economy of representation – not just criticizing it, but creating another one – and this project is exactly one of the main foci of this second school of affect theory.

I would, therefore, like to stress that this Deleuzian approach to affect with its discussions of affect/intensity/circulating energy/sensation/rhythms, that which escapes capture (of language), holds important affinities with a tradition of poststructuralist and postmodern feminist aesthetic, which attempts to create/gesture to a feminine language/symbolic through concepts such as *écriture féminine* (Cixous 1976) and the Kristevan semiotic (Kristeva 1984). It is for this reason that I believe this school could be extremely useful for feminist love studies. I am struck especially with how often the discourse of 'energy' is used to discuss affect within this school, and how 'energy' becomes a major way in which power, life, creativity, and love are linked. Contemporary new materialist and affect theorists are, of course, not the first to suggest using the discourse of 'energy' to discuss affect/emotions in general or love in particular. In many instances, these theorists are merely continuing the psychoanalytic discourse that discusses affect as 'cathected energy'. However, while psychoanalysis may discuss energy, it is a very specific kind of energy on which it focuses and its origins a very narrow one (libidinal); in contrast, this second branch of affect theory is interested in many kinds of affective energy and finds their origins in multiple locations.

My main argument in this chapter, then, is that 'affective energy', a concept that some theorists in both feminist love studies and feminist affect theory share, is one possible way of linking these two areas and provides a promising possible basis for a productive dialogue between these fields. I am not suggesting that this is the only possible basis, nor am I limiting the analysis of love solely to the concept of 'affective energy'. I am also not arguing that love is the only kind of emotion that can be described in terms of affective energy. My hope is that future studies from many different perspectives that depart from this basis could perform important analyses and help us to understand the particular qualitative affective energies that circulate and which go by the name of 'love'.

Love as an affective energy

In this section, I will foreground feminist theorists who use the discourse of energy to describe love, affect, or both. I begin by examining Lucy Goodison's contribution to feminist theories of love and romance in the 1980s in her argument for a feminist theory of love rooted in a discourse of 'energy'. I then move to Patricia Clough's contributions which intertwine Freud, Marx, and Weiner to theorize affect in terms of psychic, social and informational energy. I conclude by turning to feminist affect theorist Teresa Brennan, who contributes to both fields in her gendered theory of the transmission of affect, her theory of 'energetics', and her theorization of how gendered bodies are used as emotional 'dumping grounds'. I have chosen these particular examples in order to highlight unique contributions from three separate areas of 'study' that could benefit from being in dialogue: feminist theory, affect theory, and feminist affect theory.[10]

Lucy Goodison and love as energy

In terms of establishing a history of feminist theories of love, it is worth noting British feminist Lucy Goodison's (1983) nicely named essay, whose title is taken from a Situationist pamphlet lying on her floor, 'Really Being in Love Means Wanting to Live in a Different World'. While Goodison's work is not well-known within contemporary feminist theory, this essay, anthologized in the collection of feminist writing on love, *Women and Romance*, is notable. As Susan Ostrov Weisser comments in the introduction to the collection (2001), it importantly departs from most Anglo-American feminist considerations at that time, which tended to consider love as a harmful force in women's lives. Goodison not only theorizes love as a complicated phenomenon and one that provides for the possibility for growth and change, but she also raises questions about the relationship between love and politics as a productive alliance and, important for our discussions, suggests the usefulness of the discourse of 'energy' to discuss the phenomenon of love.

Goodison starts with the argument that discourses around falling in love make one speak in a way in which 'feelings are rendered passive' and operate within the presumption that emotions 'just happen' (1983: 158). Yet, at the same time, she calls attention to the sense of power that someone in love carries: 'we are undoubtedly the carriers of some huge power' (160), including the sense of 'the ability temporarily to transcend personal limitations and boundaries' (166). Goodison suggests that we should think about love as a physical experience and that our five senses are involved in this experience. She encourages us to become more precise about the way we describe our feelings, and that we develop the ability to compare them. Her argument is based in her desire for us to become more aware of the way we speak about these feelings and to become more literate about our emotions. She argues that we need to become more aware of the particular sensations that arise around the experience of falling in love as well as how much we only label these sensations as 'falling in love' when it is socially acceptable to do so.

Within this discussion, she turns to 'another vocabulary' that exists to try to describe the sensations that one has when in love: 'Radar, electricity. A contact which zooms, races, penetrates, undulates like radio waves' (1983: 167). For Goodison, this vocabulary defamiliarizes speaking about love in a passive way and instead is linked to everyday discourse, for example of 'good vibes' or 'being drawn' to someone. However, she also notes its similarity to 'the kind of language used by esoteric anatomy to describe the phenomena of the 'energy body' which is thought to interpenetrate and surround our physical body' (167). While such a discussion might sound a little 'new-agey', it is significant for the purposes of this chapter to foreground that Goodison is interesting in terms of her emphasis on the *usefulness* of this set of discourses, as well as any theoretical perspective we might employ rather than on its *truth value*: 'it provides a language for certain aspects of the experience which other theories ignore. We do not have to "believe" in it [...] but we can explore the usefulness of each framework' (167).

I will continue to draw attention to the politics of the employment of discourses of energy; for the moment I want to underline Goodison's important, almost Foucauldian point, about discursive strategies/usefulness rather than truth value, as well as how the discourse of energy might help as a defamiliarizing technique to see aspects about love that we might not be able to see without this discourse. One aspect that Goodison's discourse of energy accomplishes, which is important especially within a discussion of romantic love, is that it enables a desexualization of the concept of 'falling in love'. She suggests that we 'broaden the scope of our loving feelings' by realizing that 'we 'fall in love' in situations far from the socially recognized romantic or sexual ones. Because our culture does not validate such feelings, we tend to dismiss them ourselves'. She lists examples such as a teenager falling in love with a horse, a scholar falling in love with ideas, a protester engaged in a demonstration, or a grandmother's excitement when her grandson who is caring for her at the end of her life arrives, wherein the connection is full of 'intimacy, excitement, interest and tenderness'. Goodison argues that this examination could help to transform our concept of falling in love 'from a bewildering passion for one person to a deep-rooted lust for all of life' (1983: 171). Her argument pairs nicely with Grossi's arguments in this volume about theorizing love as a revolutionary force.

Important aspects of Goodison's unusual early essay on feminist theories of love include her emphasis on the discursive usefulness of discussing love as 'energy', and the way this discourse locates energy in the body. It shares, with the first strand of feminist affect theory, an attention to discrete affects and the importance of developing a precise vocabulary for describing each complex affect. The practice of awareness of one's body, the precise tracking of the circulation of energy in one's body, and the growing ability to distinguish and to name these different energies that Goodison calls for sound similar to the kinds of practices involved in, for example, Buddhist meditation. In a more developed theory of love as affective energy, it would be interesting to investigate other theorists who are also exploring these kinds of practices of tracking embodied affective energy, including, for example, Irigaray's recent work (2002) that is informed by eastern practices of yoga (see Stoller this volume) or Sedgwick's work on Buddhism (2003).

Clough and affective energy

It is in Clough's introduction to her edited collection (2007) that she ties together many discourses that need to be used when theorizing the complicated and complex world in which we live. She joins together a number of disciplines/areas through the vocabulary of affect, energy, etc. In particular, I noticed the usefulness of the ways in which she discusses psychoanalytic and Marxist concepts within a global context with a similar vocabulary, so as to make them logically inform one another and work as tools that can easily be brought together to discuss this larger context. Clough herself discusses a graduate course she taught in which she brought a range of material together: The course was 'to think about the postcybernetic bodies of the early 21st century by means of reconsidering the relationship of energy, entropy, work, information, and capital' (21). Clough links Freud's theory of psychic energy with Deleuze's theories of affect and Shannon and Wieners' theory of information as an open system, and examines Marx's theory of capital and labor and the shift from a Foucauldian disciplinary society to a Deleuzian control society. She discusses the circulation of psychic energy, labor power, and information circulation through organic and cyborg bodies. The discourse of 'energy' is crucial for rethinking and linking all of these systems.

An important contribution to the discussion of affect in terms of energy can be found in Clough's discussions of information theory. A change has occurred within this field, which shifted from physics' classical laws of thermodynamics that describe closed systems, to new physical theories of open systems. Articulating this theoretical shift, Clough argues, allows us 'to understand the changing relationships of information to bodies, labor, and energy, from industrial capitalism, from the nineteenth century elaboration of the first and second law of thermodynamics to the late-twentieth-century elaboration of complexity theory' (2007: 17). A closed mechanical system follows the second law of thermodynamics, which states:

the increase in entropy is inevitable as an irreversible process of heat-death. Here entropy is defined as energy that can no longer be put to work, no longer organized to do something, having become chaotic, lie microparticles moving out of order, without aim or purpose. Entropy is the measure of turbulence or disorder in a closed system.

(2007: 18)

She points out that Freud works within a concept of a closed system: 'the discussion of trauma as the excess of in-flowing energy and of traumatic repetition as a curative rebinding of energy that tends toward the preservation of the equilibrium or homeostatis of the body ego' (10). She argues: 'For Freud, as for Butler, and for theorists of trauma generally, the body is the body as organism, a closed system, seeking homeostasis and equilibrium'. In contrast, she suggests that by drawing on new physical theories we can discuss energy in relationship to open systems. The implications, for Clough, of these theoretical shifts are enormous: 'To think the body differently is to rethink matter and the dynamism inherent to it. It is to rethink the evolution of the species as well' (11).

Whatever the nature of the material relationship amongst physical, psychic and social energies, the question of using a model of closed or open systems when it comes to talking about any of these energies is a worthwhile consideration, and especially around theories of love as a gift or a kind of 'surplus' outside of a use/exchange value economy. Even a mainstream children's song approach suggests an open system: 'love is something if you give it away, you end up having more. It's just like a magic penny/hold it tight and you won't have any/lend it, spend it and you'll have so many/they'll roll all over the floor'. Indeed, as we shall see in the section below, more than one theorist underlines lacunae in Brennan's otherwise interesting theories around the transmission of affect in terms of her use of a closed rather than open system model.[11]

It is important to situate the discussion of the discourse of 'energy' within affect theory or the connected area of the new materialism within a longer, rather polemical debate between sciences and the humanities and social sciences regarding how the latter are interpreted by the former as 'taking up' 'their' concepts incorrectly. Developing a theory of love as affective energy will need to address more fully the ways in which the discourse of 'energy' is and is not being used. Do Clough and others mean to suggest they are also referring $E=mc^2$ when they discuss affective, informational, or labor energy? Or is their use what some call 'metaphorical' or 'figurative?' Are inter-disciplinary discussions of 'psychic energy', 'social energy', 'electrical energy', and 'subatomic energy' discussing anything similar, or is the use of the term 'energy' in each of these terms coincidental? Do the physical sciences own the term? Are social science discussions borrowing the term or is it a matter of just a different parallel vocabulary? Dorothea Olkowski (2012) summarizes Alan Sokal's and Steven Weinberg's positions as articulating the most extreme end of the debate in their claim that natural scientists and physicists 'continue to reject the notion that the disciplines concerned with social and cultural criticism can have anything to contribute, except perhaps peripherally to their research'. Olkowski refers to an intervention by Weinberg in the *New York Review of Books*, where he argues that:

> Those who seek extrascientific messages in *what they think they understand about modern physics* are digging dry wells. I think that, with two large exceptions, the results of research in physics (as opposed, say to psychology) have no legitimate implications whatever for culture or politics or philosophy.
>
> (In Olkowski 2012: 1–2, emphasis in original)

In contrast, postmodern feminist Donna Haraway's response (1997) foregrounds a much more complex theory of language and culture than Sokal presumes, and also questions his and others' attempts to police who is allowed to make proclamations about science: 'Science is revisable from what its practitioners like to think of as 'outside' as well as from 'inside'. What counts 'semiotically' as inside and outside is the result of hard, ongoing work, work deeply inflected by and constitutive of power of all sorts' (1997: 126). Significantly, she also changes the mode of discourse around what she refers to as the 'so-called Science Wars', by shifting away from the combative 'ripe exchanges and the body counts of the fracas' (123) rooted in discourses of war to tell, instead, a story of love – 'love of science in general, and biology in particular' (123).

Teresa Brennan, affect, and 'energetics', and love as 'living attention'

Teresa Brennan's work also emerges from psychoanalysis, but like Tomkins and Deleuze she expands and criticizes this basis. Like many 'affect theorists', Brennan does not distinguish between affect and emotion – she writes that 'emotions are basically synonymous with affect' (2004: 6); however, she tends to use the term 'affect' more than 'emotion' and discusses their similarity to 'the passions'. For Brennan, an affect is a 'physiological shift accompanying a judgment' (5). She stresses the importance of this judgmental component – affects, for her, are 'any evaluative (positive or negative) orientation toward an object' (5) – which differs from the more common expressive understanding of emotion.

Brennan's work has had an important impact on contemporary theories of affect in terms of her discussions of the circulation of affect and its relationship to subjectivity. Pointing out that psychoanalysis and metapsychology locate the origin of affects in the individual experiencing them, she argues instead that not only are we 'not separate from others', but we are 'not self-contained in terms of our energies' (2004: 6). Brennan discusses 'the transmission of affect' in terms of the circulation of energy, or what she has called 'an energetics', which is the belief that all beings, 'either naturally or artificially forged are connected energetically' (40). She describes an 'inter-active economy of energies' around and through individuals. For Brennan, emotion is exchanged as a bodily energy and our ego-boundaries are actually shaped by this energetic field shared with others.

Brennan's revolutionary theories rooted in both relational ontology and relational ethics challenge a western liberal humanist understanding of the subject, which forwards a concept of 'individuality' and assumes that we are discrete individuals, separate from others, and where our discrete emotions that we each own emerge from within this unique self. Instead, her theories challenge our sense of ourselves as individuals, in their suggestion that this sense is a mere fantasy (she calls it the 'foundational fantasy'), an effect of the borders and boundaries that we create to contain psychic energy. Further, and significantly, we continue this practice of projecting when it comes to the circulation of negative affect. She suggests that rather than owning our part in the circulation of negative affects, we tend to project its origin onto an other and then force this other to carry these affects. We come to believe that the one that we are projecting our negative affects onto is actually where the negative affects originated.

It is important that, unlike many contributors to affect theory, Brennan offers us a *gendered* theory of affect and considers the *gendered* nature of this energetics. She points out that the first being in whom we locate negative affects and on whom we dump our unwanted affects is the mother. Afterwards, and aligned with classic psychoanalysis, we replace the mother with a substituted mother/woman/feminine subject. For Brennan, femininity is not linked to sex but rather to *this position* within the energetic transmission of affect: 'femininity [...] should be approached as transformation of energy, a disposition, possibility or modality in the relation to the other that can be assumed or actualized by any subject at a particular moment' (2004: 74). She goes so far as to suggest that maybe the reason why our society has so many malaises of depression, anxiety, etc. is that it lacks enough feminine beings/racialized subjects who are willing to be the depositers of negative affect (15). Further, it is important to note that her energetics, which concentrates on the depletion of affective energy, is interested in more than just gendered subjects but also encompasses a concern regarding the depletion of the earth's resources.

As a counter to this depletion, she develops a concept called 'living attention', which Brennan herself glosses as 'love', and which is also a gendered concept. As Kelly Oliver observes, for Brennan, those who 'occupy the feminine position give living attention to others but do not receive it themselves' (2007: 14). There is a resulting harmful impact on feminine subjectivity. If a feminine subject is a subject whose energetic resources are depleted, because, by definition, she serves as the dumping ground for others' affects, then she would therefore have no energy to sustain herself. Oliver foregrounds that Brennan, therefore, suggests an ethical and political ecology regarding the circulation of energy and transmission of affect that is influenced by this gendered perspective: 'we shall not use energy or living attention at a rate faster than they can replenish themselves or be replenished' (2007: 18). Brennan's concept of living attention and her call for another economy of energy – an economy of generosity – also extends beyond intersubjective relationships as a criticism of global capitalism and the ways in which energy is transferred from 'creativity and love to conquest and war' (Oliver 2007: 17) Significantly, Brennan does not just gender the destructive energetics as masculine; she identifies the 'feminine fantasies' that she also sees as destructive and suggests, in a similar way to Janice Radway's criticism of popular romance (1991), that the pursuit of feminine fantasies within patriarchal culture can divert important political energies.

Brennan's work joins together affect and love in exciting, productive ways. Her gendered theory of living attention, energetics, and love call attention especially to expectations about feminine subjects as the source of and givers of energy, but also to the fact that this aspect can lead to their oppression. Her concern with the affective treatment of such subjects who are 'dumped on' and whose energies are drained from them highlights the cultural need to develop places for them to 'recharge'. This gendered theory of love as energy is really important for calling attention to what, for instance, Irigaray has theorized in terms of 'love as labor'.[12]

Another important contribution that Brennan gives us is a controversial, and yet compelling, *material* – at the level of matter – description of affect in ways that are often not considered. This is not a metaphoric energy transfer that she is forwarding. She discusses material 'chemical changes in the body transmitted atmospherically [ ] through smell, subtle rhythmic vibration, and waves such as tension', which gives us the actual materiality of the body and not the discursive body. She even turns the discussion of vision into the material movement of electrons/waves, or 'spectrum vibrations at various frequencies' (2004: 10).

However, there are some concerns. Similar to the issues Clough raised above around a theory of energy rooted in an open rather than closed system, Oliver (2007) and Kalpana Seshadri (2007) discuss how Brennan's theories, and perhaps psychoanalysis more generally, are limited in that they operate within classic closed systems of thermodynamics rather than the more open systems that quantum physics offers. I also wonder how much her division of affects into clear categories of 'positive' and 'negative affects' is limiting, especially for the study of love, which I believe needs to involve a complicated discussion about what gets included as positive and negative and by whom (see note 7). Further, while Brennan's discussion of neuroscientific concepts is compelling, how much she has researched and grounded her theories in this area has been questioned.

Despite its problems, Brennan's work has important implications, including in terms of developing a political and ethical understanding of affect, and love in particular. Oliver points out that one of the political and ethical implications of Brennan's work is that 'we not only need to take responsibility for negative affects but also acknowledge the positive effects of the transmission of affect that create a surplus of living attention and energy' (2007: 22). Brennan also provides us with an interesting way of rethinking affect and community. A theory of the circulation of energy implies 'that we can get more than we put in, that the whole is larger than the sum of its parts, when it comes to people working or playing together' (Oliver 2007: 22). Further, it changes common assumptions that the circulation of energy and the transmission of affect come from an individual ego or consciousness and, instead, suggests that group dynamics could help to contribute to a political notion of love – the responsibility of circulating affects in certain ways is not just an individual decision but a collective one.

Conclusion

I have suggested here that recent insights within feminist love studies regarding the need to re-evaluate the concept of love for feminism, and the contributions of 'feminist affect theory' to rethinking emotion in general as well as discrete affects, could have an enormous impact on rethinking the concept of love if they were to enter into a committed dialogue. Two possible barriers to this dialogue include different understandings of what counts as a feminist materialist approach and different senses of the aesthetic and the role it plays in theorizing love. I have argued that the discourse of 'energy' could be useful for dialogue between the two fields, in large part because of the ways in which a discussion of 'energy' helps us to defamiliarize some of the ways in which 'love' has been talked about. It also helps us to form a complex theory of love because of the commonality of the discourse of 'energy' to psychoanalytic theories of the psyche; neurological research on the brain; Marxist theories of the social, including labor, and power and politics; informational and posthuman networks of global communication; and discussions amongst non-western theories of energy and bodies. If this 'energy' is not the same material phenomenon, at least discursively it allows for productive dialogue and aims at the interdisciplinary complexity needed to come to terms with this concept. Discussing love in terms of its energetic component also roots love in the body, as a sensual experience. Love as energy calls out for a theory of ontology and politics that suggests contagion, transmission, networks, transformation, and creation. Much still needs to be investigated but my main point has been to demonstrate that exciting work is being done in many places and that we could all learn from these conversations.

Notes

1 Even Allison Jaggar's early 'Love and Knowledge', often pointed to as one of the first works to reconsider emotion in a way that led to the development of 'feminist affect theory', does not, despite her title, spend much time addressing 'love'.

2 My argument that those working in feminist love studies and feminist affect studies need to converse more does not ignore that some contributors to feminist love studies have been in dialogue with scholarship described as 'affect studies';

however, the majority have tended to engage with the non-feminist versions. Hardt and Negri's *Commonwealth* has been a focal point, mainly from a critical perspective, most likely because of its widespread circulation within post-Marxist discourse and their infamous call for rethinking love has had a widespread impact on what is being received as 'love studies'. Many essays (Jónasdóttir, Ferguson, Hennessy, and Wilkinson) in Jónasdóttir and Ferguson (2014b) engage in important feminist criticisms of this work. In her contribution to this volume, Kathleen B. Jones widens this criticism of affect theory to include many theorists, both feminist and non-feminist, although ultimately her focus is on the latter, in her assessment that thinking about emotion at a 'sub-personal, non-intentional, autonomic level' is dangerous. On a different note, Adriana García-Andrade and Olga Sabido-Ramos build on, rather than criticize, the work of Antonio Damasio, while Ferguson mentions, although does not develop, the importance of Deleuze as a materialist thinker. The only other contributor to engage with *feminist* affect theory and its potentially productive contributions to rethinking love in this volume is Lena Gunnarsson, who sets her work into dialogue with Sedgwick's concept of paranoid and reparative reading.

3 Jónasdóttir's essay in that volume provides an important overview of this scholarship.

4 Some contributors have defined themselves in opposition to, or, at least, as diverging from, feminist poststructuralist theory (e.g. Jónasdóttir and Ferguson 2014a; Gunnarsson 2014).

5 For example, Ahmed (2008) is a prominent feminist affect theorist who has criticized some of the tendencies in 'the new materialism' and, arguably, from a feminist poststructuralist materialist perspective.

6 The addition of a significant third school, informed by Raymond Williams' work on 'structures of feeling', needs to be included as a third important influence alongside these other two pillars, and, increasingly, reference is being made to a fourth significant tradition, Alfred North Whitehead's work.

7 This approach, whose roots go back to Spinoza, tends to label one set of affects/emotions as 'positive', which are aligned with the hegemonic, and another set as 'negative', which are aligned with the counter-hegemonic. Love is labeled as 'positive' by many affect theorists and ends up getting short shrift by those searching for a resistive base. The approach I am suggesting rethinks these binary oppositions of 'positive' and 'negative' affects and does not stop at an analysis of hegemonic uses of our traditional concepts of love, but emphasizes rethinking and reshaping what counts as 'love'.

8 Mapping this diverse body of work into two approaches with two main figureheads is not meant to be a hard and fast drawing of borders and boundaries; in doing so, I am following suggestions in the review of the literature. There are many theorists who contemplate affect in more generalized terms than just Deleuzian inspired theorists, including Sedgwick, whose work, especially 'Dialogue on Love' (1998) and her work on Buddhism (2003), would fall more into this second approach.

9 Grosz (1994) notes how comparatively few feminist theorists in the 1980s and early 1990s had commented on the work of Deleuze, which was striking, given so much scholarship on other French theorists. She indicates the early negative reception by Alice Jardine and Luce Irigaray of Deleuze's concept of 'becoming woman'.

10 There are many other theorists who need to be included in a more detailed investigation of this subject; a significant contributor who could be placed alongside these thinkers is Ann Ferguson who, in this volume, expands on her earlier concept of 'sex/affective energy' (1989), which she now distinguishes from another kind of energy called 'love affective energy' (see also Jónasdóttir's similar use of the term 'energy' in this volume). It is noteworthy that in 1989, Ferguson was discussing 'affective energy' by bringing the discourses of Marx and Freud together, while

also mentioning the contributions of Deleuze; her discussions which bring together these theorists predate similar discussions within 'affect theory'. In turn, a dialogue with the theories foregrounded in this chapter might be helpful for Ferguson's elaboration of concepts, especially in terms of clarifying the sources for and the differences among the theories of energy in which her work is based.

11 For a discussion of love as a depletable resource vs. love as infinite and self-generating from a different perspective, see Gunnarsson (2014).

12 As an example of the dialogue I am encouraging among feminist love studies and feminist affect theory, a comparison of Brennan's gendered energetics with Ferguson's (1989, this volume) and Jónasdóttir's (1994, this volume) Marxist theories of men's exploitation of women's loving energies, could be productive.

References

Ahmed, Sara (2008) 'Open Forum: Imaginary Prohibitions. Some Preliminary Remarks on the Founding Gestures of the 'New Materialism'', *European Journal of Women's Studies* 15(1): 23–39.

Barad, Karen (2007) *Meeting the Universe Halfway.* Durham, NC: Duke University Press.

Barriteau, Eudine (ed.) (2012) *Love and Power.* Kingston, Jamaica: University of the West Indies Press.

Braidotti, Rosi (2006) *Transpositions.* Malden, MA: Polity Press.

Brennan, Teresa (2000) *Exhausting Modernity.* London: Routledge.

Brennan, Teresa (2004) *The Transmission of Affect.* Ithaca, NY: Cornell University Press.

Cixous, Hélène (1976) 'Laugh of the Medusa', trans. K. Cohen and P. Cohen, *Signs* 1 (4): 875–893.

Clough, Patricia Ticineto (2007) 'Introduction', in P. T. Clough with J. Halley (eds) *The Affective Turn.* Durham, NC: Duke University Press.

Coole, Diana and Samantha Frost (2010) 'Introducing the New Materialisms', in D. Coole and S. Frost (eds) *New Materialisms.* Durham, NC: Duke University Press.

Davis, Dawn Rae (2002) '(Love Is) the Ability of Not Knowing: Feminist Experience of the Impossible in Ethical Singularity', *Hypatia* 17(2): 145–161.

Ferguson, Ann (1989) *Blood at the Root.* London: Pandora.

Ferguson, Ann and Margaret E. Toye (eds) (2017) 'Feminist Love Studies', special issue, *Hypatia* 32(1).

Goodison, Lucy (1983) 'Really Being in Love Means Wanting to Live in a Different World', in S. Cartledge and J. Ryan (eds) *Sex and Love.* London: The Women's Press. Reprinted in S. O. Weisser (ed.) (2001) *Women and Romance.* New York: New York University Press.

Gorton, Kristyn (2007) 'Theorizing Emotion and Affect: Feminist Engagements', *Feminist Theory* 8(3): 333–348.

Gregg, Melissa and Gregory J. Seigworth (eds) (2010) *The Affect Theory Reader.* Durham, NC: Duke University Press.

Greyser, Naomi (2012) 'Beyond the "Feeling Woman": Feminist Implications of Affect Studies', *Feminist Studies* 38(1): 84–112.

Grosz, Elizabeth (1994) *Volatile Bodies.* New York: Routledge.

Grosz, Elizabeth (2008) *Chaos, Territory, Art.* New York: Columbia University Press.

Gunnarsson, Lena (2014) *The Contradictions of Love.* New York: Routledge.

Haraway, Donna (1997) 'enlightenment@science_wars.com: A Personal Reflection of Love and War', *Social Text* 50(1): 123–129.

Hardt, Michael (2007) 'Foreword: What Affects Are Good For', in P. T. Clough with J. Halley (eds) *The Affective Turn*. Durham, NC: Duke University Press.

Hardt, Michael and Antonio Negri (2009) *Commonwealth*. Cambridge, MA: Belknap Press of Harvard University Press.

Hemmings, Clare (2005) 'Invoking Affect: Cultural Theory and the Ontological Turn', *Cultural Studies* 19(5): 548–567.

Hemmings, Clare (2011) *Why Stories Matter*. Durham, NC: Duke University Press.

Irigaray, Luce (1993) *An Ethics of Sexual Difference*, trans. C. Burke and G. Gill. Ithaca, NY: Cornell University Press.

Irigaray, Luce (1996) *I Love to You*, trans. A. Martin. London: Routledge.

Irigaray, Luce (2002) *Between East and West*, trans S. Pluháček. New York: Columbia University Press.

Jaggar, Allison (1989) 'Love and Knowledge: Emotion in Feminist Epistemology', *Inquiry* 32(2): 151–176.

James, Susan (2007) 'Repressed Knowledge and the Transmission of Affect', in A. Jardine, S. Lundeen and K. Oliver (eds) *Living Attention*. New York: SUNY Press.

Jónasdóttir, Anna G. (1994) *Why Women Are Oppressed*. Philadelphia, PA: Temple University Press.

Jónasdóttir, Anna G. and Ann Ferguson (2014a) 'Introduction', in A. G. Jónasdóttir and A. Ferguson (eds) *Love: A Question for Feminism in the Twenty-first Century*. New York: Routledge.

Jónasdóttir, Anna G. and Ann Ferguson (eds) (2014b) *Love: A Question for Feminism in the Twenty-first Century*. London: Routledge.

Klesse, Christian (2014) '"Loving More Than One": On the Discourse of Polyamory', in A. G. Jónasdóttir and A. Ferguson (eds) *Love: A Question for Feminism in the Twenty-first Century*. New York: Routledge.

Kristeva, Julia (1984) *Revolution in Poetic Language*, trans. M. Waller. New York: Columbia University Press.

Lorraine, Tina (1999) *Irigaray and Deleuze*. Ithaca, NY: Cornell University Press.

Oliver, Kelly (2007) 'Living A Tension', in A. Jardine, S. Lundeen and K. Oliver (eds) *Living Attention*. New York: SUNY Press.

Oliver, Kelly (2015) *Earth and World*. New York: Columbia University Press.

Olkowski, Dorothea (2012) *Postmodern Philosophy and the Scientific Turn*. Bloomington: Indiana University Press.

Pedwell, Carolyn and Anne Whitehead (2012) 'Affecting Feminism: Questions of Feeling in Feminist Theory', *Feminist Theory* 13(2): 115–129.

Radway, Janice (1991) *Reading the Romance*. Chapel Hill: University of North Carolina Press.

Rudy, Kathy (2011) *Loving Animals*. Minneapolis: University of Minnesota Press.

Sedgwick, Eve Kosofsky (1998) 'Dialogue on Love', *Critical Inquiry* 24(2): 611–631.

Sedgwick, Eve Kosofsky (2003) *Touching Feeling*. Durham, NC: Duke University Press.

Seshadri, Kalpana Rahita (2007) 'After Teresa Brennan', in A. Jardine, S. Lundeen and K. Oliver (eds) *Living Attention*. New York: SUNY Press.

Strid, Sofia and Anna G. Jónasdóttir (eds) (2011) *GEXcel Work in Progress Report IX. Proceedings from GEXcel Theme 10: Love in Our Time – A Question for*

Feminism. Conference of Workshops 2–4 December 2010. Örebro, Sweden: CFS Report Series no. 14; and Linköping, Sweden: Tema Genus Report Series no. 12.

Toye, Margaret E. (2010) 'Towards a Poethics of Love: Poststructuralist Ethics and Literary Creation', *Feminist Theory* 11(1): 39–55.

Weisser, Susan Ostrov (2001) 'Introduction', in S. O. Weisser (ed.) *Women and Romance: A Reader*. New York: New York University Press.

6 From murderous love to worldly love?

Affect theory, violence against women, and the materiality of love

Kathleen B. Jones

In *The Transmission of Affect*, Teresa Brennan embarked on an ambitious project. Repudiating the idea that 'the subject is energetically and affectively self-contained' as 'a residual bastion of Eurocentrism in critical thinking' (2004: 2), she cited clinical research, social science studies of crowds, and other neurological findings to support the development of a new paradigm to overcome the split between the biological and psychosocial explanation of behavior. Her intention was to make the case for 'how the transmission of affect occurs in relationships' (2004: 3) and, by implication, to lay the groundwork for exploring further how this transmission process also operates at the social level as one factor contributing to group or crowd phenomena. For Brennan, affects are

> constant potentials [...] that devolve from the quasi-geometric positioning of human perception that occurs as humans come to see the world from their own standpoint [...]. [S]uch positioning becomes material and physical when it is constructed in external reality. *It can be constructed in the external realities of social and economic orders.*
>
> (2004: 22, emphasis added)

Brennan's work is situated among a proliferation of studies of affect in the humanities and social sciences that call for a renewal of these disciplines 'based on the findings of scientists working in the emotion field' (Connolly 2002, 2005; Leys 2011: 435; Thrift 2004). Many of these newer materialist ontologies of affect[1] either explicitly or implicitly aim to contribute to rethinking the political in ways that can further some kind of globally democratic project (Barad 2007; Berlant 2011; Braidotti 2013; Connolly 2002; Thrift 2004). Can this line of ontological thinking provide adequate normative justification or reasons for linking a reordering of affective transmission with more inclusive, democratic practices?

To explore this question, I evaluate the impact of this 'affective turn' on understanding the energetics of love and power in interpersonal relations and connect the analysis to efforts to develop a more politicized concept of love, or what Ella Myers (2013) has termed a concept of 'caring for the world' or, to be more consistent with Hannah Arendt's concept of 'amor mundi', what I call 'worldly love'. Myers' defense of worldly care, or, in my formulation worldly love, is resonant with Michael Hardt's effort to articulate a 'political concept of love' that betrays 'conventional divisions between personal and political, and grasp[s] the power to create bonds that are once intimate and social' (2011: 677). In addition to this characteristic, for Hardt a properly political concept of love would also 'operate in a field of multiplicity and function through not unification but the encounter and interaction of differences'. Finally, it would be transformative, 'such that in love, in our encounter with others we constantly become different' (678).

I proceed paradoxically, by examining love's failure in cases of violence against women. Examining extreme cases of love's failure, where divisions between personal and political seem to be forcibly installed, where unification aims to prevail over multiplicity, and where an encounter with the other can lead to annihilation, might enable us to consider better the political possibilities and limitations of affect theory's account of love as a particular, complex kind of affect, which Brennan defined as a 'physiological shift accompanying a judgment' (2004: 5), and assess its relevance for the development of a political or worldly concept of love.

For Myers, worldly care or love 'is meant to describe an emotional investment in and deep affection for something other than human selves, namely, for the extrasubjective 'web' that constitutes the conditions of our lives' (2013: 87). Defined as an expanded practice of 'recognition',[2] or what Brennan called 'the deployment of living attention or love' (2004: 139), worldly love is both an interpersonal and political activity.[3] At the level of the interpersonal, 'love or living attention' recognizes the fundamental associative or interactive dimensions of human existence. Brennan explained this as a kind of gift, or '[a]ttention to something other than oneself, or the living energy that enlivens another without affective penalty' and distinguished this from 'an affect directed toward another' that also 'carries a message of self-interest along with the attention it rides on' (2004: 41). Politically, Myers connected 'caring for the world' (2013: 109) with a 'democratic ethics' as an 'orientation or mode of being that can inspire participation in associative efforts to shape worldly conditions' (2013: 51).

In social/political theory a long trajectory of arguments has drawn attention to how the failure of recognition of 'the other' as an equal at an interpersonal level conditions and is conditioned by the failure of recognition of groups of 'others' at a socio-structural level. Such conditioning does not constitute a causal relation, as if one necessarily led to the other, but signals that displacement of the sovereign subject by a fundamental ontological intersubjectivity or interdependence contains an ethical core with political potential.[4] As Judith Butler puts it,

> It is not just a question of finding that what I am depends upon a 'you' who is not me, but that my very capacity for attachment and, indeed, for

love and receptivity requires a sustained dispossession of this 'I' [...]. [W]e have to consider what it is that one can finally love in order to move outside the claims of nationalism.

(2014 [2012]: 51)

Does affect theory account for not only *how* but *why* we should move 'outside the claims of nationalism'?

The affective turn

Introducing the essays in *The Affective Turn: Theorizing the Social*, Patricia Clough describes the shift in socio-political critical theory toward studying affect as one where scholars across a range of disciplines have defined 'affectivity as a substrate of potential bodily responses, often autonomic responses, which are in excess of consciousness' (2007: 1–2). Put differently, Clough explains, affect theorists understand affect as the 'pre-personal or pre-individual bodily capacity to affect and be affected or the augmentation or diminution of a body's capacity to act' (2007: 1).

Commentators have applauded this shift in focus, suggesting, for different reasons, that it brings much needed attention to the role of the emotions and feelings[5] in human (and other animal) behavior, while broadening our understanding of that behavior to include the non-intentional, corporeal experience of material life processes (Bennett 2010; Berlant 2011; Brennan 2004; Connolly 2002; Massumi 2002; Sedgwick 2003).[6] In particular, many have welcomed the renewed emphasis on the material or bodily experience of feelings (see Toye's review in this volume). Yet, others (Barnett 2008; Leys 2011) have raised concerns about affect theorists' understanding of affective responses as reactions occurring at the sub-personal, non-intentional, autonomic level of material existence. Shifting attention away from meaning in favor of a non-representational conceptualization of affect, in Barnett's view, means that 'the critical account of affect makes it difficult to avoid a sense that politics is all about interventions that go on below the threshold of explicit articulation' (2008: 195) and, without consent, becoming potentially a decidedly anti-democratic way to create an affinity for 'worldly love'.

Does affect theory help us understand better the dynamics of attachment at work in love? In other words, does affect theory's ontological proposition that affect is about the body's pre-conscious attunement and adjustment to its environment offer a sound theoretical foundation for developing an understanding of the energetics of love? What are the political implications of its ontological claims?

Affect theorists interested in politics have concentrated largely on classical activities and arenas of politics, such as the impact of media on shaping public opinion and voting behavior (Connolly 2002), or the design of urban public space (Thrift 2004). Most affect theories of politics have not sufficiently analyzed the gendered dynamics of love and power. Considering the implications of an application of affect theory to the analysis of gender-based violence might help demonstrate the stakes involved in adopting its approach to explain, and ultimately transform, the dynamics of intimate interactions.

Violence against women: perspectives and strategies

Defined by the Convention for the Elimination of Violence Against Women (CEDAW) as 'violence that is directed towards a woman because she is a woman or that affects women disproportionally' (1992), gender-based violence[7] takes many forms, both public and private. At one end of the continuum are acts of violence against women where the state itself specifically targets women not only to prevent their further participation in activities considered subversive but also to send a warning that a regime would stop at nothing to maintain its control. At the other end is intimate partner violence, the most common type of violence experienced by women globally, usually in the private sphere of their own home. Intimate partner violence ranges from emotional or psychological abuse to physical abuse that may be repeated or even become lethal.

As Gillian Youngs noted, although 'patriarchal systems have traditionally classified violence against women as private [...] the protection of the private sphere from the intrusion of public (state) interference has traditionally worked against women exposed to the excesses of unfettered male dominance and violence' (2009: 275). Recognizing how the lack of public concern and public policy has 'privatized' the social problem of intimate partner violence led Amnesty International, among others, to redefine the problem of intimate violence, tying 'issues of private pain to public peace by identifying a holistic definition of torture as acts by public officials *or* private individuals across all settings, including the home and community' (Youngs 2009: 276).

The percentage of women experiencing intimate partner violence varies widely within and across countries. Regardless of differences in frequency, no community is exempt from the occurrence and consequences of men's violence against women. Given the general presumption that the elimination of women's legal subordination and systemic intersectional inequalities will reduce the risk of violence against women, the persistence of gender-based violence in more egalitarian communities challenges the assumption that women's integrity and peace can be secured effectively through a combination of legal and socio-economic change. As a result researchers continue to explore ways to explain the persistence of violence against women under conditions of formal equality.

Stories of lethal intimate partner murder-suicide violence are not common; yet, they form a recognizable pattern and occur not only in places where gender inequality is prevalent but also where the law proscribes sex-based inequalities. Referred to in the literature as 'dyadic deaths', these cases stand at the extreme end of the continuum of intimate partner violence. Although their incidence is much less frequent than other forms of violence, such cases

cast into relief the dynamics of control found in almost all heterosexual intimate partner violence situations: when the relationship starts to break down,
when the man suspects that his wife/partner is about to leave, or imagines she
has become involved with someone else, he becomes enraged and lashes out
to regain control. Under extreme circumstances, his violence causes a loss from
which he cannot recover, and he then kills himself. What might these cases
represent? I argue that using these 'outlying' or 'pathological' cases of the
dynamics of love and its 'failure' can provide a way to analyze the possibilities
and limits of affect theory's account of love.

In particular, one fact about such extreme cases stands out: homicide-suicides
are overwhelmingly committed by men fearful of abandonment and mainly
occur in the private space of the home. Anomalous in terms of rates of
occurrence and different from patterns of homicidal or suicidal behavior
alone, these events are starkly intimate and dynamically inter-subjective.
Their anomaly provides an opportunity 'for reconstructing theory', acting as
a kind of 'signpost calling for a more integrated theory' (Woo 2004: 279)
about men's violence against women.

To begin with the obvious, in these extreme cases men's murderous violence
against women is an extreme, though paradoxical, instrument of control; a
violent attempt to secure recognition, once and for all. As Jessica Benjamin
put it, 'the need of the self for the other is paradoxical, because the self is
trying to establish himself as an absolute, an independent entity, yet he must
recognize the other as like himself in order to be recognized *by* [her]' (1998:
31–32). 'Recognition is the essential response, the constant companion of
association' (21). This paradox is redoubled by another in the case of murderous
violence. Fatal violence deprives a man who commits such an act of the most
important 'object' of his attachment – the woman, who is the source of his
recognition as a man, that is, as sovereign owner of gendered power. And so,
his unmodified rage at the ultimate loss of what he depends on for self-affirmation
can lead to his own self-destruction.

Most men don't experience the loss or withdrawal of women's 'love power'
(Jónasdóttir 1991) as inciting violence. Yet, these 'outlying' cases suggest a
way to understand the persistence of inequality in otherwise legally equal
societies. Both men and women express a desire for self-assertion and recognition. Yet in a society and culture structured by 'sexism and family relations
in which men can achieve independent existence only by separating themselves psychologically from [first] their mothers', and then from those activities of erotic care that symbolize the feminine, 'domination [or exploitation]
and submission are the products of the inevitable failure to achieve mutual
recognition' (Downs 1996: 94) in heterosexual relations under these conditions. Put differently, the institutionalization of heterosexual love relations in
contemporary society occurs under conditions of social-systemic inequality
even when legal or formal equality exists. The systemic inequality at the heart
of the social relations of heterosexual love pits loving care against erotic
desire in such a way that men's erotic self-concept depends on women's loving

care and is sustained without reciprocity (Jónasdóttir 1991: 109). As Anna G. Jónasdóttir argued, women and men may enter into these relations 'freely' (1991, this volume). Yet, because, in heterosexual relations, men's erotic self-concept as men depends on women's continued caring love, if women's care is withdrawn, it may frustrate some men's self-concept as men, lead to a decrease in men's gendered 'power' and increase the possibility of violence.

In her essay *On Violence*, Arendt made important, often overlooked, distinctions between power, strength, and violence.

> *Power* corresponds to the human ability not just to act but to act in concert. Power is never the property of an individual; it belongs to a group and remains in existence only so long as the group keeps together [...]. *Strength* unequivocally designates something in the singular, an individual entity; it is the property inherent in an object or person [...] which may prove itself in relation to other things or persons, but is essentially independent of them [...]. *Violence* [...] is distinguished by its instrumental character. Phenomenologically, [violence] is close to strength, since the implements of violence [...] are designed and used for multiplying natural strength.
>
> (1970: 44–46)

It is tempting, Arendt wrote, to 'think of power in terms of command and obedience, and hence to equate power with violence'. Yet, she cautioned against it. Violence, she argued, 'appears as *a last resort to keep the power structure intact against individual challenges*' (1970: 47, emphasis added). Through this lens, extreme cases of intimate violence suggest a way to understand the subterranean structure of men's gender power in modern societies, and what happens when this structure of power meets individual challenges in the form of a woman's resistance to it or attempt to escape it altogether. As Jeff Hearn put it, 'In seeing men in terms of both plurality and what is in common across social divisions, men's violence to known women may assist maintenance of masculine identity, while seeming on the surface to undermine it' (2012: 601).

Applying Benjamin's theory of 'the bonds of love' to understanding battering relationships, Donald Downs writes:

> On the one hand, batterers' needs for power and control [...] seem to embody deep and powerful needs for recognition and dependency, for everlasting devotion to counter the fear of abandonment. On the other hand, battered women might seek recognition in the forms available to the oppressed. They often love their mates, however traumatically, and attempt to salvage respect and recognition in a variety of seemingly self-destructive ways. Like good mothers, they acknowledge and serve their man's desperate need for recognition [...]. In some cases, the circle of [...] domination leads to numbness, deadness, and even death; the tension

between domination and recognition is too hard to sustain, and satisfaction seeks deeper abuse, a process that furthers the obliteration of the object of recognition.

(1996: 95–6)

In this reading, men's violence against known women indicates a response to a threatened or perceived loss of their gendered power. Let me stress this is a loss experienced in gendered terms, that is, as a loss of 'status' as a man (Hearn 2013: 5).

Recall Arendt's definition of violence as the instrument of 'last resort to keep the power structure intact against individual challenges'. Power, for Arendt, belongs to a group and disappears when the group is no longer together. Since men's deadliest violence against women occurs most frequently when women leave or attempt to leave their abusive partners, these extreme situations indicate that violence is being used to sustain a system of gendered power that formal, legal equality otherwise has mitigated. This perspective avoids defining men who exercise violence as deviant. Rather than dissociating the man who uses violence to sustain his gender power from the so-called average man, who has access to this power without violence, cases of extreme violence expose the otherwise hidden and quite ordinary psychodynamics of gender in modern, egalitarian societies, which continue to assign men the position, in the sphere of love and intimacy, of being the one with the 'right' to erotic desire and love/recognition and to take these 'things' by one means or another (Hearn 2013; Illouz 2012). Jane Caputi put it similarly when she wrote, 'Violence is both the paradigmatic means of 'proving manhood' and the last resort of those without other forms of social power to accomplish that end' (2003: 3).

If murderous love represents an extreme instance of the breakdown or failure of love, implicit in this judgment is an alternative ontology of love as mutual recognition or 'accommodation to accommodation' (Benjamin 2006: 134) or love as living attention (Brennan 2004: 139). Benjamin articulated this concept of love as 'the intersubjective third' or the 'moral third' and describes it as 'the ability to maintain internal awareness, that is, to sustain the tension of difference between my needs and yours while still being attuned to you' (2006: 128). Recognition, she wrote, is 'an energetic principle and [...] its economy is laid down in *organic* imperatives we have yet to understand [...]. [E]nergy – vitality, motivation, drive – is created through [...] attunement and recognition' (132–133, emphasis added). Although humans seem to experience a 'deep pull to get that energy' (133), there is nothing about this pull toward vitality, or life itself, that guarantees its fulfillment, much less that it will be obtained through recognition and surrender to intersubjectivity. Based largely on object-relations theory in psychoanalysis, Brennan conceptualized living attention as an energetic dimension of the (positive) affect of love, which enhances the other to whom it is directed. It is an 'energetic and profoundly material additive' that adds to the well-being of its recipient (2004: 34–36).

Under historically and culturally constituted conditions, the inherently 'precarious business' of mutual recognition (Benjamin 2013: 7) carries different dangers for women and men in the spheres of intimate love. That recognition entails both 'inevitable tension' and 'the idea of mutual recognition as something that necessarily breaks down' (6) also suggests that love need neither be idealized as a merging of two (or more) partners into one nor become stuck in complementary 'doer and done-to' scenarios. Rather, 'mutual accommodation and correction become the name of the game [...] resilience and attachment are built on *imperfect unions*' (6, emphasis added).

The inability to sustain this 'inevitable tension' in the process of mutual recognition lies at the heart of the failure of love in domestic violence situations. Yet, this begs the question: what factors and forces contribute to this inability to sustain the tension at the heart of recognition? A major contribution affect theory claims to make is to explain the transmission process as an embodied, energetic, physiological exchange grounding the unconscious dynamic in the 'circle of domination' through the flesh (García-Andrade and Sabido-Ramos this volume).

Margaret Toye has suggested that the turn to affect can be 'extremely useful for feminist love studies' by 'offering important and complex insights about the particular affect/emotion of love' (this volume). Proposing a more mind/body integrative, bio-social explanation of how we attach ourselves to or desire things that can actually act as obstacles to our flourishing, or what Lauren Berlant has called 'cruel optimism' (2011: 1), affect theory claims to provide a more coherent account of how the material dynamics of attachment work in love.

While assessing how the 'transmission of affect' might explain love's success or failure, I remain equally concerned with what kind of politics follow from an emphasis on the 'ontology of bodily matter' (Clough 2007: 6). In other words, what kind of politics might be entailed in the shift from the concept of 'subjects' to the concept of 'organisms' or even 'machinic assemblages' whose emotions are conceptualized as non-intentional bodily reactions to external sensorial stimuli? Despite its potentially effective interventions, might there yet be strong reasons to resist certain versions of affect theory's corporealization of politics?

While considering these questions, I recognize distinctions between affect theorists relying more on interpretations of recent neuropsychological research, and other affect theorists who have placed emphasis more on the development of an intersubjective ontology of the human person. Although, as Toye notes in this volume, such distinctions are not absolute, they represent starkly different approaches to thinking about politics and political change. In particular, political theorists of affect (Connolly 2002; Thrift 2004), as opposed to cultural theorists, have relied heavily on selective interpretations of the work of neuroscientists, such as Antonio Damasio. Cultural theorists, such as Eve Kosofsky Sedgwick (2003), have drawn more on the work of the psychologist Silvan Tomkins, while Teresa Brennan has taken inspiration from research on the transmission of hormones and pheromones.[8] Such olfactory transmission, Brennan wrote, repudiates the notion of the self-contained subject because '[p]heromones act as direction-givers which, as molecules, traverse the physical space between one subject and another, and factor in or determine the direction taken by the subject who inhales or absorbs them' (2004: 75).

In place of intentionality, certain affect theorists, such as Nigel Thrift (2004), Brian Massumi (2002) and Patricia Clough (2007), drawing inferences from neuropsychological research, treat behavior/(re)action as an autonomic effect of affect, where affect/emotion is understood as the body/brain response to external stimuli. In Thrift's formulation, for example, 'an action is set in motion [by stimuli affecting the body/brain] *before* we decide to perform it [...]. Thus we can now understand emotions as a kind of *corporeal thinking*' (2004: 67, emphasis added). Damasio's (2005 [1994]) explanation of the relationship between emotions, or autonomic corporeal responses to external stimuli, and consciously perceived 'feelings' describes the same 'delay' between the body/brain's automatic response to stimuli or triggers and corporeally registered sensory perceptions of these responses, which he calls 'gut reactions'. Although Damasio ascribed cognitive capacity to emotion, cognition here is understood as information registered, initially without our awareness, in the body/brain, which *only later* becomes consciously perceived as a bodily feeling.

Bio-scientifically informed affect scholars in social and political theory have placed considerable emphasis on affect as a bodily response occurring below the level of consciousness, and hold the corresponding view that thinking 'comes "too late" for reasons, beliefs, intentions, and meanings to play a role in action and behavior usually accorded to them' (Leys 2011: 443). Although Brennan drew on different scientific studies to support her defense of a new paradigm of the 'horizontal line of affective transmission' (2004: 79) across the boundary between one subject and another, her argument about hormonal entrainment still rested heavily on a largely autonomic, stimulus–response model of behavior. Hence, part of my criticism below of Damasio applies to Brennan's affect theory.

Damasio's studies of patients with prefrontal lobe damage led him to conclude that a distinctive collection of neural systems controlled the processing of feelings, separate from emotional processing centers, and were located in particular areas of the brain. Damage to these neural systems impaired reasoning and decision-making because the feeling processing centers of the brain had been impaired (2005 [1994]: chs 1–4). As he concluded, 'bilateral prefrontal damage [...] precludes normal emotional display and [...] causes abnormalities in social behavior' (74). But Damasio's conclusions and the implications he drew from them beg two questions: What constitutes *normal* emotional display or *normal* social behavior (or, where do culturally inflected judgments of behavior come from)?[9] What is the reason to conclude that if emotional display or behavior is biologically dependent on brain functioning then 'normal' emotional displays or their lack should be understood as the non-intentional, automatic product of physiological processes?

In addition, Damasio's moving the mind 'from a non-physical *cogitum* to the realm of biological tissue' and his corresponding relation of this 'body-minded brain' to a 'whole organism possessed of integrated body proper and brain and fully interactive with a physical and social environment' ultimately rests on an ontology collapsing the mind into the body. The result merely reverses the Cartesian dualism. It replaces the so-called disembodied thinking ego that creates an awareness of being with an equally dualist postulation that the body-minded brain's feeling (sensation) of being creates subjectivity as an image in the brain of a 'self' – a meta-self produced by the brain as an image 'of an organism in the act of perceiving and responding to an object' (2005 [1994]: 243). And it asserts that this image arrives 'hopelessly late for consciousness' (240).[10] As Ruth Leys noted, the conclusions drawn about the 'half-second' lapse in time between affective and reflective responses rest on the dubious assumption that the mind is 'a purely disembodied consciousness' (2011: 456). The so-called 'late arrival' of conscious intentionality in the causal chain of motor movements under investigation in various neuro-scientific experiments leads affect theorists 'to conclude in dualist fashion that intentionality has no place in the initiation of such movements and that therefore it must be the brain which does all the thinking and feeling and moving for us' (457).[11]

The conclusions Damasio reached about affect in his studies of both motor and emotional bodily responses to stimuli entail an assumption of our material predisposition for 'attunement' or responsiveness to the world that leaves little place for willful intentionality with regard to the objects of our affection. Objects come to us arbitrarily and from outside ourselves; we merely react to them in innate and habituated ways. What are the implications of this and related theories of affect with regards to intervention in broad areas of social conflict and suffering? I take this up in connection with the issue of violence.

> Both pain and pleasure are the levers the organism requires for instinctual and acquired strategies to operate efficiently [...] The configuration of stimuli and of brain-activity patterns perceived as pain or pleasure *are set a priori* in the brain structure [...]. Although our reaction to pain and pleasure can be modified by education, they are prime examples of mental phenomena that depend on the activation of *innate dispositions.*
> (Damasio 2005 [1994]: 262, emphasis added)[12]

Under normal circumstances, Damasio wrote, pain functions as an involuntary corporeal trigger, acting as 'a lever for the proper development of drives and instincts, and for the development of related decision-making strategies'. Suffering is the feeling the body attaches to pain. It is 'what puts us on notice' and 'offers the best protection for survival, since it increases the probability that individuals will heed pain signals and act to avert their source or correct their consequences'. If there have been 'alterations in pain perception' (2005 [1994]: 264) then the normal, appropriate decision-making strategies are also impaired.

But what if 'suffering' does not trigger automatically a response to avoid the pain it signals? Could it be hypothesized that what has occurred is parallel to Damasio's analysis of individuals who are born with a congenital absence of pain and do not acquire 'normal behavioral strategies' (2005 [1994]: 264)? In fact, this is precisely how many domestic violence victims have been viewed – she stayed because she lacked the ability to behave 'normally', i.e., to leave.

By seeing women who have experienced violence and don't leave immediately as lacking in agency or the cognitive ability to make the 'correct' decisions in response to pain, a rhetoric of victimization congeals around them similar to Damasio's description of patients with neurological damage. They become victims of faulty decision-making, trapped in their suffering because their brains have failed them. They need to be fixed. This representation can act as its own form of social control, with concrete consequences in terms of how women's actions or inactions are interpreted by police officers, in criminal justice proceedings, or civil decisions about children's protective custody (Downs 1996).

Despite Damasio's cavalier warning that taking a medical approach to resolve the 'suffering that arises from personal and social conflicts outside the medical realm' may wind up treating the symptom but not 'the roots of the disease' (2005 [1994]: 267), certain treatment programs designed to 'fix' victims of violence seem to do that exactly. Neuropsychological research on post-traumatic stress disorder (PTSD) has documented that trauma can lead to or exacerbate cognitive impairment of the 'executive' or decision centers of the brain, inhibiting the ability to develop and implement goal-directed behavior (Aupperle et al. 2013). Within the last two decades, this research has been applied to domestic violence victims, demonstrating that those experiencing PTSD from repeated abuse evidence impaired cognitive functions. Such research has led to the development of cognitive trauma therapy protocols to alleviate symptoms (Kubany and Watson 2002), along with neuroimaging studies of treatment effectiveness (Aupperle et. al. 2013). Research on the neuropsychological impact of abuse remains important for the development of appropriate individual treatment regimens. The risk, however, is that placing emphasis on countermanding the individual, corporeal effects of violence leaves the systemic basis of the problem unaddressed. Despite its attention to corporeal effects, does Brennan's analysis of the transmission of affect provide an alternative angle of view on the question of violence and what to do about it?

Attempting to identify the roots of the 'disease' she might have called the modern 'resentment of dependence', Brennan integrated research in psychoanalysis with political economy and neurophysiology to postulate the 'foundational fantasy' or the 'fantasy of self-containment' (2004: 13) as this resentment's origin:

> [T]he self-contained Western identity has to be a construction and [...] this construction depends on projecting outside of ourselves unwanted

affects such as anxiety and depression in a process commonly known as 'othering'. To be effective, the construction of self-containment also depends on another person (usually the mother, or in later life, a woman, or a pliable man, or a subjugated race) accepting those unwanted affects for us.

(2004: 12)

Instead, Brennan argued, 'all beings, all entities in and of the natural world, all forces, whether naturally or artificially forged, are connected energetically' in an 'interactive energetic economy' (2000: 51). Elsewhere, she termed this the 'chain of communication and association in the flesh (with its own anchors in the brain) that is also structured like language and functions in a parallel way' (2004: 23). In Brennan's account, this fleshly language is not determined biologically, that is, through a 'generational line of inheritance' (75), but is shaped interactively through an exchange, or transmission, between the socio-cultural 'environment', beginning with the maternal environment, and the human-in-formation. By implication, for Brennan, the denial of energetic interconnectedness and the interdependence it presupposes, along with the projection of negative affects onto those whose 'feminized' position serves to remind us of our dependence on others, explains the basis of violent aggression.

Two characteristics distinguish Brennan's interpretation of affect theory from its more deterministic alternatives. The first is her stress that the identity of those who become the bearers of negative affects is not accidental:

Women, I hazard, regardless of whether they are mothers, have carried the negative affects. But a better term than 'women' would be 'feminine beings', by which I mean those who carry negative affects for the other. These are most likely to be women, but the disposition of negative affects varies, especially when racism is a factor.

(2004: 15)

The second is that Brennan refuses to jettison some notion of intentionality from her account of the transmission of affects.

Leys contended that we need an adequate account of the emotions that would do justice to the fact that '[e]motions appear to be at once intentional and corporeal behaviors involving the organism's embodied disposition to act toward the objects in its world' (2007: 141). Brennan's account comes closest to offering a materialist theory that remains sympathetic to some concept of intentional human agency, while, at the same time, acknowledging an inherent activity in matter, which de-centers the fantasy of the self-contained subject as the sole source of all forms of 'intentionality'. She wrote:

[N]atural matter is active in certain natural cycles; it is only passive to the extent that it does not have free will [...] and is not individual; its intentional activity does not place it at odds with its surroundings. Only humans have intentions at odds with the scheme of things, but those intentions do not originate within them.

(2004: 93)[13]

Insofar as the individual will acts against the body's intelligence, Brennan contended, we persist in erecting 'self-contained barriers against feeling the other's affects and/or feelings' (2004: 197). Against the subjective standpoint of the willful ego, Brennan postulated an 'other I' of discernment 'able to be alert to the moment of fear or anxiety or grief or other sense of loss' and 'allied to a position in which one receives and processes without the intervention of anxiety or other fixed obstacles in the way of the thinking process' (119–120). Developing this capacity for discernment depends on a re-education of the senses and a re-interpretation of the flesh 'through the deployment of living attention or love' (139; cf. Gunnarsson 2016). And this discernment, in Brennan's perspective, entails both political and personal attention (139).

I return now to some questions raised at the outset: What connections might be drawn between both Benjamin's and Brennan's analysis of the tension-filled process of intimate intersubjectivity in love and its failures and what Myers has called 'worldly ethics?' And how can these connections be related to the 'politicization of love?' Myers wrote of a specifically democratic worldly ethos as 'care for the world', where care is a collaborative project, 'expressed in joint action by plural participants' and the

> recipient of care is not another person or even persons, but the world understood as the array of material and immaterial conditions under which human beings live – both with one another and with a rich variety of nonhumans, organic and technological. More specifically still, coaction among citizens is directed not at the world per se but at particular worldly things that become objects of shared attention and concern.
>
> (Myers 2013: 86)

I suggest the possibility of developing a theory of worldly love by translating onto the socio-political terrain the dialectic of intersubjective 'recognition' Benjamin has called the 'double directionality of recognition' (2006: 119) as a 'two way street' (116) involved in the re-creative process of an 'intersubjective third' (121). This translation is sympathetic with, yet departs from, Brennan's identification of the practice of 'discernment', which she defines as a process of detachment from possession by negative affects, a 'deployment of sensation, meaning feeling', so as to be 'open to others in a way that wishes them well and would dissipate their anxiety or sorrow if one could' (2004: 123).

Discernment 'presupposes a different sense of self or boundary than the boundary the ego manufactures by projecting out' (Brennan 2004: 123). '[T]he boundaries that matter, and the only ones that work, are those that shield the organism from dead matter by surrounding it with a field of living attention directed outward in a perpetual act of love' (116–117). Such discernment engages with feelings of connection, a 'feeling of kinship' with another 'as a fellow living, suffering, joyful creature' (119). In Brennan's view, the development of discernment depends on both cultural and personal practices. Brennan associated cultural practices with 'religious codes and codes of courtesy [...] and the virtues embodied in those codes' (122). Among those virtues, Brennan cites 'faith, hope and love' (131) and related codes, such as forgiveness (133). She connected personal discernment with 'personal practices of comparison [with a religious or ethical ideal], recollection and memory, and detachment' (126).

As if imagining a situation of violent aggression stemming from a perceived challenge to a man's gendered status, Brennan described a process of redirecting energy through personal discernment in this case:

> When a man realizes that there is grief behind his anger, and that what he felt when he heard this or that is not the passionate affect that possessed him at the time, but something finer, how does he do so? He remembers. Then he outwits the affects by comparing the state in which he was possessed by the othering affects with the state in which he discerned and felt [...]. He follows an essentially historical procedure to recover a truth, and he does so with loving intelligence rather than wallowing in judgments of himself (guilt and shame) or others (fear and paranoia).
>
> (2004: 121)

It would be interesting to explore the extent to which such processes have been reflected in programs designed to 'rehabilitate' aggressive offenders, especially given current research raising questions about extant programs' effectiveness (Eckhardt et al. 2013).

Can we extrapolate from the realm of intersubjective discernment to the realm of the political? It was precisely the intimacy of the dyadic relation of love that led Arendt to declare love to be the most antipolitical of human forces (1958: 242). Private intimacy made the world disappear, she argued. Nonetheless, the dialectic of relationality Benjamin identified as 'intersubjective recognition', and Brennan implied in her critique of the 'foundational fantasy', can have political resonance, while avoiding the pitfalls of a more manipulative approach to politics advanced by other affect theorists.[14]

As Benjamin wrote,

> I believe these insights can be extrapolated and hold good for politics as they do for analysis. In politics, as in analysis, we should learn to distinguish true thirdness from the self-immolating ideal of recognizing the other in a form that demands self-erasure [...]. The political activist, like the analyst, needs to work through fears of blame, badness, and hurtfulness that leads to a simple reversal of the power relations one is trying to oppose. The oppressed cannot be relieved of their responsibility to

recognize the humanity of the Other; otherwise, they succumb to the identity of victim such that dignified assertion of rights and agency, rather than reactive rebellion and defiant demand, become quite difficult.

(2006: 122)

The stress on the dynamic interaction between 'victim' and 'perpetrator' reflected in Benjamin's insight demands emphasis.

Intersubjective recognition can have political consequence provided recognition is not conceived as the sole end or purpose of politics. Yet, just as intimate love is more than recognition of the other as distinct from me, as a subject in herself, but also as one who co-exists *with* me in a shared world preceding and exceeding us and on which we both depend for life, so also is worldly love more than recognition of the plurality of others as subjects in themselves, but also as those who are *with* me in this shared world. The emphasis on being *with* gestures toward the conflicts that can and will arise in both intimate and worldly love around struggles of belief, interest, passion, and ideology about how to live and shape the same world as 'home'.

Translated into the socio-political context of worldly plurality, where each subject could be understood, in Arendt's phrasing, to have the 'right to have rights', activities of worldly love are directed to 'worldly things that become objects of shared attention and concern [practices, places, laws, habits, events] [...] around which people gather, both in solidarity and division' (Myers 2013: 86). As Arendt made clear in *The Origins of Totalitarianism*, the idea of the 'right to have rights' by no means limits the concept of rights to juridical terms, but invokes the idea of the 'right' of a plurality of others to be at home in a world we share in common. This right, she contended, can only be guaranteed by the actions of humanity as whole, a guarantee Arendt saw as 'by no means certain' to be possible (2004 [1951]: 379). In this sense, Arendt's acknowledgment that it is by no means certain that what I am calling 'worldly love' will succeed dovetails with Benjamin's sense that 'understanding of co-creation and intersubjectivity [of recognition] should make more palpable how the two-way structure is indeed fragile, highlighting its susceptibility to a kind of breakdown in which the pattern of 'doer and done to' predominates' (2006: 119). In other words, worldly love represents a political 'movement from breakdown to renewal' that is a continuous, dynamic process of negotiations toward recognition and concerted action instead of a final achievement.

Both Benjamin's and Brennan's ontological perspectives remain less capable, however, of articulating reasons why a commitment to personal or political discernment should be undertaken in the first place. To move from the descriptive ontological plane to the normative requires additional steps missing in both accounts. The critical task is not only to acknowledge our interdependence and mutual vulnerability, but also to 'engage the risky business of democratic contestation, publicizing and casting as changeable those specific harms that are systematically and unnecessarily wrought on some human beings and not others' (Myers 2013: 81). And that entails, among other things, the 'conventions of justification, that is, the giving and asking for reasons' in order to account for 'why the contemporary deployment of affective energy is bad for democracy' (Barnett 2008: 190).

The descriptive dimension of intersubjective relationality as worldly love needs supplementing with a prescriptive or normative dimension – worldly love is the activity of fostering the conditions enabling the world to be a 'shared home' 'common to all of us' (Myers 2013: 112–113; cf. Arendt 1958: 52). As Myers has demonstrated so clearly, the normative dimension of worldly love as a democratic ethos 'is enacted in part through collaborative efforts directed at creating material conditions that make the world a home to all people. Minimally, such home making requires transforming collective arrangements so as to secure basic needs', by focusing not only on human needs, but 'on the world in which [...] many selves and others [non-human] live' (121–122). Equally important is the idea of the activity of worldly love as 'fostering practices and building institutions that provide as many citizens as possible with meaningful opportunities to articulate their innumerable perspectives in the presence of one another and to influence the conditions under which they live' (125).

Notes

1 Not all new materialist thinkers take the turn toward the political in ways I articulate below. Karen Barad (2007), for instance, considers the relevance of quantum physics for articulating a philosophy of matter that ends up suggesting an ethics of pluralism is already built into matter, once we understand matter as an evanescent becoming. More recently, both William Connolly (2011) and Jane Bennett (2010), among others, have employed the perspective of new materialism as vitalism to argue against anthropocentric accounts of politics in favor of post-humanist politics.

2 Although focusing on the dynamics of recognition, my intention is not to emphasize the singularity of the subject's 'identity' but the concept of a relational subject-in-the-world, i.e., the subject as an agent, with needs, desires, drives, and interests of her own, connecting and conflicting with those of others. Thus, I stress politics as an arena of inter-action as opposed to a space of recognition beginning and ending with affirmation of one's unique identity. Recognition entails a willingness to be and to act in the world with others, and not simply to acknowledge difference per se. In this regard, I mark my work off from Sedgwick's recent celebration of difference as queerness in identitarian terms in her *Touching Feeling* (2003).

3 The leap that I take in this essay from the analysis of intersubjective recognition to the level of social theory finds its echo in Jessica Benjamin's (2006) preoccupation with the practical question of how to restore recognition in arenas of social and political conflict. Benjamin had in mind the Israeli–Palestinian conflict when she wrote that 'with some mediation' understanding intersubjective recognition 'might be susceptible to translation from clinical to social theory' (2006: 121; cf. 143 note 4). Brennan extended Benjamin's insight into the connection between the intersubjective and the socio-political in both *The Transmission of Affect* (2004) and *Exhausting Modernity* (2000).

4 Myers rejects the tendency in Foucault-influenced accounts of the development of a democratic ethos, such as that of Connolly (1995), to accord causal precedence

to the 'micropolitics' of self-care (Myers 2013: 45–52). While calling attention to the relationship between love as living attention and worldly love I reject any implication of causality.

5 Considerable debate exists about the terms 'emotion' and 'affect' in affect theory. Some scholars use them interchangeably, while others insist on clear distinctions. Among the leading neuroscientists whose work has been cited frequently, Antonio Damasio asserted an absolute distinction between emotion and affect because he locates the operation of these two bodily responses in different areas of the brain, which communicate, in ways not made absolutely clear, to enable decision-making (see García-Andrade and Sabido-Ramos this volume). In normal brain functioning, emotions are hard-wired bodily responses to sensorily perceived external stimuli. Feelings are the perception of bodily changes. Corporeal responses (emotions) are detected and processed by the brain's limbic system, which triggers the 'enactment of a body state characteristic of the emotion fear, and alters cognitive processing in a manner that fits the state of fear' (Damasio 2005 [1994]: 131). Yet, at base, this complicated description conceptualizes emotions as conditioned reflexes occurring below the level of conscious thought and without regard for the content or meaning of the stimulus to the subject. As Ruth Leys has put it, in Damasio's view 'affects are only contingently related to objects in the world; our basic emotions operate blindly because they have no inherent knowledge of, or relation to, the objects or situations that trigger them' (2011: 437). By contrast, Brennan's interpretation of affect theory introduced a more nuanced account of the interaction between affects and feelings, crediting the specificity of the 'objects' or stimuli that generate affects with the production of particular physiological responses.

6 Brennan's account is distinct among this group because she differentiates between unconscious intentionality and conscious agency, or the subject's conscious response to a sensed affect. 'The measure of agency in an action is its degree of conscious intentionality [...]. Yet intentions by this definition are linked to both the voluntary and autonomic nervous systems [...]. [F]eelings are tied to voluntary intention. They are, therefore, conscious and thoughtful. Affects are conscious as states discerned by feelings, but their production is involuntary and unconscious. Affects are thoughtless' (2004: 183). Still, it is the 'thoughtlessness' of affects that makes them a dangerous substratum for democratic politics, if we conceptualize democratic politics as demanding justification for particular commitments (Barnett 2008: 192).

7 It is important to note that this definition has been challenged by activists and theorists over the years.

8 For a critical discussion of how affect theorists' selective appropriation of new studies in biology and neuroscience rest either on misinterpretations of the research or uncritical endorsement of their findings, see Hemmings (2005), Leys (2011) and Papoulis and Callard (2010).

9 Discussing the difference between all living organisms' built-in, instinctual biological mechanisms for survival and the existence in human societies of 'social conventions and ethical rules over and above those biology already provides' (Damasio 2005: 124), Damasio attempted to sidestep reducing cultural phenomena to biological phenomena with the caveat that 'culture and civilization could not have arisen from single individuals and thus cannot be reduced to biological mechanisms and, even less [...] to a subset of genetic specifications. Their comprehension demands not just general biology and neurobiology but the methodologies of the social sciences as well' (124). Yet, he attached social rules and norms to basic survival instincts and located the dynamics of their sustenance in the 'neural representations of the wisdom [these norms and rules] embody', asserting that 'the means to implement that wisdom [...] are inextricably linked to the neural representations of innate regulatory biological processes' (125).

10 Although Damasio's distinction between the body's material response to stimuli and the subject's self-perception as an 'organism in the act of perceiving' appears similar to what Brennan called the 'foundational fantasy' that we pre-exist as self-contained, independent 'subjects', differences in these materialist accounts remain.

11 For Brennan, intentionality can be both conscious and unconscious (2004: 75; see note 6 above and note 13 below).

12 Unlike Damasio (and Tomkins, on whose work Sedgwick heavily relies), Brennan insisted that the affects, and the feelings evoked by them, are not innate; or, as she puts it, they are 'not only inherited' (2004: 75). 'What is at stake with the notion of the transmission of affect is precisely the opposite of the sociobiological claim that the biological *determines* the social [...]. [S]ocial interaction shapes biology. My affect, if it comes across to you, alters your anatomical makeup for good. This idea [...] stands neo-Darwinism on its head' (74). Yet, even this new gloss on the lineage of affects and their transmission fails to surmount linear, stimulus–response thinking. Something outside the subject (a transmitted affect) triggers a response in the subject in a casual chain. But if this affect has been corporeally produced intentionally, though involuntarily and unconsciously, as Brennan claimed, how to account for that production in the first place remains unexplained. Brennan attempted to preserve some notion of agency that can interrupt or elude the direction toward which negative affects would otherwise drive us (76). She tied this agency to the operation of 'the faculty of discernment' (118–120).

13 Although I generally agree with Brennan's formulation, I would say intentions do not *only* originate within the subject. Her use of 'intention' to describe the activity of matter is imprecise. 'Intention', in general usage, connotes a 'willfulness' or 'purposefulness' different from an automatic, albeit active, response to stimuli. Connolly's formulation of 'modes of agency' to counter the 'transcendental [human] subject' falls into a similar confusion (2011: 31–32).

14 Some theorists advancing 'non-representational ontologies' (Barnett 2008: 186) use affect theory to claim that better understanding of how power circulates below the level of consciousness can enable the development of affective adjustments supporting more progressive democratic politics. Connolly and Thrift both argue in favor of learning how to manipulate affects to this end, to facilitate the sedimentation of an ethos of democratic pluralism in the bodies of (unsuspecting) political subjects, thereby sidestepping the messy politics of deliberation and decision-making among antagonistic publics (Barnett 2008: 192). Yet, as Clive Barnett (2008: 186) has argued, because 'assertions of the political relevance of ontologies of affect rhetorically appeal to norms that are not [and cannot be] explicitly avowed from these theoretical perspectives', materialist ontologies of affect provide no reasons for justifying an allegedly more democratic mode of affective intervention in the arena of politics over some other mode, except an instrumentalist reason: affective manipulation is effective.

References

Arendt, Hannah (1958) *The Human Condition*. Chicago, IL: University of Chicago Press.

Arendt, Hannah (1970) *On Violence*. New York: Harcourt, Brace, Jovanovich.

Arendt, Hannah (2004 [1951]) *The Origins of Totalitarianism*. New York: Schocken Books.

Aupperle, Robin L., Andrew Melrose, Murray Stein and Martin Paulus (2012) 'Executive Function and PTSD: Disengaging from Trauma', *Neuropharmacology*, 62: 686–694.

Aupperle, Robin L., Carolyn B. Allard, Alan N. Simmons, Taru Flagan, Steven R. Thorp, Sonya B. Norman, Martin P. Paulus and Murray B. Stein (2013) 'Neural Responses During Emotional Processing Before and After Cognitive Trauma Therapy for Battered Women', *Psychiatry Research: Neuroimaging*, 214: 48–55.

Barad, Karen (2007) *Meeting the Universe Halfway: Quantum Physics and the Entanglement of Matter and Meaning*. Durham, NC: Duke University Press.

Barnett, Clive (2008) 'Political Affects in Public Space: Normative Blind-Spots in Non-Representational Ontologies', *Transactions of the Institute for British Geography*, 33: 186–200.

Benjamin, Jessica (1998) *The Bonds of Love: Psychoanalysis, Feminism, and the Problem of Domination*. New York: Pantheon.

Benjamin, Jessica (2006) 'Two-Way Streets: Recognition of Difference and the Intersubjective Third', *Differences*, 17: 116–146.

Benjamin, Jessica (2013) 'The Bonds of Love: Looking Backward', *Studies in Gender and Sexuality*, 14: 1–15.

Bennett, Jane (2010) *Vibrant Matter: A Political Ecology of Things*. Durham, NC: Duke University Press.

Berlant, Lauren (2011) *Cruel Optimism*. Durham, NC: Duke University Press.

Braidotti, Rosi (2013) *The Posthuman*. Cambridge: Polity Press.

Brennan, Teresa (2000) *Exhausting Modernity*. New York: Routledge.

Brennan, Teresa (2004) *The Transmission of Affect*. Ithaca, NY: Cornell University Press.

Butler, Judith (2014 [2012]) *Parting Ways: Jewishness and the Critique of Zionism*. New York: Columbia University Press.

Caputi, Jane (2003) '"Take Back What Doesn't Belong to Me": Sexual Violence, Resistance and the "Transmission of Affect"', *Women's Studies International Forum*, 26: 1–14.

CEDAW (Convention for the Elimination of Violence Against Women)General Recommendation no. 19, 1992. Available at: www.un.org/womenwatch/daw/cedaw/recommendations/recomm.htm (accessed 28 November 2016).

Clough, Patricia Ticineto (2007) 'Introduction', in P. T. Clough with J. Hally (eds) *The Affective Turn: Theorizing the Social*. Durham, NC: Duke University Press.

Connolly, William (1995) *The Ethos of Pluralization*. Minneapolis: University of Minnesota Press.

Connolly, William (2002) *Necropolitics*. Minneapolis: University of Minnesota Press.

Connolly, William (2005) 'The Media and Think Tank Politics', *Theory and Event*, 8 (4). Available at: https://muse.jhu.edu/article/192270 (accessed 28 November 2016).

Connolly, William (2011) *A World of Becoming*. Durham, NC: Duke University Press.

Damasio, Antonio (2005 [1994]) *Descartes' Error: Emotion, Reason, and the Human Brain*. London: Penguin.

Downs, Donald (1996) *More Than Victims: Battered Women, the Syndrome Society, and the Law*. Chicago, IL: University of Chicago Press.

Eckhardt, Christopher I., Christopher M. Murphy, Daniel J. Whitaker, Joel Sprunger, Rita Dykstra, and Kim Woodard (2013) 'The Effectiveness of Intervention Programs for Perpetrators and Victims of Intimate Partner Violence', *Partner Abuse*, 4: 175–195.

Gunnarsson, Lena (2016) 'The Dominant and Its Constitutive Other: Feminist Theorizations of Love, Power and Gendered Selves', *Journal of Critical Realism*, 15(1): 1–20.

Hardt, Michael (2011) 'For Love or Money', *Cultural Anthropology*, 26: 676–682.

Hearn, Jeff (2012) 'A Multi-Faceted Power Analysis of Men's Violence to Known Women: From Hegemonic Masculinity to the Hegemony of Men', *The Sociological Review*, 60: 589–610.

Hearn, Jeff (2013) 'The Sociological Significance of Domestic Violence: Tensions, Paradoxes and Implications', *Current Sociology*, 61: 152–170.

Hemmings, Clare (2005) 'Invoking Affect: Cultural Theory and the Ontological Turn', *Cultural Studies*, 19: 548–567.

Illouz, Eva (2012) *Why Love Hurts*. Cambridge: Polity Press.

Jónasdóttir, Anna G. (1991) *Love Power and Political Interests*. Örebro Studies no. 7. Örebro, Sweden: Örebro University.

Kubany, Edward and Susan Watson (2002) 'Cognitive Trauma Therapy for Formerly Battered Women With PTSD: Conceptual Bases and Treatment Outlines', *Cognitive and Behavioral Practice*, 9: 111–127.

Leys, Ruth (2011) 'The Turn to Affect: A Critique', *Critical Inquiry*, 37: 434–472.

Massumi, Brian (2002) *Parables for the Virtual: Movement, Affect, Sensation*. Durham, NC: Duke University Press.

Myers, Ella (2013) *Worldly Ethics: Democratic Politics and Care for the World*. Durham, NC: Duke University Press.

Papoulis, Constantina and Felicity Callard (2010) 'Biology's Gift: Interrogating the Turn to Affect', *Body and Society*, 16: 29–56.

Sedgwick, Eve Kosofsky (2003) *Touching Feeling: Affect, Pedagogy, Performativity*. Durham, NC: Duke University Press.

Thrift, Nigel (2004) 'Intensities of Feeling: Towards a Spatial Politics of Affect', *Geografiska Annaler. Series B, Human Geography*, 86: 57–78.

Woo, Deborah (2004) 'Cultural "Anomalies" and Cultural Defenses: Towards an Integrated Theory of Homicide and Suicide', *International Journal of the Sociology of Law*, 32: 279–302.

Youngs, Gillian (2009) 'Private Pain/Public Peace: Women's Rights as Human Rights and Amnesty International's Report on Violence Against Women', in A. G. Jónasdóttir and K. B. Jones (eds) *The Political Interests of Gender Revisited: Redoing Theory and Research with a Feminist Face*. Manchester: Manchester University Press.

Part III
Togetherness and its forms

7 Feminist visions and socio-political meanings of non-monogamous love

Justyna Szachowicz Sempruch

[Our] bodies are made up of multiple species (parasites, symbiotes), our cultures created through the crossing of borders, the mixing of identities.

(Barker et al. 2013: 201)

The understanding of love bonds has over the centuries undergone various conceptual splits vis-à-vis the changing geopolitics of family structure. It is certainly worthwhile to remember that the early Europeans adopted hetero-geneous meanings of love, such as homoerotic enactments inherited from ancient Greece Roman and (early) Christian polygamy, troubadour/chivalry romance, or love based on the arranged marriage. These distinct yet all patriarchal traditions grew into the European mold of 'family' serving as a socio-political counterpoint to the polluting effects of encounters with differ-ence (Nocentelli 2014). Safeguarding lineage, class and property, the socio-political liaison of the 'love-family' culminates in the sixteenth and seven-teenth century, subordinating its meanings to the masculine parameters of reason, liberty, and the superiority of whiteness. During this period, 'family' consolidates itself as a structure of intimate sociality based on monogamy, individuality, and a sense of European integrity that may, but does not need to, embody the experience of love as an emotional affect. In fact, relying on such a rationale, 'family' and close hetero-mono-normative relationships begin to undermine the power of love as a social act of sharing, transforming intimate life into a system of privilege and accumulation.

The twentieth-century western aesthetics of love, which becomes of impor-tance to my further discussion, is foremost preoccupied with individual loss, anxiety, and alienation, building on the symbolical 'matching halves': 'anima and animus', 'logos and eros' (Jung, Freud, Fromm). During this period, the ideas of partnership begin to appear on the grounds of individual choice, suggesting that the 'westerners' have moved from conjugal relationships towards 'pure' (confluent) love as a subject of free negotiation between autonomous partners (Giddens 1992: 94). Following this shift towards indi-viduality but also, quite clearly, towards commodification of individual desires, relationships turn into life style preferences and love becomes a pri-vate affair, whereby sexuality and erotically satisfying partnerships are most fundamental, overlapping with the Freudian libido, a mental/erotic force that stands against the death drive. From this privacy-focused perspective, desire as well as the fantasy about desire, becomes the focal point of bonding; and this happens at the time when multicultural, homosexual, and interracial identity begins to enter the public sphere, gaining both cultural validity and political prominence. What is thought-provoking about this transformative process is that the post/modern conceptualization of love as the archetypal union continues to build on the notion of scarcity and the deeply rooted belief that the beloved/missing half can become our 'possession', that we can mark our ownership, be suspicious or even hostile towards others because of the fear that they could take our 'love' away (Barker et al. 2013).

The possessive dimension of love as the most intense form of human bonding has been a key source of contestation in the first- and subsequently second-wave feminist critique of patriarchal structures. In Europe, the explicit tensions between the idealized longing for a union based on mutual possession and women's realities were particularly strong in early twentieth-century feminist Marxism (Goldman 1910; Kollontai 1932; Zetkin 1895). Formulations of 'free love' offered in this period decisively reject the privatization of affects, locating the roots of women's oppression in the libidinal economy and thus playing an important, but largely overlooked, role in shaping the subsequent feminist-conscious close relationship ideals. In particular, Clara Zetkin and Alexandra Kollontai recognized that women's subordination within the family is a larger societal issue than just the so-called 'woman's question', and needs to be approached as part of an overall societal transformation that opens broader political horizons of love as a form of spiritual abundance to be shared with everyone. In resonance with parallel intercontinental 'first wave' feminism (e.g. de Beauvoir, Drucker, Fuller, Stanton, Woolf), 'bourgeois love' is said to rest on the oppressive structure of the patriarchal family, at best referenced as duty, at worse as an emotional entrapment, manipulation and madness within the normative confines (Zetkin 1895; and later e.g. Friedan, Irigaray, Kristeva, Rich). Against these stifling family scenarios, 'red love' reclaims the emotional spontaneity of love, liberates the concepts of gender, friendship, and care from the state-controlled family in the romantic sense of revolution and solidarity between classes, sexes, and nations (Goldman 1910; Kollontai 1984; Luxemburg 1918).

Simultaneously, as part of the political necessity to formulate class-conscious ideals, the envisioned 'New Woman' is said to enrich (proletarian) spontaneity with a sexual liberty that abandons monogamous ideals and strives towards autonomous socialist-conscious independence from capitalist production. This transference of the romantic logic into social dialectics becomes possible under the premise that 'red love' is not about carnal promiscuity, carnivalesque temporality, or anarchy, but foremost about the conviction that social equality and love for the community cannot be achieved without eradicating the property-related oppression of female sexuality and love (Kollontai 1972). In consequence, and arguably more explicitly today than it was possible in the early twentieth century, the difference between the revolutionary socialists and the 'bourgeois' intellectuals was not due to minor strategic standpoints, but based on crucial political and philosophical decisions as whether to fight for global or partial class- and race-related women's suffrage. In recognizing such differences, feminist socialists created the most radical vision of the global societal transformation, which they believed could only be achieved gradually, through a process of socio-political revolution of the monogamous family structure. Amounting to a fundamental milestone on the path to the societal liberation of affects, 'free love' requires an end to the global devaluation of care work and labor inside the family, an issue still unresolved today (Bjørnholt and McKay 2014) and thus of particular significance for my discussion of non-monogamous formulations of love as a creative, socio-emotional, and revolutionary power.

While contemporary family research has begun to engage in the subject of love power, the undeniable validity of early socialist proposals for the twenty-first century should be seen in light of the continued tensions between Euro-centric individualization (the increasing instability of nuclear 'romance') and contemporary eco-political forms of collective sustainability (communities, groups, cooperatives). The latter, as a socialist 'legacy of love' towards society, derive from and illustrate the urgency with which to approach 'family' as a 'love bond' that is based on choice and capacity to transcend its nuclear entrapment. The contemporary changes of living conditions in Europe, especially in large urban spaces of which Warsaw serves in my discussion as an empirical example, certainly suggest that attitudes to and understandings of love bonds are becoming more diverse and elastic, but also more politically charged than ever. Rising divorce rates, LGBTQ and other non-traditional forms of relationship, extramarital births, adoptive parenting, and assisted reproduction have clearly begun to signal new patterns of family formation, which might significantly revolutionize the normative model (Eurostat 2017).

To conclude my introduction, it is certainly difficult to speak about a common imagery of bonding in light of the vulnerability and commodification of love as well as the decline of the normative family model in the twenty-first century. Inquiries into whether there exist any new, contemporary cutting-edge concepts of love are very significant. Following especially on the questions of why the socialist feminist ideals are interesting to compare with the current decentralization of the family structure, and how this transformation of intimacies converges with current feminist-informed spiritual awakening (Anzaldúa 1997; Barker et al. 2013; Gunnarsson 2014; hooks 2000),[1] I have become interested in whether the growing precariousness of bonding implies increasing uncertainty, instability and temporality, or whether such precariousness might become a precondition for its actual sustainability. In particular, I believe that we might find some interesting elements of such sustainability in the practice of polyamory understood as multiple loves based on consensual agreement among all partners involved. The underlying question which I attempt to answer is whether love, as affected by current politically compressed and unresolved tensions, can be defined as a concept based on co-existence and solidarity with others beyond the privacy of the individual household. It is perhaps important to specify what kind of love is referenced here, and I believe that it is neither exclusively the capitalist nor socialist notions of it, but all that embrace the significance of care, friendship, and ecstasy/eroticism in the feminist ethical and socio-political sense. In developing my argument throughout this chapter, I rely on my empirical research on alternative bonding conducted in Warsaw, in order to show how the growing fragility of the family structure might correlate with contemporary trans/feminist exchange across socio-political and emotional frontiers. In this, I follow recent feminist-informed formulations of love as a subject of knowledge that move beyond earlier Eurocentric traditions, paying tribute to 'red love' as well as laying further gender-sensitive foundations for a 'new' sociality based on love as a socio-emotional power (Ferry 2013; Illouz 2007; Jónasdóttir et al. 2011).

Contemporary bonding, plurality of love

The enormous ethical work of the early twentieth century with respect to the recognition of love for sociality is currently reflected and finds its revival in the growing visibility of non-hetero-mono-normative bonding across Europe (Gabb 2008; Kulpa and Mizielinska 2011; Santos 2013; Weeks 2007). The proliferation of LGBTQ relationships and of polyamorous love based on friendship and commitment attest to the rising alternatives to traditional family models (Labriola 2010; Morgan 2011; Roseneil et al. 2013). While I have already argued that the early twentieth-century feminist thought broke new grounds in the perception of close relationships, the beginning of the twenty-first century reveals an even more complex vulnerability of bonding in the face of the continued bio-social and political forces of commodification (Bauman 2003; Ferry 2013; Kristeva 1995). Following on these manifestations of change, I do not mean that the traditional meanings of family are dying, or that there is less need for stability in love bonding as such. Rather, the changing conditions of life (migration, mobility, internet, local/global inequalities) are causing cracks in the old, existing forms of bonding under the strain of internal and external conflicts, while, simultaneously, new forms are emerging.

Above all, and before I continue with any (cultural) analysis of non-monogamous bonding, I would like to emphasize that non-monogamy has never been, straightforwardly, friends with any form of feminism. This is due to the overwhelming phenomenon of historical and contemporary polygamy, which – with few globally registered exceptions – subjugate(d) a number of socio-economically dependent women (slaves, servants) to privileged men (patriarchs), who could/can afford such female groups (Zeitzen 2008). Having said that, the newly emerging socio-political meanings of love, frequently articulated in connection with contemporary contestations of the family structure, have much more in common with the early twentieth-century feminist collective consciousness than any non-monogamy practiced under patriarchal law. The reason why contemporary non-monogamous bonds might be different, and therefore relevant to my discussion, stems precisely from their potential connections with the early feminist awareness of responsibility and care for the community, i.e. something larger than the private (nuclear) love.

Among the various non-monogamous intimacies, I emphasize the consensual polyamorous relations, i.e. bonds open for multiple romantic and sexual partners, which seem to have received most acute feminist attention in the last decade and are continuously re-shaping their own socio-political semantics (Barker et al. 2013; Barker and Langdridge 2010; Haritaworn et al. 2006). At the moment, I would refer to polyamorous constellations practiced across Europe by individuals representing various and sometimes conflicting views on the actual meanings of their experience, and who most often simply identify with the process of 'becoming polyamorous' (NMCI 2015). I therefore discuss the visions and socio-political potential – rather than any outcome – of such bonding practices in terms of building new forms of emotional sustainability. This is significant both in light of the current structural precariousness of non-normative bonding and in light of the political urgencies across and beyond European borders, attesting to the growth of economic and cultural inequalities. In my further discussion, I follow up on contemporary expressions of polyamory relying on my empirical research samples collected in the region of Warsaw from 2013 to 2016.[2]

While the phenomenon of polyamory has become a popular subject of research in Western Europe, it has also been increasingly discussed in various studies concerning alternative forms of family life in Poland (e.g. Andrzejczyk-Bruno 2012). However, polyamory is still utterly controversial in the Polish discourse, which continues to take certain models of non-hetero-monosexual behavior as a sign of inability to create a family as such (FCBOS 2004). In Poland, there is no civil partnership act, no recognition of same-sex or any other non-standard families. In 2013, three bills were discussed for the very first time by the Polish parliament but did not pass, and they were met with a vulgar response from the public (Mizielińska and Stasińska 2017).[3] Since the victory of the conservative party (PiS) in 2015, the level of verbal aggression in the media towards any form of 'abnormality' that extends beyond the Catholic tradition does not cease to surprise. The word 'gender' has in itself become a trigger to divide the nation into those who stand for 'healthy, Polish family values' and those who import 'abject' elements into the otherwise 'true national culture'.[4]

In contrast to such public construction of the family landscape, my overall research (RS 1–3, see note 4) contains a detailed material on the growing precariousness of the nuclear family structure and the significance of other forms of bonding in relation to love, friendship, and trust. My research subjects are representative of these new types of relationships, since they were not recruited in mainstream places and are not homogeneous in terms of class, nation, or race (some are not Polish, some are not heterosexual, some are openly polyamorous). The category 'polyamorous' refers to an open-ended definition of bonding in terms of its socio-emotional stability, whereby relationships are negotiated as a response to 'the stifling mono-normativity' (RS2), and to the many other precarious, temporary, and non-committal bonding arrangements, such as swinging or having 'friends with benefits'. Indeed, out of 68 research participants who defined their bonds as 'casual, plural, bi-sexual and/or polyamorous' (RS2), 59 described them as 'uncertain (undocumented, undefined, changing in terms of definition), yet stable (remaining intact)' (RS2); 53 referred to the need for a 'consensual contract', i.e. an agreement on what is and is not acceptable within the given constellation; 48 emphasized that it is an open attitude to new possibilities, equal for all partners, that ensures trust, commitment, and stability of the relationship; and 17 found stability in a closed bond ('poly-fidelity'), in which no other sexual or emotional relationships are accepted. Out of these, only 15 declared to have founded their relationship on a 'freedom from contract', i.e. the acceptance of any choices made by partners independently of what these might imply for the relationship. Overall, the growing emotional need for freedom to express affects connects in my research directly with the ability to follow one's passions (desires, ideals) and to maintain a psycho-economic independence from the partner/family or bond (RS1–3). The most attractive bonding 'trends' among younger partners (up to 35 years of age) are in fact characterized by 'spontaneous uncertainty', a phenomenon based on openly declared freedom and respect for choices among partners, which includes their emotional and financial ability to leave the bond at any moment of life, if desired. Such 'uncertainty' should not be confused with generally more researched instability (psychological and/or physical violence, economic poverty, addictions), but rather represents a manifestation of human capacities for psychic advancement in bonding.

Rather than attempting to condense polyamorous bonding into any binding definition, my analysis focuses on the question of why such open-ended relationships have gained so much popularity over the last decade. I find this question of crucial importance in light of research that warns us against over-romanticizing the political potential of polyamory; there is some awareness of new sexual hierarchies in which non-monogamy is positioned as unquestionably better, or perhaps politically more valid than monogamy (Barker et al. 2013; Easton and Liszt 1997). Following both theory and research, polyamorous enactments indeed vary to such an extent that categories, especially those based on values, are difficult to establish due to differences generated by age, family status, social belonging, and income. A young unmarried and childless person is usually much more willing to enter a multiple bonding ('play with the possibilities', RS2) than a married and/or divorced person of 45+. Economic independence from a current and/or former partner also impacts on the willingness to 'experiment with freedom of choice' (RS2). Some prefer to gather around a poly-community, some avoid groupings and remain in private/closed relationships, and some practice both, depending on their 'current emotional needs, which are often changing' (RS2). Independently on these differentiations, polyamorous love is recurrently identified as 'uncertain', and yet – due to its risky (shifting) status – 'deeply engaging', because it abandons granted attachments and privileges in the hope of 'gaining more emotional freedom' (RS2). The latter involves the ability to make decisions, choices, and commitments following one's heart and 'one's own convictions', rather than any 'socially-approved prescriptions for happiness' (RS2):

> [Our love] is not a smooth process [...] but I think it's worthwhile. With respect to [M] – when I look back at what I know about her, I marvel at her desire to find the definition/experience of utopian love. To learn as to what that is. She is [still] learning to love and I believe her path is dependent on developing the thing that she lacks most – intuition and self-love [...] I think her frustration is that she sees this great energy between me and my other partner – this love that we have [had] for each other for many years [and] that we often waste on being angry and unhappy about things that lack significance when compared to our love and passion for each other. We lose our track on that and there she is right. We need to teach [one another] to live without limits on love and with full compassion, understanding, and self-devotion. When we achieve this, then [we] all will be free to make [our] own decisions and go if required to follow [our] own paths.
>
> (RS2)

Interestingly, the majority of research participants define their bonding as 'happy' only as long as they maintain a well-balanced socio-emotional connection both within and outside the bond, e.g. friendships, working environment, communities (RS1–3).[5] Bonding through openly manifested physical touch (patting, hugging), flirting, and empathy 'at home, work, and elsewhere' are often referenced as crucial not only to the overall 'healthy atmosphere' but also to 'a thought-inspiring, creative spirit' shared by family members, employees, and friends (RS1–3). Other committal and non-committal connections, e.g. culturally sanctioned, financial, political ('because we are married', 'have children', or 'believe in similar values'), appear rather secondary and insufficient to build a bond, except through enforcement, convenient arrangement, and/or manipulation (RS1–3).

In my research, these types of insufficiencies amount to the average emotionally disengaged landscape (72 percent of those interviewed had at least one experience of a serious bonding failure; 47 percent had experienced stagnation, anxiety, and depression; 82 percent displayed curiosity about other bonding options and a willingness to change). Moreover, conflicts, abuse, and inequality appear to exist across the axis of differences based on culture, nationality, race, sexual orientation, religion, health, and age. Those who declared their longing for or had already practiced bonding as an alternative to normativity (76 percent) expressed an exposure to existential precariousness but also a willingness to act together (RS1–3), e.g. 'a need to meet on a regular basis in order to discuss and compare their bonding/family experience' (RS2). Most interestingly, in challenging the common imagery of traditional belonging, polyamory (at least it its theoretical conjecture) appears to radically diverge from other forms of non-monogamy, such as cheating, swinging, or having other 'disposable' relationships. The question, therefore, which also became important early in my work, is about the consensual bonding as such: What makes it different? What, if at all, makes it last?

Placed in a broader societal context than the usually discussed neoliberal commodification of emotional values, polyamory involves the acceptance of uncertainty in terms of belonging, property, and exclusivity, i.e. in terms of values that dismiss any playfulness or spontaneity of love beyond the normative bond. Therefore it is important to distinguish between the experience of love as 'a sheer openness to possibilities' (e.g. spontaneous in/stability, playfulness, trust) and as 'an act of securing belonging of all partners', which might derive from emotional insecurity or mistrust displayed by one or more partners (RS2). The disparity between these two actualities becomes evident in moments of conflict, frustration, or other challenges related to jealousy and rejection – the two commonly referenced emotional states (52 out of 68 respondents in RS2). One might therefore argue that while the emotional acts of insecurity (e.g. hiding/suppressing undesirable emotions) validate rather than challenge the normative value of property, polyamorous ideals based on the consensual acceptance of uncertainty – (and I emphasize ideals rather than practice, RS2) – do not just simply challenge, but truly revolutionize the mononormative model of bonding. Plurality of love can therefore serve as a useful point of reference for further discussion of contemporary feminist-informed visions of love power.

Simultaneously, my findings indicate that polyamorous bonds can but do not always imply a higher, i.e. unencumbered and therefore more advanced or more ethical sexual order, as formulated by the early feminist Marxist ideals. Inadvertently, polyamorous constellations can become a form of idyllic manifestation of love, which in reality contains exclusion and disappointment, often related to 'superficial bonding with too many partners' or to 'difficulties with maintaining a truly loving and truly open love bond' (RS2). While commercialization of polyamory is by far not the case in my research location, where such bonding arrangements represent a marginalized lifestyle, the lifestyle as such can fail to consider deep socio-personal attachments, mirroring contemporary romantic love enactments of rejection, jealousy, and control:

[So you want to punish me for the trip?]
    Not the point [...]. This does not mean that I do not love you nor that I am not happy for you but it does put us on opposite sides when it comes to our common decision-making processes – it's like your whole

thing with polyamory: you just did things without explaining and under-standing the risks and even when something happened you did not tell [me] about it. Classic example is your trip to [D] where you were to heal yourself together with [K] while at the same time you were all over Facebook showing off your trip. It's also like the statement that I am never around (not on holidays but working) but without that you would not be able to go to [D]. Life is not about saying I love you and then doing your own thing – it's about compassion and understanding and most of all about empathy. I did not feel any when you picked the time that you picked to go on this trip – it was a decision that did not consider the timing from my perspective – a time where I spent most of the time in the house [...] something that I have been accused of not doing enough.

(RS2)

Building on Eleanor Wilkinson's argument that our need to believe in love makes us at times accept or endure 'things we should not have to endure' (2016: 8), hostility or fear of being hurt and abandoned are well-known emotional complexities, applying in fact to any kind of loving situation (nuclear bonding, love among friends, parents–children). The plurality of loving partners, however, makes it all the more intersectional and complex in terms of desires, demands, or expectations involved, as these may be 'different each time' and 'complicated in practice' (RS2). Thus, in agreement with Meg Barker, Jamie Heckert, and Wilkinson, I believe 'that there is no one way of doing polyamory' (2013: 198) and that the understanding of its advancement depends on a careful delineation of its heterogeneity. It is the plurality of bonding rather than some rules that constitute its structure and which embo-dies the actual challenge to 'the norms of monogamy' and, more importantly, to 'the politics of mononormativity' (2013: 198). I would also highlight the uniqueness of each bonding partner, whereby the uniqueness is not exclusive to polyamory, but is in fact valid for all human bonds, including the nuclear model. What appears more intense and sometimes perhaps more excessive in polyamory is the complexity of emotional interchange based on plural inter-actions among multiple and consensually acknowledged fascinations, loves, partners. What I find most important is that polyamory 'can potentially blur the definition between sexual and non-sexual, the romantic and non-romantic, especially when we shift its meaning away from having "multiple lovers" to "multiple loves"' (Barker et al. 2013: 198). It is precisely in such a generous sense of loving that the usually unnoticed multiplicity of loves becomes apparent, i.e. that one can be simultaneously in love with plural partners, plural works of art, plural landscapes, and plural philosophies.

This argument, in turn, allows for a theoretical interpellation about poly-amory (plural love) as something more advanced than monogamous and non-monogamous scripts in general, building on the experience of in/stability understood as resistance to financial or emotional dependency on one's part-ner (e.g. 'I can't leave [him] because I don't have my own money', RS1), and allowing for a connection based on 'trust in' and 'commitment to more than just one person' (RS2). Here multiplicity stands in direct opposition to nuclear property, need for domination, and control in the Marxist sense. For some such resistance might come easily, for some it might become a serious challenge that leads them into a continuous process of giving up dependency through emotional work involving assertiveness, self-reliance, and self-love, and oftentimes also professional therapy as well as other forms of healing, or building alliances and identifications.

For example, my research samples contain a spectrum of references to 'the overall quality of life' and 'alternative lifestyle' (e.g. sustainable consumption, meditation, love of animals, nature, RS2), as part of a larger picture of practicing polyamory. In light of such recognition, communities seem to emerge and constitute themselves not only through people who represent the same bonding ideals (e.g. who practice polyamory in consensual ways), but also through those who are attracted to and affiliate with the overall socio-emotional environment that the community represents, e.g. 'bonding as an antidote to mono-normativity' (RS2). Although there might be some danger in such identifications, they undeniably converge in self-awareness and a need for in-depth communication (interconnection, interchange) with partners and communities (59 out of 68 researched bonds, RS2). My research in fact reveals two parallel socio-emotional needs: the need for acceptance within the relation itself (e.g. to make sure that 'emotionally speaking, we are all on the same page', as 'a form of securing one another a space for safety and comfort within the bond', or as 'a constant process of negotiating terms and conditions of the relationship', RS2) and the need for acceptance within the overall sociality (during public events, with respect to legal regulations, custody, RS2). These characteristics parallel in many ways what Anthony Giddens (1992) describes as 'pure relationships', yet these become more complicated once approached from the feminist-informed, equality-sensitive, and plural partnerships angle.

Although as yet fragmented and under-documented, contemporary polyamory in Europe, with particular emphasis on the Central and East European region, marks a significant turning point in the history of the family, most obviously with respect to gender relationships vis-à-vis a wide variety of bonding possibilities via friendships, sexualities, affects, material properties, and socio-political coalitions. This speaks foremost to theory, as research shows that practice can always surprise us with much more complexity. Thus, a distinction between practice and theory will be necessary in my further discussion, and I will refer to 'polyamory' as practice and to 'consensual plurality' as an abstraction that builds upon existing literature and research that order the existing practices into some theoretical framework. Overall, I will look at 'consensual plurality' of love as the most significant and transformative potential of bonding, as well as a possible point of departure to explicate its sustainability – especially the emotional and ethical values which make love power lasting and fair from a trans/feminist perspective.

Consensual plurality and sustainability of bonding

This final section addresses consensual bonding in terms of its socio-emotional but also political power. I will attempt to define these two aspects of power through the possible meeting points of the feminist-Marxist, global trans-feminist, and ecological positions. In its ethical conjecture, I understand the consensual plurality of bonding as a precarious and peripheral transgression of normativity that seeks to undermine the dominant codes of culture, such as the patriarchal preservation of the nuclear family (Sempruch 2008). To begin with, the pejorative understanding of precariousness as heresy or deviance, goes back to the beginnings of European philosophical thought and the wes-tern construction of intimate life as a system of accumulation (family based on property and belonging), which I addressed in the first part of this chapter.

Here, I would like to consider the precarious traits of bonding in light of the emerging feminist-informed theories on love power (Gunnarsson 2014; hooks 2000; Jónasdóttir and Ferguson 2014). This set of theories reflects on the current dissemination of cultures, in which identities are useful as strategic identifications in the areas of socio-political significance, e.g. in the face of tensions with respect to gender, nationality or religion, in Poland and across Europe. At the same time, it attests to the growing need for sustainability of the affects that govern those identifications, as such offering a constructive divergence from the cultural (conservative) order.

Tracing especially the expanding feminist interest in love as a socio-emo-tional power, a worldwide awareness of this affect has begun to emerge in the form of interdisciplinary knowledge with significant consequences for indivi-dual bonding and for societies at large.[6] Most interestingly, researchers are beginning to realize that next to socio-political and psychic transformations there exists a domain of spirituality, which, besides in theological studies, has not been discussed as a valid reference in a secular environment (academic scholarship, politics). Barker et al. formulate, for example, 'a (r)evolutionary love ethic', a new political economy 'unbounded by classical notions of revo-lution', in which the early feminist/anarchist thought of 'changing the world' connects with 'letting love blossom and persist within oneself' (2013: 199). These spiritually enriching associations between 'the world' and 'the selfhood' interlink the unencumbered spirit of 'red (proletarian) love' with such pro-foundly important processes of bonding as caring, building bridges and alli-ances, negotiating, or even flirting with the sociality. In this, admiration – the subtlest, and, ontologically speaking, the purest aspect of love – begins to unfold in unpredictable, multiple directions. The ability to admire (marvel, wonder) brings us back to childhood and indicates losing oneself in sponta-neous beauty without the urge to control or even understand. And, thus, in the state of admiration, sociality too, as we know it from the post-Marxist landscapes, begins to grow and expand, transforming the ways in which bio-logical, geographical, and social bodies interact with the capitalist rationale. Love, especially in these socio-emotional aspects, begins to transgress towards other kinds of logic, shifting from the nuclear experience between individuals towards other beings, human and non-human alike, and towards the earth as a life-giving energy (Anzaldúa 1997). In this spiritual encounter, love is borderless, without aim or even shape, but persists as a very tangible experience. Some might know this kind of love from art, poetry, or literature, some might have experienced it more directly through various acts of creativity, through solitude, meditation or even illness and death.

Feminist preoccupations with spirituality echo, in this respect, the Hegelian understanding of love as a form of new potentiality and a force of resistance that infinitely acts against 'the terror of one's emptiness' (Sosnowski 2011: 22). Such emptiness is often experienced through one's inability to find a loving partner or a life companion, or after loss, divorce or other forms of separation from them. In a broader sense, this experience might also include living in a place without support and recognition from the society (e.g. as a result of enforced emigration) or with someone one does not desire (e.g. due to some contract or financial obligation). Indeed, without socio-emotional support the subject is homeless and alienated, but not immobilized. Following feminist thinking on love power, there is an immense potential in homelessness and transgression (Kristeva 1995; Spivak 2012), suggesting ways in which stigma and recognition are perennially translated one into the other, and allowing precisely for a spiritual awakening. Of importance here are such projects as bell hooks' vision of 'selfless love', Audre Lorde's 'erotic power' or Gloria Anzaldúa's 'queer ontology', all three discussing transgression as a transformative power: transgression of one's own possessiveness towards the other, which activates selflessness and love for oneself (hooks 2000), transgression of the suppressed passions and desires within oneself, which activates the erotic power (Lorde 1984), and, finally, transgression understood as a constant intermingling of all forms of living without discrimination (Anzaldúa 1997).

Once perceived from this socio-emotional angle, transgression provides us with a useful theoretical and practical ground to explicate the potential of love power in contemporary precariousness and plurality of bonding. The common feature of such forms as intermingling short-term relationships, multiple on-line dating, promiscuity, or polyamory, is that they rest on the acceptance of uncertainty: first, because they challenge the normative family/ bonding structure based on property and exclusivity of belonging; second, because they challenge emotions based on control and domination, such as jealousy and rejection, which are inherent to mono-normativity; and, third, because they occur and operate in the world with no or very limited legal regulations with respect to property, heritage, and representation. Following the transformative potential of homelessness and transgression, the very meanings of uncertainty undergo simultaneously a '(r)evolutionary' (Barker et al. 2013: 199) shift towards power as a space without judgment, where caring and responsibility for the other(s) meets with self-care and responsibility for oneself. The very intensity of plurality (the multiplicity and intermingling of loving subjects-objects) enables a whole spectrum of unruly, and, in that sense, also revolutionary affects, e.g. excitement, pain, joy, sorrow, fear, or hope. The semantics of precariousness might therefore suggest that bonding does not require security, borders, or divisions in order to last and endure, and, hence, to sustain its power. One can love a person despite sharing everydayness with somebody else, one can love more than two (Veaux and Rickert 2014), or even share love with many, which reflects on the fact that love relationships can be enacted as very subjective socio-emotional performances that reject structural, property-based constrains. What is needed, however, is a careful delineation of the kind of power that these performances propose, and I will explicate this thought in the remaining part of this chapter.

Following on 'love power' as a specific human creative power/productivity, to me it is foremost the question of what we can do with the loves we have, and, more specifically, with the powers the loves might and oftentimes do relinquish in terms of the socio-sexual, erotic (ecstatic), and/or care relations we build. Following on these three intersecting dimensions of power (Jónasdóttir 2011: 47), a polyamorous, or simply open-ended and plural, concept of love is not only transformative in the Marxist sense of labor or in its socio-emotional potential, but it is also – and needs to be – politically empowering: enabling transitions from (capitalist) domination towards spiritual inter/connections and interdependencies among individuals, communities, movements, and systems (Anzaldúa 1997; hooks 2000). Returning to the various enactments of consensual plurality (e.g. polyamory) of bonding, as discussed in light of my research findings, what seems to me the most crucial in defining love as power is its socio-emotional sustainability. In this context, I first suggest Anna Jonasdóttir's Marxist-feminist work on love in relation to current feminist explorations of affects, friendships, ecological care, and solidarity with the world (Messina-Dysert and Ruether 2015; Wilkinson 2010), all arguing for broader formulations of love extending beyond the romanticized nuclear union.

Jónasdóttir, in particular, has long argued for the understanding of love as a systematic work (involving time, energy, emotional and physical engagement of partners/lovers), which eventually leads to the accomplishment of unity, solidarity, and partnership as a vital site of collective transformation. In 'What Kind of Power Is "Love Power"?' Jónasdóttir elaborates on the concept of 'political sexuality' as the 'production point of entry' rather than 'reproduction per se', within which she frames her feminist intervention with historical materialism. This approach allows for the assumption that human love, similar to human labor, should be understood as a 'practical, human-sensuous activity' with creative capacity in a Marxist sense (Jónasdóttir 2011: 45; cf. Chapter 2 this volume). In an attempt to explicate the intersections between heteronormativity and other forms of love bonding, she also suggests that 'sexual love', and the ways it is practiced, 'influence [...] significantly the way other love relations are practiced, for instance those between parents and children', as well as 'the way people tend to practice person-to-person relations in other social contexts' (2011: 46). This observation expands the feminist work on how the cultural order and belonging dominates other kinds of love, enabling more complex 'intersectionality' as applied to sexual subjectivities and 'multi-dimensional social processes and contexts' (46).

Thus, in order to explicate some possibly political meanings of a consensual plurality of bonding, I believe that love, as a socio-emotional affect, has never been fully disciplined by capitalist endeavors. In agreement with Srecko Horvat, in my view love has more to do with a revolutionary tension between dynamism and fidelity; it is a constant re-invention that resists the force of habit: 'The moment when a revolution stops to reinvent, not only social and human relations, but stops reinventing its own presuppositions, we usually end up in a re-action, in a regression' (Horvat 2015: 4). This thinking returns both to Kierkegaard's reading of love as work against stagnation and Jónasdóttir's notion of 'love practices', speaking, in that sense, against the very structure of love subordination through the libidinal economy. The political potential lies in the metamorphic process of love as 'becoming', most tangibly as an experience of evolution that conquers our fears and obsessions with (economic) power for the sake of our psychic advancement (Heckert 2010; Wilkinson 2010). In this process love power becomes spontaneously un/ stable and more vulnerable than ever, but its meanings no longer remain confined to the sphere of private European homes. Following hooks, but also many other non-academic writers, love becomes in this sense 'selfless' (hooks 2000; McWhorter 2004), enabling its sustainability precisely through openness and vulnerability. Consequently, in its theoretical frames, a plurality of love (polyamory, spontaneous social friendships, multiplicity of admirations) aims at open coalitions based on ethical treatment, echoing themes of self-awareness, self-love, feminist-informed autonomy with respect to decisions of personal space, self-development, as well choices with respect to involvement of others (Mint 2010; Wilkinson 2016). Such paradigms of bonding values reflect the growing recognition that the world is one and that humanity, in the interest of its cultural survival, is bound to work together across various personal, cultural, national, and religious boundaries in order to settle the rising ecological, socio-economic, political, and security issues (Barker et al. 2013; Bjørnholt and McKay 2014; Illouz 2007). In particular, important voices emerge in research on the human right to love (care, preserve, sustain), the right to values globally eroded through enforced migrations, deteriorating labor contracts, and various denials of affects (Ferry 2013; Lynch et al. 2009).

Following up on these social/collective meanings of bonding on a more theoretical note for the twenty-first century, I have built my argument on a view of love as not only a socio-emotional, but also political power, as active will, knowledge, and awareness of being together in the world. Despite the idealistic, if not utopian undertones of this interpellation that echoes the early feminist formulations of unrelenting love power, I believe that to look at contemporary bonding enactments is to look at the significance of building and maintaining their power in cosmopolitan relation to the community, city, nation and beyond. In resonance with these and many other feminist accounts, rather than an idyllic vision, the agenda of such 'togetherness' needs to be seen in relation to divergent and unequal subject positions as constituting its substance. As already discussed in the context of polyamorous constellations, some can be happy living in a 'tri-some', some need an exclusive partner or a 'patchwork family', and some need a nation to feel being loved. What this means is that the key to any political positioning of 'togetherness' is its own heterogeneity/subjectivity, allowing for a re-formulation of transgression into an empowering, albeit not always happy affirmation of difference. As referenced by Barker et al. (2013), Derrida's project of 'unconditional hospitality' discernibly reminds us that cross-encounters can be ecstatic, but they are also 'unbearable', requiring that we 'give up mastery of [our] space, [our] home, [our] nation' (Derrida 1999: 70). In its radical delineation, 'togetherness' is therefore philosophical and political at once: it speaks about its own inherent incompatibility and the conscious, subjectively defined enactments of resistance, the practices of freedom, which, to paraphrase Luxemburg (1918), is always the freedom of those who think differently.

Finally, in the light of the intensification of conservative and neoliberal thinking in Poland and Europe at large, the coupling of 'plurality' and 'togetherness' offers an interesting intervention into the field of social justice. I draw here on Nancy Fraser's concept of 'misframing', which is central to present-day struggles for the political visibility of marginalized groups, and which means that when 'political space is unjustly framed', it results 'in the denial of political voice to those who are cast outside the universe of those who "count"' (2008: 147). Placing this political dimension of justice in the world of practice, what is needed is a greater visibility of transformative action, which would enable the multiple potentials of many unaccounted voices of love (Bjørnholt and McKay 2014; Lynch 2009; Waring 1988). The uneven terrain on which these reflections take place speaks volumes about 'the nature' of the politics of love. It also explains the actual political potential of such a transformation as undeniably immense. Since 'togetherness' involves sustainability of love in its multiple practice of difference, it creates no space for any political tactic of division. Self-love (self-respect, self-consciousness) therefore becomes a vital part of this transformation. To draw on Wilkinson, love integrity (sustainability) might be destroyed if it enters into an encounter with another more powerful body: 'If a coalition or encounter decreases our capacity to act then we should refuse to engage' (Wilkinson 2016: 9).

Thus, rather than dismissing the relation between domination and love, it is important to consider our own histories, which also shape our fears of rejection and hence our need to take control (Benjamin 1988; Gunnarsson this volume; Wilkinson 2016). Since our experiences of alienation, depression and incapacity to act border on the experiences of control and domination, love power – in its most political aspect – should be placed in the context of its own unruliness. Contemporary polyamory, especially as consensual plurality, therefore serves as a vivid example of building different (multiple) intimacies and modes of bonding (Labriola 2010). In this light, the growing precariousness of bonding might also imply that categorizing love bonds into any exclusive definitions as stable, rigid, or lasting (be it a nuclear, single parent, blended, same-sex, polyamorous, or any other) can be very limiting. Such understanding projects love as borderless and fluid (Diamond 2008), containing all or any of these categories as intersecting in a given cultural, socio-emotional, but also temporal arrangement. Accordingly, individuals might be able to 'move' from hetero-mono-sexual (nuclear) relations to various intersecting forms of love bonds that involve a broader community and friendship with animals and non-human nature, based on respect and expanding beyond the human desire to protect, sustain, and control. Whether they do, and under what conditions, is a question for further investigations with significant impacts on ways through which to understand contemporary bonding.

Current European revisions of thinking and practices related to marriage, sexuality, and intimacy are inevitably linked to broader socio-economic and political transformations. In line with feminist discussions of intersectionality within their specific theoretical frameworks (postsocialist, poststructuralist, postcolonial), a consensual plurality of bonding represents difference, giving rise to discursive innovations that subsequently can be normalized in the form of modified signifying practices. To quote Barker et al.:

> capitalism is not the truth of the world economy, nor the State the truth of politics. Exchanges based not on profit or power games, fear or greed, but on love, solidarity, mutual aid and recognition of our 'embodied interdependence' abound.
>
> (2013: 201)

What I thus have here attempted to convey is that the concepts of 'family' and 'love bonding' are continually redefined through increasingly interlocking global–local interdependencies of cultures and economies. It is compelling to formulate love as a bio-socially embedded, but subjectively defined capacity/power of individuals, a subject that cannot be studied through separately existing family models but in relation to their current heterogeneity and opened-ended structure. Such a love-centered, but also difference-sensitive, perspective defines bonding as an affect based on care and responsibility, that is not only a concern for individuals who are in love with one another, but a broader social issue that extends beyond private households and affairs. In this, revisions of thinking and practices related to marriage, family, sexuality, and intimacy are inevitably linked to broader socio-economic and political transformations necessitating new policy regulations with respect to wide-ranging rights of individuals, such as the right to same-sex marriage, abortion, consensual non-monogamies, and protection from domestic violence.

Notes

1 Throughout the history of feminist thought there has been a growing interest in spirituality corresponding directly or indirectly to missing or forgotten feminine

values and the politics of their representability (Christ 1997; Clément and Kristeva 2001; Klassen 2009; Ruether 1992; Messina-Dysert and Ruether 2015).

2 Funded by the Women Matter Foundation, the three year-long research (2013–16) was conducted by volunteers with social and anthropological studies in the Warsaw region. Methods involved questionnaires, open-ended in-depth interviews, semi-participant observation, and analysis of Instant Messaging samples. Altogether 208 active research participants presented their views on the subject of their past/current love bonding experiences and described their family situation. Participants were recruited from various support groups and multi-cultural communities (women's groups, poly-groups, international families, expat groups, and two programs run by the Women Matter Foundation). Participants represented different cultures, nationalities, age, and sexual orientation, whereby 64 per cent declared to be Polish and permanent residents of Poland, 15 per cent declared to be Polish living in the UK, Germany, or Switzerland, and 21 per cent declared to be of other European nationality than Polish. Within bonds there were plural and possibly intermingling participants (43 semi-active participants were observed, semi-interviewed in pairs/groups, and 104 passive actors were related to by their partners). Percentage refers to active research participants – based on the overall number of 208 participants: Participants were grouped into three categories of bonding: RS1 = hetero-mono-normative insecure and stable bonds based on 108 samples; RS2 = insecure/casual and stable polyamorous bonds based on 68 categorized and 11 non-categorized samples; RS3 = LGBTQ (mono) bonds based on 21 samples.

3 There has been a growing hostility in Polish public discourse to any form of non-hetero-normativity, especially towards LGBTQ families. In the most influential journals and newspapers (both the more liberal, pro-EU *Gazeta Wyborcza*, *Newsweek* and *Polityka*, and the conservative pro-Polish Catholic Church *Rzeczpospolita* and *Gazeta Polska*) same-sex relations are treated as a sexual and psychological disease which degenerates the Polish nation. Here, also, the word 'gender' has become a signifier for the entire political left, usually portrayed as very powerful and with feminist, pro-gay and lesbian, abortionist, pro-Western, and anti-Polish implications. An example offering an interesting synthesis of this discourse appeared on an anti-gender demonstration poster from 2015, warning 'healthy Poles' against 'gender': 'the ideology of spineless Westerners [is] not for our hardy Poles. Homosexual bonds are to be cured and not sanctioned' (in Graff and Korolczuk 2017: 27).

4 Over the last years I have been invited to give public lectures on the subject of gender outside of the university environment, which were met with open resentment and aggression. Recently (March, 2017), I was invited to a Polish National TV show about the funds allocated to so called left-oriented organisations, a show which I found utterly shocking and was clearly based on manipulated statistics (video available at http://wpolityce.pl/media/333690-dzis-w-warto-rozmawiac-kto-decyduje-o-tym-ze-m iliony-trafiaja-do-organizacji-gejowskich-i-feministycznych (accessed 4 June 2017)).

5 The concepts 'healthy', 'voluntary' and 'happy' have been defined and differentiated by cultural and national belonging, sexual orientation, and other individually defined preferences.

6 See the Love Research Network (University of Hull), http://lovenetwork.hull.ac.uk/; the Feminist Love Studies Network (Örebro University), https://www.oru.se/english/research/teams/humus/the-feminist-love-studies-network2/; and the International Association for Relationship Research, www.iarr.org/about/ (accessed 4 June 2017).

References

Andrzejczyk-Bruno, Grzegorz (2012) *Philia*. Available: www.philianizm.pl/publikacje (accessed 4 June 2017).

Anzaldúa, Gloria (1997). *Borderlands: The New Mestiza: La Frontera*. San Francisco, CA: Aunt Lute Books.

Barker, Meg and Darren Langdridge (2010) 'Whatever Happened to Non-Monogamies? Critical Reflections on Recent Research and Theory', *Sexualities*, 13(6): 748–772.

Barker, Meg, Jamie Heckert and Eleanor Wilkinson (2013) 'Polyamorous Intimacies: From One Love to Many Loves and Back Again', in T. Sanger and Y. Taylor (eds) *Mapping Intimacies: Relations, Exchanges, Affects*. Basingstoke: Palgrave Macmillan.

Bauman, Zygmunt (2003) *Liquid Love: On the Frailty of Human Bonds*. Cambridge: Polity Press.

Benjamin, Jessica (1988) *The Bonds of Love: Psychoanalysis, Feminism, and the Problem of Domination*. New York: Pantheon Books.

Bjørnholt, Margunn and Ailsa McKay (eds) (2014) *Counting on Marilyn Waring. New Advances in Feminist Economics*. Bradford: Demeter Press.

Christ, Carol P. (1997) *Rebirth of the Goddess: Finding Meaning in Feminist Spirituality*. New York: Addison-Wesley.

Clément, Catherine and Julia Kristeva (2001) *The Feminine and the Sacred*. [*Le féminin et le sacré*, 1998]. Translated by Jane Marie Todd. New York: Columbia University Press.

Derrida, Jacques (1999) 'Hospitality, Justice and Responsibility: A dialogue with Jacques Derrida', in R. Kearney and M. Dooley (eds) *Questioning Ethics: Contemporary Debates in Philosophy*. London and New York: Routledge.

Diamond, Lisa (2008) *Sexual Fluidity. Understanding Women's Love and Desire*. Cambridge, MA: Harvard University Press.

Easton, Dossie and Catherine A. Liszt (1997) *The Ethical Slut: A Guide to Infinite Sexual Possibilities*. San Francisco: Greenery Press.

Eurostat (2017) Available: http://ec.europa.eu/eurostat/statistics-explained/index.php/Marriage_and_divorce_statistics; http://ec.europa.eu/eurostat/statistics-explained/index.php/People_in_the_EU_–_statistics_on_household_and_family_structures (accessed 4 June 2017).

FCBOS (Fundacja Centrum Badania Opinii Społecznej) (2004). Available: www.cbos.pl/SPISKOM.POL/2004/K_004_04.PDF (accessed 4 June 2017).

Ferry, Luc (2013) *On Love: A Philosophy for the 21st century*. Cambridge: Polity Press.

Fraser, Nancy (2008) *Scales of Injustice: Reimagining Political Space in a Globalizing World*. Cambridge: Polity Press.

Gabb, Jacqui (2008) *Researching Intimacy in Families*. Basingstoke: Palgrave Macmillan.

Giddens, Anthony (1992) *The Transformation of Intimacy*. Stanford, CA: Stanford University Press.

Goldman, Emma (1910) *Anarchism and Other Essays*. New York: Mother Earth Publishing Association.

Graff, Agnieszka and Elżbieta Korolczuk (2017) 'W Stronę Antyliberalnej Przyszłości: Antygenderyzm i Antyglobalizacja', *Globalny Dialog*, 7(1): 27–29. International Sociological Association/Sage.

Gunnarsson, Lena (2014) *The Contradictions of Love: Towards a Feminist-Realist Ontology of Sociosexuality*. New York: Routledge.

Haritaworn, Jin, Chin-ju Lin and Christian Klesse (2006) 'Poly/logue: A Critical Introduction to Polyamory', *Sexualities*, 9(5): 515–529.

Heckert, Jamie (2010) 'Love Without Borders? Intimacy, Identity and the State of Compulsory Monogamy', in M. Barker and D. Landridge (eds) *Understanding Non-Monogamies*. New York: Routledge.

hooks, bell (2000) *All About Love: New Visions*. London: Women's Press.

Horvat, Srecko (2015) *The Radicality of Love*. Cambridge: Polity Press.

Illouz, Eva (2007) *Cold Intimacies: The Making of Emotional Capitalism*. Cambridge: Polity.

Jónasdóttir, Anna (2011) 'What Kind of Power Is "Love Power"?' in A. G. Jónasdóttir, V. Bryson and K. B. Jones (eds) *Sexuality, Gender and Power. Intersectional and Transnational Perspectives*. New York: Routledge.

Jónasdóttir, Anna G., Valerie Bryson, and Kathleen B. Jones (eds) (2011) *Sexuality, Gender and Power: Intersectional and Transnational Perspectives*. New York: Routledge.

Jónasdóttir, Anna G. and Ann Ferguson (eds) (2014) *Love: A Question for Feminism in the Twenty-first Century*. New York: Routledge.

Klassen, Chris (ed.) (2009) *Feminist Spirituality: The Next Generation*. London: Lexington Books.

Kollontai, Alexandra (1932). *Free Love*. Translated by C. J. Hoghart. London: Dent.

Kollontai, Alexandra (1972) *Sexual Relations and the Class Struggle: Love and the New Morality*. Bristol: Falling Wall Press.

Kollontai, Alexandra (1984) 'The Social Basis of the Woman Question', in *Selected Articles and Speeches 1872–1952*. Moscow: Progress Publishers.

Kristeva, Julia (1995) *New Maladies of the Soul*. New York: Columbia University Press.

Kulpa, Robert and Joanna Mizielinska (eds) (2011) *De-centring Western Sexualities: Central and Eastern European perspectives*. London: Ashgate

Labriola, Kathy (2010) *Love in Abundance: A Counselor's Advice on Open Relationships*. Emeryville, CA: Greenery Press.

Lorde, Audre (1984) *Sister Outsider. Essays and Speeches*. Berkeley, CA: The Crossing Press.

Luxemburg, Rosa (1918) *The Russian Revolution*. Chapter 6: The Problem of Dictatorship. Available: https://www.marxists.org/ (accessed 21 June 2017).

Lynch, Kathleen, Maureen Lyons and John Baker (eds) (2009) *Affective Equality. Love, Care and Injustice*. Basingstoke: Palgrave Macmillan.

McWhorter, Ladelle (2004) 'Sex, Race, and Biopower: A Foucauldian Genealogy', *Hypatia*, 19(3): 38–62.

Messina-Dysert, Gina and Rosemary Radford Ruether (2015) *Feminism and Religion in the Twenty-first Century: Technology, Dialogue, and Expanding Borders*. New York: Routledge.

Mint, Pepper (2010) 'The Power Mechanisms of Jealousy', in M. Barker and D. Landridge (eds) *Understanding Non-Monogamies*. New York: Routledge.

Mizielińska, Joanna, and Agata Stasińska (2017). 'There Is Nothing Like a Family: Discourses on Families of Choice in Poland', *Journal of Homosexuality*, doi:10.1080/00918369.2016.1267460: 1–23.

Morgan, David (2011) *Rethinking Family Practices*. Basingstoke: Palgrave Macmillan.

NMCI (1st Non-Monogamies and Contemporary Intimacies Conference, Lisbon) (2015). Available: https://nmciconference.wordpress.com/2016/05/27/archives-from -the-1st-nmci-lisbon-2015/ (accessed 4 June 2017).

Nocentelli, Carmen (2014) *Empires of Love. Europe, Asia, and the Making of Early Modern Identity*. Philadelphia: University of Pennsylvania Press.

Roseneil, Sasha, Isabel Crowhurst, Tone Hellesund, Ana Cristina Santos, and Mariya Stoloilova (2013) 'Changing Landscapes of Heteronormativity: The Regulation and Normalisation of Same-Sex Sexualities in Europe', *Social Politics*, 20(2): 165–199.

Ruether, Rosemary Radford (1992) *Gaia and God: An Ecofeminist Theology of Earth Healing*. San Francisco, CA: Harper and Row.

Santos, Christina Ana (2013) *Social Movements and Sexual Citizenship in Southern Europe*. Basingstoke: Palgrave Macmillan.

Sempruch, Justyna (2008) *The Fantasies of Gender: The Witch in Western Feminist Theory and Literature*. West Lafayette, IN: Purdue University Press.

Sosnowski, Maciej Adam (2011) *Pokochać dialektykę. O pojęciu miłości w filozofii spekulatywnej z nieustającym odniesieniem do Sørena Kierkegaarda*. Warsaw: Universitas.

Spivak, Gayatri Chakravorty (2012) *An Aesthetic Education in the Era of Globalization*. Cambridge, MA: Harvard University Press.

Veaux, Franklin and Eve Rickert (2014) *More Than Two: A Practical Guide to Ethical Polyamory*. Portland, OR: Thorntree Press.

Waring, Marilyn (1988) *If Women Counted: A New Feminist Economics*. London: Harper & Row.

Weeks, Jeffrey (2007) *The World We Have Won: The Remaking of Erotic and Intimate Life*. London and New York: Routledge.

Wilkinson, Eleanor (2010) 'What's Queer about Non-monogamy Now?' in M. Barker and D. Landridge (eds) *Understanding Non-Monogamies*. New York: Routledge.

Wilkinson, Eleanor (2016) 'On Love as an (Im)properly Political Concept', *Environment and Planning D: Society and Space*, 35(1): 57–71.

Zeitzen, Miriam Koktvedgaard (2008) *Polygamy: A Cross-cultural Analysis*. Oxford and New York: Berg.

Zetkin, Clara (1895) *On a Bourgeois Feminist Petition*. www.marxists.org (accessed 21 June 2017)

8 The invisible ties *We* share

A relational analysis of the contemporary loving couple[1]

Adriana García-Andrade and Olga Sabido-Ramos

There is no doubt that we live in what can be described as a capitalist, individualistic, and self-centered world. Despite this context, human beings strive to be in loving relationships. It is true that marriage rates are declining, but statistics on cohabitation show it is a growing phenomenon all around the world (Baker and Elizabeth 2014; Solís 2013). Puzzled by this state of affairs we ask why this is so. If 'love hurts' (Illouz 2012), if violence takes place within relationships, and if 'loving' relationships can have harmful consequences for families and society, why do we keep searching for them?

Here, we want to show that loving bonds can give joy/pleasure, personal development or a world of stable comfort; they can also give us a sense of membership and expectations that entice us to pursue them. Of course, these bonds can be both enabling and constraining. The account presented here tries to understand not only why love hurts when a relationship is called off or when the loved one dies, but also why love relationships can create bonds that are difficult to end because they involve people's own sense of being and identity.

The contemporary loving experience between lovers is a complex process. It involves sexual attraction, being in love, and having more or less stable bonds. Additionally, the relationship between lovers can be examined from numerous perspectives, which include – but are not limited to – culture, sexual preference, and a number of partakers. Given the complexity of the topic at hand, we will focus on western heterosexual couples, a contemporary version of romantic love, and the moment in which a bond between at least two persons is formed. We are aware that this is not the only relationship lovers can have but, for the time being, we shall devote our attention solely to this type of relationship.

In this chapter, we will examine the complexity of the loving relationship through the category defined as the *We*. In doing so, we want to emphasize the idea of love as a relational phenomenon; that is, as something that involves the simultaneous collaboration of at least two individuals. Here the works of Georg Simmel and Norbert Elias are relevant for us, especially when the former suggests that 'Lovers "have" a relationship (*Verhältnis*); they are as a sociological entity, "a relationship"' (Simmel 2009: 561). Following this

train of thought, we look at the loving couple through Elias' (2003) suggestion to use pronouns in order to observe social phenomena. We have thus
decided to take advantage of the *We* pronoun to explain the particular configuration of a couple's affective bonding (Elias 2003).

More specifically, our interest lies in the special bonds that result from the
We pronoun in the couple's relationship, understood as 'a specific configuration of people [...] [with] its specific dynamics, which are determined as much
by the structure of society at large as by that of the two constituents of that
society most immediately concerned' (Elias 2003: 131).

It should be noted that a couple's affective bond is different from the bonds
established amongst friends, family, and acquaintances. Following Elias, the
difference between these bonds lies in the degree of 'intensity of identification'
within the different levels of the *We*. That is, there exist different 'emotive
charges' which depend on existing degrees of integration between couples,
friends, groups, and even nations (Elias 2001: 202–203).

As it has been stated, the *We* loving relationship (from now on, *WeLR*) is
our starting point. It will be examined through three analytical levels. First,
through love as a world of meaning (the semantics of love); then through the
performative aspect of love (the situation); and finally, through the feelings
and experiences in the individual mind-body (the enminded body [Jónasdóttir
1994: 219–221, 266 note 13]). We will present each analytical level in so far as
it is related to the development of the *WeLR* and the bonds it entails.

One final remark needs to be made at this stage. The construction of the
content of each level analyzed here has been done by using the extended work
of sociologists such as Niklas Luhmann, Erving Goffman, and Georg
Simmel. Likewise, works conducted by feminists, psychologists, anthro-
pologists, and even neurologists have been included. Their contributions on
love and loving relationships were read with the following sociological questions in mind: How is the bonding between lovers possible and desirable in
our contemporary society? How do the actions of two or more participants
get linked through this loving bond (i.e. the *We*)? And, how is this related to
society in general and to experience in particular? Thus, our approach makes
use of insights from other disciplines in order to answer questions that stem
from a sociological perspective (for more on interdisciplinary dialogues see
Jónasdóttir this volume).

In what follows we present each level of analysis in order to discern what is
gained (or lost) by each member of the *WeLR* in contemporary western societies.

The semantics of love and the *We*

With the notion of semantics, we are proposing that love becomes a world of
meaning in itself. That is, it can be seen, first and foremost, as a cultural
product. Thus, love, as one social meaning amongst many others, becomes –
throughout the course of history – a sphere of separated meaning (Simmel
1971).

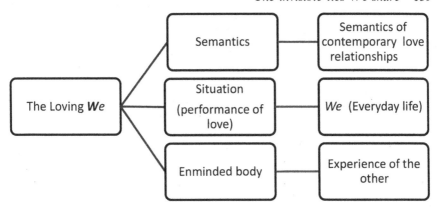

Figure 8.1 Three analytical levels of the We Loving Relationship (WeLR)

Through history, there can be found, generally speaking, and irrespective of their different names, three key semantics of love: ideal love, love as passion, and romantic love. Here we shall only focus on romantic love. Romantic love is the product of the process of differentiation in modern societies, which have constituted it as a world of autonomous meaning. It is a seventeenth-century western ideal, and most scholars currently working on the subject of love take it as a hegemonic cultural reference (Beck and Beck-Gernsheim 1995; Elias 1983; Giddens 2013; Illouz 2008; Precht 2011; Simmel 1971). In this section, we argue that the contemporary idea of the *WeLR* is related to the semantics of romantic love. However, the *WeLR* acquires particular characteristics that go beyond such semantics.

The roots of romantic love are to be found earlier in history (Rougemont 1983); however, the idea of romantic love as cultural reference reaches its point of consolidation in Europe between the seventeenth and ninetheenth centuries (Beck and Beck-Gernsheim 1995; Elias 1983; Giddens 2013; Illouz 2008; Precht 2011; Simmel 1971). The consolidation and hegemony of romantic love were possible due to certain conditions of possibility. These include *material conditions* led by a social class with enough leisure time at its disposal as well as the existence of physical spaces for love between a couple such as, for example, the bedchamber. There were also *cultural conditions,* which included the emergence of the notion of the individual; this notion vindicated the possibility of choosing the beloved person. And finally, there were *social conditions,* by which behavioral expectations regarding love were held differently for men and women and were of asymmetrical nature to the detriment of the latter. Although we cannot provide a full-fledged explanation of the development of each of these conditions, we will offer a brief description of them.

In common with several authors, we subscribe to the idea that love is the product of a distinct social class in a given historical moment. For us, it is Norbert Elias who provides the best account of the relation between romantic love and social class. For him, the *ethos* of romantic love arises within the ancien régime's intermediate courtesan stratum. Moreover, it emerges in sixteenth-century France as a form of differentiation (i.e. distinction) between the upper and lower classes. Nonetheless, Elias also argued that this *ethos* of romantic love coincides with the emergence of another *ethos* amongst the eighteenth-century western bourgeoisie (Elias 1983). The relation between the creation of a distinct social class and the idea of romantic love, helps us understand how love as experience and communication involves and depends on the existence of particular material and cultural conditions. The existence of those conditions also explains how romantic love ultimately became the hegemonic model. Thus, romantic love involves having a bedchamber of one's own, having certain emotional capital (both in terms of time and financial capital), enhancing one's linguistic skills and romantic competences (Illouz 2008: 326–327), and having 'a very refined acquaintance with situations and milieus, thus a great deal of culture, because adequately nuanced observation and attribution is only possible on such a basis' (Luhmann 1995: 226). In other words, it is not accidental that modern romantic love as experience and communication requires both cultural and social skills as well as certain material conditions.

The notion of romantic love as semantics spread to other social classes. We see how nowadays the signification of the love experience depends not on material goods or economic resources. People frame their love experiences within the semantics of love beyond the material conditions that were fundamental to the origin of the semantics itself. However, class mediation persists, both in the possibility of falling in love with those who are near in the social space (Bourdieu 1984), as well as in the practices of consumption usually associated with romantic love (Illouz 2008).

Individualization is another necessary condition for understanding love as a sphere of meaning of its own. The process of individualization, sociologically speaking, has to do with the emergence of modern society. It refers to the social transformations that allowed the individual to be liberated from certain ascriptive social bonds, on the one hand, and the emergence of new forms of relationships based on election, on the other. The emergence of social relations under the conditions of modern life promoted the creation of a distinct *self* as well as the creation of an image of the modern individual. Individualization had a direct impact on relationships based on affection such as friendship and coupledom, insofar as they were made possible via freedom of election (Simmel 2009).

For Luhmann, love as a sphere of meaning facilitates, enables, and promotes 'the communicative treatment of individuality' (1998: 14). In that sense, love works as the medium that allows the intensification of personal relations. It is through such relations that a person finds 'an unconditional confirmation of one's own *self*, of personal identity' (Luhmann 2010: 14). Accordingly, the individual as a whole and its confirmation as a special being are given by and due to the existence of love (as a medium), and find its clearest expression in the loving couple relationship.

In addition to what has been presented, a fundamental characteristic of the hegemonic model of romantic love is directly associated with what, following Luhmann, is known as *reflexive semantics*. This means *you love someone because you know you love them*. The affective bond, it follows, cannot be taken for granted, rather it is the subject of constant reflexion. Equally, for Elias an important characteristic of personal relations is their continuous evaluation. Evaluation is 'a kind of repeated inventory', 'a test of relations which is at the same time a test of themselves'. In this respect, Elias notes, '[lovers] have to ask themselves more often: how do we stand in relation to each other' (2001: 203–204).

As we have shown, the semantics of romantic presupposes certain material and cultural conditions, but gender asymmetry also plays a role – what we have named social conditions. Throughout history, love relationships and behavioral expectations associated with love have been held differently for men and women. The idea of romantic love was configured as a type of semantics based on a heterosexual relationship, where the asymmetrical relations between men and women became legitimate, usually to the detriment of women. The literature on this topic is vast, so we will only briefly describe four characteristics of romantic love and its relation to gender. First, love can be seen as a yardstick of female identity between the eighteenth and nineteenth centuries (Giddens 2013; Illouz 2012). As is well documented, cultural representations – including literature – associated with 'love stories' were sources of meaning from which women connected their everyday lives with the future and, consequently, created an individual story In contrast, male identity was associated with the public sphere. It follows, then, that love was a less prominent yardstick in the creation of an identity for men. As Shulamith Firestone has brilliantly put it, '[male c]ulture was built on the love of women and at their expense'. In other words, women did not create culture, because they were 'preoccupied with love' (Firestone 2012: 114). In the second place, the behavioral expectations regarding love have been held differently for men and women. For example, there are different ways in which men and women express their love (Hochschild 2008), the type of practices that are seen as proper to women and to men differ. We can see this differentiation of practices in courtship (Matthews 2005), in the kind of recognition that is expected from the other in a couple (Gunnarsson 2014), or in the differentiated meanings that the breaching of romantic love has, as the case of infidelity illustrates.[2] Similarly, the idea of legitimacy regarding who is acceptable to be loved, contributed to the creation of a distinction between chaste women who are eligible for matrimony and prostitutes who are ideal for sexual pleasure but remain outside of legitimate relationships (Giddens 2013). In the third place, it is important to note that the relation between romantic love and sexuality also rests on a gendered-differentiated code; that is, on a code that values sexual practices differently (Rubin 1992). Research shows that women require ascribing sex within the discourse of love; whereas men are not obliged to abide by any conduct that legitimates their sexual practices

(Bourdieu 2001; Jones 2010; Sosa 2005). By the same token, the discourse on romantic love can turn into an obstacle for 'safe sex' practices amongst women (Sosa 2005: 37). Also, the representation of romantic love has had an impact on the negative value that is attached to women's autoerotic practices such as masturbation and the consumption of pornographic material (Jones 2010). Finally, love can be seen as a form of exploitation. As Anna Jónas-dóttir has shown, the love of women has been exploited by men in a fashion similar to Marx's account of the 'labor force' with its alienation and exploi-tation traits (Jónasdóttir 1994). Hochschild, in turn, showed pristinely that love and caring practices had been monetized. This has gone to such an extent that we are, in this globalized time, faced with a combination of class, national origin, and the emotional exploitation of women, as the cases of prostitutes, *au pairs*, and maids illustrate (Hochschild 2008).

The revision of each of the particularities that explain both gender differ-entiation and gender asymmetry demands a wider approach than we can offer here. However, it should be sufficient, for the time being, to state that this is a feature of romantic love that should not be overlooked.

We hope the above snapshot will be enough to sustain our argument that the semantics of romantic love involves a process of individualization, the existence of material and cultural conditions, as well as differentiated gender positions. The loving couple is formed, in this semantics, by two heterosexual individuals that select each other and are expectant of the mutual recognition of their individuality.

Those are the grounds where the semantics of romantic love emerged. Now we would like to present how this semantics orients the contemporary *WeLR* and the benefits the individual may expect from it. We start from the notion that semantics of love historically guide expectations about how the *WeLR* must be expressed; that is, through the current cultural expectations regarding a love relationship. But, it is important to note that the semantics of the contemporary *WeLR* entail the re-signification of two elements that are con-stitutive of romantic love, namely (a) the semantics of the loving relationship is not exclusive of the heterosexual couple; and (b) there exists, at least as cultural expectation, a certain balance between the differences of power in the couple, which is different to what happened in the semantics of romantic love that predominantly rested on male domination.

What are the promises (expectations) that the contemporary loving rela-tionship aims to fulfill? As we have shown, a distinctive trait of a couple's affective bond is that it enables the expression of individuality (Luhmann 1998: 14) and makes possible an ego-confirmation of the *self*. At the same time, it also constitutes a world that is neither in the *I* nor in the *You* nor in the world (Luhmann 2010: 17) but in the 'proximate world of daily living' shared by *ego* and *alter* (2010: 15). Besides this trait, the notion of sexuality and sexual pleasure is introduced (Jónasdóttir 1994: 102), at least as a 'pro-mise'. Sexuality and sexual pleasure are mechanisms that help persuade the body of the communication of love and the materialization of the other

(Luhmann 2010: 59). Moreover, the affective bond allows the acting of the *ego* (of the loved one) to be experienced as love (Luhmann 1995: 187) and, consequently, facilitates the experience of love in general. The *WeLR* constitutes itself when ego takes into account the information that alter provides and this information is interpreted in the light of the experiences in the world they have as a *We*, and vice versa.

Affirming that the *WeLR* constitutes itself presupposes the construction and maintenance of a reality that is particular and meaningful to the couple (Berger and Kellner 1993). This constructed, and meaningful reality involves a process of re-socialization that is as important as the stages of adolescence and childhood (Berger and Kellner 1993: 128). The world of meanings of the *We* includes a process of re-interpretation of the past of the person in love in the light of a projection of a future together (Alberoni 2008: 36). In other words, the couple creates its own history. This creation supposes the revision of the personal past and the creation of a new version of the present and the future. It is in this sense that both the personal past and the couple's present-future are restructured through a process that takes place through the couple's time (Alberoni 2008: 71). Within the *WeLR*, individuals who are 'heirs of their societies of origin, of the traditions that gather their personal stories and their cultural heritage' meet and create something new (Alberoni 2008: 20). This new history by no means implies that the couple's history is exempt from gender asymmetries. The existence of hegemonic semantics with a differential of power is ever-present. In that way, the couple's history can be constructed from the perspective of one of its members, but it tends to be perceived and experienced as something created by both members of the *WeLR*. [3] Similarly, the level of elaboration and reflexivity will be subject to class positions (cf. Skeggs 2004).

With the traits presented before, it can be stated that the semantics of love involved in the creation and sustaining of a *WeLR* presents for the individual, at least five surpluses: (1) affirmation of identity in an impersonal world; (2) the experience of love (through and thanks to the actions of the other); (3) the expectation of experience of pleasure and sexual exchange; (4) the creation of a shared world (a shared history and a sense of belonging as *We*); and (5) the construction (re-socialization) of new meanings (of a new culture through the conjunction of two different biographical histories).

Love in situation: the *WeLR* in motion

We use the term *situation* (Goffman 1964) to refer to the time-space in which the definition of a particular frame of meaning is established. This analytical level allows us to understand the uniqueness of a couple's affective bond and the concrete materialization of the *WeLR*. Thus, we contend that love can also be understood as *situated affection* (Wetherell 2012).

Our initial assumption is that there exist a series of cultural love codes (i.e. semantics); however, it is throughout interaction that those codes get to be re-signified. The people involved perform love drawing on their biographic trajectories and their social position. A couple that lives together or regularly cohabitates may be able to create its own history, that is, its own significant information. In that way, specific couples give value to facts that are relevant to their history and in some instances introduce meanings alien to socially shared semantics of love (Berger and Kellner 1993: 132).

Although a 'system of typifications' representations, and expectations of what love is has been already acquired, people in a *WeLR* must fill in those typifications with '*experiential content*' (Berger and Kellner 1993: 126). Individuals in a *WeLR* engage in the process of validation and re-signification of their relationship. This process 'requires ongoing interaction with others who co-inhabit this same socially constructed world' (1993: 120). It is true that any co-inhabitant can accomplish such a task. Nevertheless, there are those few who can be seen as truly significant others who are more crucial for the validation of the world, including the 'validation of identity' (1993: 120). The *WeLR* allows the individuals involved in it to validate a system of typifications, and to carry out the construction of a world in common. That is, they share a similar horizon of meaning (*Sinn*) in which they 'grow old together' and interpret the passage of time and their common space.[4] In the words of Alfred Schütz, 'consociates are mutually involved in one another's biography; they are growing old together; they live as we call it, in a pure *We-relationship*' (Schütz 1982: 16–17, emphasis added).

According to Peter Berger and Hansfried Kellner (1993), this is possible through conversation, for it is a medium by which the biographies of two different people are 're-interpreted'. However, conversation for these authors is not limited to people's disembodied communication. Rather, such conversational exchanges require the existence of physical space that enables bodily contact. That is, communication and the body are constitutive elements in the construction of a world of shared meanings, which allows the formation of *situations* that are meaningful to a couple sharing an affective bond.

The spatial dimension then, becomes relevant to the existence of *meaningful situations*. Those sharing an affective bond structure their joint project into one single space, and more precisely, in places that are 'charged with meaning' (Alberoni 2008: 67) and which will become relevant to their cohabitation. Therefore, some places acquire a particular symbolism for the love relationship. Through cohabitation, couples 'acquire a harmonious resonance, they vibrate in a common fashion' (Alberoni 2008: 54). Cohabitation also involves 'practical knowledge' that is 'almost automatic in character' (Berger and Kellner 1993: 130). This practical knowledge is encrypted in the body and involves the 'know how' of the daily life with the other in which practices may clash, oppose, be modified or negotiated.

To explore how love is enacted in the situation, we use the concept 'sensible proximity'. It was coined by Simmel to refer to a specific relation between the body (sensitivity/sensory) and space (proximity) (Simmel 2009: 607; Sabido

Ramos 2008, 2012). Through this notion it is possible to observe what kind of bonds are created in a *WeLR*, and how they are created in the situation. The bonds created in a *WeLR* depend on four features, although they are not limited to them. The first one is the creation of intimacy. Intimacy enables the modification of the social rules of disgust and shame, as well as the eroticization of seemingly unimportant gestures by the people involved in the relation (moreover, this intimacy is understood as something more than sexuality). The second one includes the creation of the boundaries of the *We*, and consequently, the exclusion of others. The third feature involves the analysis of the 'somatic modes of attention' (Csordas 1993: 135) between lovers. Finally, the fourth relates to the analysis of the selection of *the* lover. The selection is usually made through the perception of the other, but always and from the outset involves a sensitive perception that may be shaped by class, ethnicity, gender, and other structural conditions.

The interaction between bodies that share an affective bond creates situations of intimacy that include but are not limited to sexuality. Cohabitation is an important element of this interaction. Actions that involve sharing time and space and 'growing old together' (Schütz 1982) contribute to the creation of sites that are charged with meaning and with practical knowledge that is cognitive and affective. In turn, those shared meanings and practical knowledge play a role in the creation of significant information about the *WeLR* and the bracketing of existing social rules concerning bodily and sensory contact.

For instance, societies influenced by the bodily and sensory habits of the west attribute close and prolonged olfaction only to lovers, not to strangers and not even to friends. In the semantics of romantic love, the act of smelling another person is a sign of closeness and intimacy. Lovers can endure levels of disgust not usually accepted. The *WeLR* re-signifies the meanings of bodily excretions in a number of situations like kissing (saliva, breath); sharing a bed (human warmth and odor); and love-making (sweat, odor, semen, menstruation blood, urine). Thus, bodily fluids and their by-products become symbols of love and not excretions subject to spurn.

Intimacy, however, is not only related to the contraction of the boundaries of disgust but also, following Viviane Zelizer (2005), to the mutual knowledge of the bodies of the lovers. On this, William Ian Miller adds that love leads to the suspension of the rules of disgust as it allows your loved one to see you in a way that otherwise would be 'shameful' or 'disgusting' (Miller 1997: 202). Also, daily practices like touching the other's arm in the living-room can be translated into an 'authentic declaration of love' (Kauffmann 2010: 172–173). As Helmut Schelsky points out, every social structure and social behavior where human beings 'establish a reciprocal contact through their bodily presence' can be eroticized (1962: 16).[5] Eroticism in the *WeLR* is created not only through contact and bodily presence, but through a particular reading of those contacts in the light of the meanings elaborated by and through the couple's history.

The *WeLR* can create its territory in the situation. For western societies, gazing at each other is a symbol of intimacy and close communication, it creates boundaries between the 'gazers' and the ones left out. Within the semantics of romantic love, gazing or looking at each other figures as a recurring bodily sign between lovers (Le Breton 2006). This is why 'eye-language' is understood as the 'language of love', the revealing of one's soul to another (Luhmann 1998: 25). Gazes are associated symbolically with the sense of touch: some gazes feel as if they could touch or, as Le Breton puts it, touching is an 'affective experience' (2006: 195).

Erving Goffman spoke about couples using 'withness cues', to tell others (an audience) that they are together (Goffman 1979: 227, quoted in Guerrero and Hecht 2008: 211; Collins 2005). Illouz, in turn, has referred to the situation when lovers find themselves amid a crowd of people and 'they symbolically construct their space as private and isolated from the surrounding people' (1997: 115). Although 'withness cues' tend to change over time and cultures, it is still true that the bodily contact has substantial effects both for the *We* relationship and the individuals' bodies. For example, Laura Guerrero and Michael Hecht have found that married couples (i.e. cohabiting couples) convey a 'behavioral matching', a high level of synchronization between them. This finding 'supports previous research [...] suggesting that nonverbal communication becomes more similar and synchronized as a relationship moves from an impersonal to a personal level' (2008: 217–222).

In a similar vein, Geoffrey Beattie has asserted that '[w]hen people are being naturally intimate they often synchronize the timing of small movements, and this is done at a very unconscious level, this is called interactional synchrony' (2004: 4). The possibility of synchronicity is relevant in the study of the interaction order because it emerges from interactions that take place on the participants' level of proximity and intimacy (Illouz 2012). Meanwhile, Randall Collins (2005) highlights the fact that, in couples, some of the signs of this synchronicity involve almost unnoticeable bodily movements (such as blinking or nodding), vocal intonations, or even conversational turn-taking, which makes *rhythmic entrainment* possible between them. In short, the *WeLR* creates its territory through the exchange of glances, different ways of touching (kissing included), and its interactional movement in the situation.

The meeting of the bodies in the *WeLR* can also be analyzed if we look at the role bodily senses have in physical co-presence. Some authors have suggested that we tend to radicalize our attention to someone's body in relationships with strong affectivity in which, unsurprisingly, the importance of body communication is quite significant (Guerrero and Hecht 2008: 395). Love in the *WeLR* is acted through the senses. However, the role of the latter and their relation to specific parts of the body is shaped in and by the historical semantics of love. Our sense of perception is enabled and guided by that semantics, and it generates concrete 'somatic modes of attention' (Csordas 1993: 135). Thomas Csordas claims that somatic modes of attention are ways in which our perception is directed towards certain movements, gestures, odors and aromas that are significant to the loving interaction. That is to say: there exists a 'cultural elaboration of an erotic sensibility'. Thus, we pay attention towards certain body shapes and movements that are considered attractive. In his words: 'Attending to others' *bodily movements* is even more clear-cut in cases of dancing, making love, playing team sports, and in the uncanny sense of a presence over one's shoulder' (Csordas 1993: 139).

Finally, the selection of the lover (that initiates the possibility of a loving bond) entails perception of the other. But, following Bourdieu, perceiving in itself involves positive and/or negative evaluation. It is not a natural process. It begins with *schemata* that we have incorporated into an endless process of socialization and is combined with the specific interactions in which we find ourselves situated. In that way, beyond the socio-historical and cultural moulding of our sensory perceptions, each one of us has a particular biographical trajectory. This biography modifies our social positions, practices, and worldviews. Taste, understood as 'elective affinities' is 'what brings together things and people that go together' (Bourdieu 1984: 241). Therefore, choosing a loved person is an elective affinity. What seems to be a spontaneous event (i.e. a crush) is a sample of socially oriented elections in which knowledge that is in the body goes unnoticed.

Through the four features mentioned before, the bonds in the *WeLR* can be observed in the situation, and involve the creation of a *sui generis* reality: they create intimacy and a territory of the *We*. The territory of the *We* delineates an intimate space where what is permissible goes beyond the standardized social limits of disgust and embarrassment; it also re-creates daily materials and practices as forms of eroticization.

Likewise, sensitive perception is also mediated by social categories such as social class, gender and ethnicity. In that way, the sensible affinities that help create the loving bond of the *We* are socially constituted and narrow the possibilities of who can be a subject of love. These sensory restrictions are reasonably stable because they are non-conscious; they are part of an embodied knowledge that is pre-reflexive – yet that does not mean they are fixed. Finally, it is important to state that the semantics of love also redirects the perception, meaning, and hierarchy of the senses in the loving interaction.

What happens to an individual at a neurobiological level cannot be disregarded either. In the case of those who form an affective bond, neurobiology is relevant if we want to have a thorough understanding of the love phenomenon. That is why we consider it pertinent to talk about the idea of 'enminded bodies'. We direct our attention to this concept in the next section.

Enminded bodies in the *WeLR*

As shown earlier, a situated *WeLR* may, in practice, modify the cultural meanings of love. However, such a performance is made by individuals who are already structurally positioned (within a class, an ethnicity, or a gender). We can gather from this that the practices of those individuals are shaped both by their conceptions of what counts as attractive or repulsive, and by their own life stories. By looking at this analytical level, we seek to understand how those social meanings become embedded in the *enminded body* and the consequences this brings to the experience of oneself in relation to the loved one.

While the idea of embodied minds is mentioned in different works regarding the body, Anna Jónasdóttir's (2014) wordplay *enminded bodies* is more convenient to illustrate the pre-eminence of the body. It is useful for us because it emphasizes the importance of the situated bodies (bodies that, of course, have a mind); and how they are co-constituted in and with a social and natural environment.

Enminded bodies are constituted both by brain and soma (muscles, skeleton, viscera etc.), hence it is important to complement social perspectives about the body with current works on neurology, which suggest that for the brain to exist as such – with all its conscious processes – an environmental and constitutive relation with the body is needed.[6] The neuronal connections and processes developed in the brain take place due and thanks to the existence of the body. In that way, we can see a link between Merleau-Ponty's phenomenology and current neurological studies: the formation of knowledge occurs through a body that is spatially situated. Here, it is important to take a look at this connection given that it understands love not only as something exclusively ideational, but also as the constant body-and-mind feedback that occurs in the enminded bodies.

Antonio Damasio's distinction between emotions and feelings is adequate to comprehend how the experience of love takes place in the enminded bodies. For him, emotions refer both to processes of evaluation vis-à-vis a given situation such as unnoticeable bodily states (physical changes in heartbeat, breathing, etc.), as well as noticeable states such as the making of some gestures. On the other hand, feelings involve awareness of particular events, people, or objects that produce physical and mental changes in us. Thus, feelings have to do with awareness as an idea of the *self*. In this case, we can suggest that love has both emotional and feelings-based dimensions.

Thus, love as an emotion lived in the enminded body, involves a bodily state, a reaction from the body. Love is an emotion that requires the symbolic processing of bodily states. More precisely, it includes noticeable changes in the body such as blushing, trembling, as well as subtle neurochemical brain variations in the blood flow, or musculoskeletal rearrangements, and even the generation of substances like oxytocin (cf. Damasio 2005). Feeling love, in turn, involves the perception of changes in the bodily state and a relation to the other(s) (Damasio 2005: 139). It '*is the experience of* [bodily] *changes in juxtaposition to the mental images that initiated the cycle*' (Damasio 2005: 139). We can extract from this that 'feeling love' is the attribution of meaning that we create in regards to the emotions and states that certain people trigger in us. Or, as Luhmann puts it, love is 'interpreted biochemistry' (1995: 274).

For Damasio, feeling love is related to positive states such as pleasure and joy. Social sciences have taught us that frames of cultural meaning inform those states; nonetheless, with Damasio we could also add that they are not only marked in a person's consciousness but also in their body. Damasio coins the term 'somatic marker' (2005: 173)[7] to account for a record of emotional experiences that remain in the brain, and that involve specific bodily reactions – neural and chemical – which are associated with concrete situations. Under particular circumstances, options to which we 'automatically' attribute a certain pleasant, or unpleasant feeling will come to mind. The automatic nature of this process supposes that we have previously lived and experienced situations that have 'marked' our body at chemical and brain levels.[8] Therefore, somatic markers are acquired by experience (Damasio 2005: 179) and, more specifically, 'during the process of education and socialization, by connecting specific classes of stimuli with specific classes of somatic state' (2005: 177).

The idea of somatic states as a neuronal fixed product supports Csordas' anthropological take on 'somatic modes of attention' discussed earlier. For Csordas, let us recall, cultural elaboration accompanies attention, and this helps explain how and why the latter is directed towards specific aspects of the body.

In regards to our discussion on the *WeLR*, we can see that the selection of a partner is – in part – a process that goes beyond the threshold of our consciousness and is based on embodied experiences as well as on neural processes. It is connected to both 'somatic markers' and 'somatic modes of attention'. Accordingly, selecting, accepting, and saying 'yes' to the loved person, involves a decision that is not 'somatically marked' as unpleasant, and implies attention to features of the other person's body and their environment. In the same way, the continuation of a relationship would be influenced by the existence of somatic markers. Such continuity enables, so to speak, emotional guarding, that is, the keeping of familiar emotions. Therefore, we would feel somatically attracted to (though not determined by) repeatedly observed situations that have marked us positively during the process of socialization.

Finally, we shall have a look at the impact the relationship with a significant other has on the *enminded body* itself. According to Damasio, 'one can die of a broken heart' (2005: 205). Such a possibility exemplifies not only the strong relation between the body and the brain, but also our relations with others. Psychiatrists Thomas Lewis, Fairi Amini, and Richard Lannon suggest that '[w]hen somebody loses his partner and says a part of him [sic] is gone, he is more right than he thinks. A portion of his neural activity depends on the presence of that other living brain' (2000: 205).

These neurology-based views of love are also similar to Elias' sociological perspective discussed above. We can see love as a relational phenomenon, from the I perspective, when facing the death of a loved person. If the death of the loved person:

> 'causes' illness [in the survivor] [...] is because an integral part of his [sic] self, his 'I-and-we' image has been broken off. [...] The particular

figuration of all the survivor's valencies is altered, and the balance of his whole web of personal relationships is changed.

(Elias 1970: 136)

To conclude this section we can say that, on this analytical level, it can be observed how creating, sustaining and breaking a *WeLR* involves the individual enminded body in that it marks one's body/mind and it becomes part of the perceived and lived environment (part of their reality). Breaking a loving bond entails not only ideational changes (mentality changes), but also bodily and experiential changes in our relation with the world.

Final remarks: the bonds the *WeLR* creates

In this chapter, we have shown how the meanings of love, love in situation, and the processing of emotions and feelings in the body/mind have consequences and are implicit in a contemporary loving relationship. More importantly, we have also shown that such conditions can explain how a couple's loving bond, the *We*, is made possible and is desirable.

We want to emphasize that we are not concerned with providing a checklist of how the *WeLR* should be. Rather, we wanted to explain the social conditions that make it possible for people to keep establishing loving relationships. We asked what conditions within our contemporary society and within the loving bond itself allow for the continuity of this type of relationship and what is gained from it. This can explain why, sometimes, the bonding lasts even though the relationship is not at all satisfactory for its partakers or when that satisfaction is merged with asymmetrical conditions. It seems to us that, for the time being, the analytical levels proposed in this article shed some light on those questions. More specifically, we think that in contemporary western societies, the *WeLR* fosters the creation of four surpluses of bonding:

1   *Identity*: it involves an acknowledgment of personal identity. The *WeLR* becomes the site for identity self-realization (Luhmann 1998). Thus, people get involved in a loving *We* in order to be recognized as particular individuals. On the one hand, the election of a partner represents one of the most important expressions of the modern individual, that is, their capacity to choose. On the other hand, the expectation of having or being in a *WeLR* can be so intense that the whole sense of one's existence is attributed to it. Nevertheless, as we have suggested, such an expectation is differentiated by gender.

2   *Membership*: it enables feeling part of something that goes beyond the I, and the creation and acknowledgment of a shared world (the *We*). The *WeLR* supposes the emergence of a 'new community' (Alberoni 2008: 20). That is, the *WeLR* exists beyond the people that encompass it. It involves the meeting of two personal biographies and their cultural heritages, the restructuring of social relations, and even a new ranking and description of the world. The history of the couple emerges; a history that

can be distinguished from the history of the world. Hence, splitting up involves 'change of self and loss or a reinterpretation of one's own history' (Luhmann 2010: 54). The *WeLR* creates membership, a sense of belonging and gives meaning to the world. This membership is solidified thanks to the enactment of love and the consolidation of intimacy understood as a world of shared meanings. The idea of 'growing old together' facilitates the creation of a horizon of common meaning that is automatically activated to sustain daily life, and the solution of practical conflicts. Of course, the latter will depend, in addition to the cultural capital, on the type of emotional capital and linguistic abilities possessed by those involved in the relationship (Illouz 2008).

3   *Emotional and meaningful spaces*: it enables feeling and exchanging significant emotions. Cohabiting (i.e. 'growing old together') allows the creation of spaces filled with meaning, as well as of practices that involve affective and cognitive knowledge. The everyday world generates spaces *du bonheur* (or *malheur*) in which bodies and their emotions are involved. It also allows the feeling that 'one is in the world', sharing with someone a type of sensitivity exclusive to the *We*, which excludes others, and, at the same time, re-signifies otherwise standardized rules of sensitivity. Cohabitation creates synchronization and could also generate the reiterated satisfaction of some bodily expectations. Finally, routine, as the continuation of practices, provides ontological certainty and, in this case, emotional certainty. Here it is important that we make a distinction between bodily-emotional bonds and the erotic-sexual bond, given that the lovers' bodies are recognized not only in the erotic encounter but also in their particular world of shared sensibility. Lovers can consolidate that bond through the frequency of their corporeal encounters, the creation of emotional effects (Collins 2005) and the construction of their own sensitivity thresholds. Lovers give meaning to all this. They recognize feelings that are registered in the enminded bodies via somatic markers (Damasio 2005). These feelings are manifested in modes of attention to the body of the beloved person, rituals, spaces, and objects that reinforce and symbolize the bond. The love of a couple is a bodily experience as well. It is marked in the enminded bodies through the constant interaction of the bodies and the performance of love. This characteristic of the bodily-emotional bond helps us explain its durability as well as the affliction experienced after a separation takes place.

4   *Erotic-sexual pleasure*: belonging to a *WeLR* holds a promise of sexual exchange and mutually generated experiences of pleasure. Furthermore, daily bodily contact may acquire erotic connotations depending on the frames of meaning that are produced by the loving couple itself. This type of bond is central for the couple given that it is a form of communication created by the *We* and provides the expectation of pleasure. According to contemporary conceptions of coupledom, sexual pleasure is an important expectation, yet it cannot be reduced to genital pleasure (Collins 2005). Sexual pleasure can, in fact, be opened up to a plethora of erotic

possibilities (Schelsky 1962) proper to the *We* as a couple. As we saw with Luhmann, sexuality in intimacy is a way of materializing the body of the other, a form of communication between lovers.

The analytical levels, and the surpluses and constraints the *WeLR* entails may serve as guidance for future empirical research on the permanence and non-permanence of existing love bonds. These features need to be further studied bearing in mind distinctions regarding sexual orientation, class, gender, and ethnicity. This first account, however, advances our understanding of the internal characteristics of that complex world of love formed by and around at least two lovers.

Notes

1 A previous version of this work was published in Spanish with the title 'Los amantes y su mundo. Una propuesta teórico-metodológica', in M. Pozas and M. Estrada (eds) *Disonancias y Resonancia entre la teoría social y la investigación empírica*. Mexico: El Colegio de México, 2016.
2 The breaching on exclusivity, for instance, was unlikely to raise the same type of chastisement, formal or informal, in an unfaithful man than in an unfaithful woman (Elias 1983; Giddens 2013; Perrot 2011).
3 A recent study on Mexican couples shows that before an audience, couples tend to hold a unified history. In one of the cases it was evident that the story was driven by the husband's perspective, but the wife took it as a mutual story (Tenorio 2013).
4 We understand the phrase 'growing old together' in a phenomenological perspective rather than in its common sense meaning. Thus, we take it as the shared experience within a *familiar horizon* of meanings.
5 Our translation from the Spanish. The original book (*Soziologie der Sexualität*) was first published in Germany in 1955 and ran to twenty-two editions. It was never translated into English.
6 These include works by Antonio Damasio, George Lakoff, Mark Johnson, Eleanor Rosch, Francisco Varela in collaboration with Humberto Maturana, and Gerald Edelman (Damasio 2005: 234).
7 Somatic markers are an instance of the awareness of the body generated by secondary emotions. They are marks of sensitivity that come from past events that connect an image with a bodily state. A somatic marker 'forces attention on the negative outcome to which a given action may lead and functions as an automated alarm signal' (Damasio 2005: 173). The existence of somatic markers, for Damasio, shows that decision-making does not depend on the process of reasoning but that our emotions impel it. This does not suggest a lack of rationality; rather, it suggests that the emotional input guides which options are plausible emotionally.
8 An emphasis on the automatic nature of the response can be a deterministic approach (see Jones this volume). We want to assert that there can be awareness of these processes, and they can be intentionally modified.

References

Alberoni, Francesco (2008) *Te amo*. Barcelona: Gedisa.
Baker, Maureen and Vivienne Elizabeth (2014) 'A "Brave Thing to Do" or a Normative Practice? Marriage after Long-Term Cohabitation', *Journal of Sociology* 50(4): 393–407

Beattie, Geoffrey (2004) *Visible Thought. The New Psychology of Body Language.* New York: Routledge.

Beck, Ulrich and Elisabeth Beck-Gernsheim (1995) *The Normal Chaos of Love.* Cambridge: Polity Press.

Berger, Peter L. and Hansfried Kellner (1993) 'Marriage and the Construction of Reality', in B. Byers (ed.) *Readings in Social Psychology: Perspective and Method.* Boston, MA: Allyn and Bacon.

Bourdieu, Pierre (1984) *Distinction. A Social Critique of the Judgement of Taste.* New York: Routledge.

Bourdieu, Pierre (2001) *Masculine Domination.* Stanford, CA: Stanford University Press.

Collins, Randall (2005) *Interaction Ritual Chains.* Princeton, NJ: Princeton University Press.

Csordas, Thomas (1993) 'Somatic Modes of Attention', *Cultural Anthropology* 8(2): 135–156.

Damasio, Antonio (2005) *Descartes' Error. Emotion, Reason, and the Human Brain.* New York: Penguin.

Elias, Norbert (1970) *What Is Sociology?* New York: Columbia University Press.

Elias, Norbert (1983) *The Court Society.* Oxford: Blackwell.

Elias, Norbert (2001) *The Society of Individuals.* New York: Continuum.

Elias, Norbert (2003) 'Sociology and Psychiatry', in S. Foulkes and P. G. Stewart (eds) *Psychiatry in a Changing Society.* London: Routledge.

Firestone, Shulamith (2012) *The Dialectic of Sex: The Case for Feminist Revolution.* New York: McMillan.

Foucault, Michel (1990) *The History of Sexuality, Vol. 2: The Use of Pleasure.* New York: Random House.

Giddens, Anthony (2013) *The Transformation of Intimacy: Sexuality, Love and Eroticism in Modern Societies.* Cambridge: Polity Press

Goffman, Erving (1959) *The Presentation of Self in Everyday Life.* New York: Anchor.

Goffman, Erving (1964) 'The Neglected Situation', *American Anthropologist* 66: 133–136.

Goffman, Erving (1971) *Relations in Public: Microstudies of the Public Order.* New York: Basic Books.

Guerrero, Laura K. and Michael L. Hecht (2008) *The Nonverbal Communication Reader.* Illinois: Waveland Press.

Gunnarsson, Lena (2014) 'Loving Him for Who He Is: The Microsociology of Power', in A. G. Jónasdóttir and A. Ferguson (eds) *Love: A Question for Feminism in the Twenty-first Century.* New York: Routledge.

Hochschild, Arlie (2008) *The Commercialization of Intimate Life: Notes from Home and Work.* Berkeley: University of California Press.

Illouz, Eva (1997) *Consuming the Romantic Utopia.* Berkeley: University of California Press.

Illouz, Eva (2008) *Cold Intimacies.* Cambridge: Polity Press.

Illouz, Eva (2012) *Why Love Hurts. A Sociological Explanation.* Cambridge: Polity Press.

Jimeno, Myriam (2004) *Crimen pasional. Contribución a una antropología de las emociones.* Bogotá: Universidad Nacional de Colombia.

Jónasdóttir, Anna G. (1994) *Why Women Are Oppressed.* Philadelphia, PA: Temple University Press.

Jónasdóttir, Anna G. (2014) 'Love Studies: A (Re)New(ed) Field of Feminist Knowledge Interests', in A. G. Jónasdóttir and A. Ferguson (eds) *Love: A Question for Feminism in the Twenty-first Century.* New York: Routledge.

Jones, Daniel (2010) *Sexualidades adolescents. Amor, placer y control en la Argentina contemporánea.* Buenos Aires: CLACSO, CICCUS.

Kauffmann, Jean-Claude (2010) *L'étrange histoire de l'amour heureux*. Paris: Pluriel.

Le Breton, David (2006) *Le saveur du monde: une anthropologie des senses*. Paris: Editions Métailié.

Lewis, Thomas, Fairi Amini and Richard Lannon (2000) *A General Theory of Love*. New York: Vintage.

Low, Kelvin E. (2009) *Scents and Scent-sibilities: Smell and Everyday Life Experiences*. Newcastle Upon Tyne: Cambridge Scholars Publishing.

Luhmann, Niklas (1995) *Social Systems*. Stanford, CA: Stanford University Press.

Luhmann, Niklas (1998) *Love as Passion. The Codification of Intimacy*. Stanford, CA: Stanford University Press.

Luhmann, Niklas (2010) *Love. A Sketch*. Cambridge: Polity Press.

Matthews, Sara (2005) 'Cuerpo y sexualidad en la Europa del Antiguo Régimen', in A. Corbin, J. J. Courtine and G. Vigarello (eds) *Historia del cuerpo. Tomo 1*. Madrid: Taurus.

Miller, William Ian (1997) *The Anatomy of Disgust*. Cambridge, MA: Harvard University Press.

Perrot, Michelle (2011) *Historia de las alcobas*. México: Fondo de Cultura Económica.

Precht, Richard David (2011) *Amor. Un sentimiento desordenado. Un recorrido a través de la biología, la sociología y la filosofía*. Barcelona: Siruela.

Rougemont, Denis (1983) *Love in the Western World*. Princeton, NJ: Princeton University Press.

Rubin, Gayle (1992) 'Thinking Sex: Notes for a Radical Theory of the Politics of Sexuality', in C. S. Vance (ed.) *Pleasure and Danger: Exploring Female Sexuality*. London: Pandora.

Sabido Ramos, Olga (2008) '"Imágenes momentáneas *sub specie aeternitatis*" de la corporalidad', *Estudios Sociológicos* 26(78): 617–646.

Sabido Ramos, Olga (2012) *El cuerpo como recurso de sentido en la construcción del extraño. Una perspectiva sociológica*. Madrid: UAM-Azcapotzalco, Séquitur.

Schelsky, Helmut (1962) *Sociología de la sexualidad*. Buenos Aires: Nueva Visión.

Schütz, Alfred (1982) *Collected Papers: The Problem of Social Reality*. New York: Springer.

Simmel, Georg (1971) 'Eros, Platonic and Modern', in D. N. Levine (ed.) *Georg Simmel on Individuality of Social Forms*. Chicago, IL: University of Chicago Press.

Simmel, Georg (2004) *The Philosophy of Money*. New York: Routledge.

Simmel, Georg (2009) *Sociology: Inquiries into the Construction of Social Forms*. Boston and Leiden: Brill.

Skeggs, Beverly (2004) *Class, Self, Culture*. London: Routledge.

Solís, Patricio (2013) 'Las nuevas uniones libres en México: Más tempranas e inestables pero tan fecundas como los matrimonios', *Coyuntura Demográfica* 4: 31–35.

Sosa, Itzel (2005) *Significados de la salud y la sexualidad de jóvenes. Un estudio de caso en escuelas públicas de Cuernavaca*. México: Inmujeres.

Synnott, Anthony (1991) 'A Sociology of Smell', *Canadian Review of Sociology* 28: 437–459.

Tenorio, Natalia (2013) 'Las relaciones de pareja en la sociedad contemporánea: Equipo, roles y rituales románticos'. Doctoral thesis, Universidad Autónoma Metropolitana, México.

Wetherell, Margaret (2012) *Affect and Emotion. A New Social Science Understanding*. London: Sage.

Zelizer, Viviane (2005) *The Purchase of Intimacy*. Princeton, NJ: Princeton University Press.

9 Silent love

On Irigaray's suggestion of cultivating sexual difference[1]

Silvia Stoller

> Silence is not just the absence of noise, but a quietness that allows people to open their eyes and ears for another world.
>
> (Serge Poliakoff)

Luce Irigaray is generally regarded as the main representative of difference feminism. Her theory of sexual difference has brought about an exemplary turning point in feminist theory. It is no longer gender equality that is stressed, but the establishment and cultivation of sexual difference. For Irigaray, such a cultivation should ultimately lead to an alternative culture of two sexed subjects, as opposed to the current culture that is modeled on the male sex. In her later work, Irigaray makes several unusual suggestions about how such a cultivation might be advanced. One of her proposals is the cultivation of silence, a topic that has been largely disregarded within feminist research. In this chapter I show how Irigaray's concept of silence can be connected to her theorizations of sexual difference, that is, a culture of two subjects. In particular, I want to pay attention to how Irigaray regards silence as a condition for *love* between the sexes. While Irigaray research deals increasingly with the concept of love (e.g. Gunnarsson 2014, this volume; Joy 2007; Miller 2011; Postl 2009; Secomb 2007; Toye 2010), what is less explored is how Irigaray's idea of silence in the framework of her ethics of sexual difference could shed light on her vision of love.

A culture of two subjects

If there is a major concern that has challenged Irigaray from the very beginning, it is the question of the possibility of sexual difference (*différence sexuelle*). According to Irigaray there is no sexual difference in the current phallocratic culture because essentially this culture is determined by one sex, namely the male. Any attempt to reduce the female to a single concept fails, in her opinion, because the female is subjugated to the male subject and measured accordingly. From Irigaray's point of view, a genuinely female subject, which is not subjugated to an 'a priori assumption of the same' (Irigaray 1985a: 27) but follows its own logic, has not yet emerged. For this reason,

Irigaray has raised the issue of sexual difference – and with it the establishment of a radical difference between women and men – as the key topic of the twentieth century: 'Sexual difference is probably the issue in our time which could be our "salvation" if we thought it through' (1993: 5). For Irigaray, sexual difference is a relationship essentially marked by asymmetry, differing from equality feminism, which demands a symmetrical relationship between the sexes (Stoller 2005). Her foregrounding of sexual difference corresponds to her claim about a 'culture of two subjects' (Irigaray 2004: viii), which from the beginning has accompanied her feminist philosophy: 'From *Speculum* on, my project has been how to render possible a philosophy, and more generally a culture, of two subjects' (2004: vii).

Such a culture demands a continuous *cultivation* of two subjects. In order to replace a culture of *one* subject with a culture of *two* subjects, for Irigaray, it is necessary to apply diverse means. One of the essential ways to transform the existing patriarchal culture is language, in its broadest sense. Among other things, new forms of *communication* between subjects are necessary. This includes linguistic as well as non-linguistic forms of communications. The non-linguistic forms of communication entail listening (*écouter*), which Irigaray thematized in *I Love to You* (Irigaray 1996). Here, silence – along with listening – is put into the service of cultivating two subjects.

Listening

The chapter 'In Almost Absolute Silence' in *I Love to You* opens with the question: 'how am I to listen to you?' (1996: 115). Subsequently, listening is suggested by Irigaray as an alternative form of communication between the sexes. Initially, such a proposal might seem strange. Why, in particular, should listening be useful for feminist purposes? The question is justified in that, for centuries, women have been denied the right or given only limited permission to speak. Basically, they were condemned to silence. Therefore, to put women yet again into the role of listeners, does that not mean pushing them once more into the role of passive subjects, a role that from a feminist point of view has always had to be combated? There can be no doubt about this. This is why difference feminists have recognized the necessity of feminine speech and writing, most famously expressed by Hélène Cixous in her call for women to write: 'Woman must write her self: must write about women and bring women to writing' (1976: 875). Irigaray has similarly emphasized the possibility of a *parler-femme*, that is, of 'speaking (as) woman' (1985b: 119). So why should listening be a method for feminism?

Irigaray is expressly aware of the culturally added value of speech as opposed to silence: 'In Western culture speaking is more valued than silence' (2011: 23). Nonetheless, she takes an unusual stance on silence. For her, the way forward is not to forbid the silence imposed on women in patriarchal culture and replace it with speech, but the goal is to rediscover silence in a feminist sense and imbue it with a new meaning. She clearly demonstrates that silence is not negative per se; rather, what is needed is replacing the negative connotation of silence in western culture with a positive one. This line of reasoning becomes clear in Irigaray's short essay 'The Mystery of Mary':

> Mary's silence is often interpreted in a negative manner, particularly by women. This negative judgment is inspired by western – predominantly masculine – values. Mary's silence may be understood differently. [...] The silence [...] is not necessarily negative but may represent, to the contrary, a privileged space for the preservation of self.
>
> (Quoted in Škof 2015: 189–90)

Why, in Irigaray's opinion, are new forms of communication at all necessary? Irigaray starts her reflections on this by criticizing a widespread notion of communication. Usually 'communication' is understood as the exchange of information, the transmission of messages, or at best speaking to each other. Irigaray, however, believes that this form of communication is entirely insufficient for the development of a culture of two subjects. Even though it is important in actual life to exchange data and information – for example, to know what time and place a meeting is taking place – she writes: 'Yet, this sort of communication is not enough to weave a web of alliances and histories between two subjects' (1996: 115). What Irigaray is trying to say is that the relationship between two people cannot be reduced to an exchange of words and the transfer of information, because such a reduction leads to a loss of the complexity of the relationship and – even more important – to a loss of the autonomy of the subjects involved in this relationship.

Nor does Irigaray see the language of 'subjective affects' as suitable for promoting an alternative form of communication: 'But expressing subjective affect will not manage it, either' (1996: 115). The reason is that an emotionally loaded language 'will bind one to the other, often in one direction and not reciprocally' (1996: 116). This means that such a communication could lead to an undesirable emotional dependency relationship. In this case, as well, the autonomy of the subject is jeopardized.[2]

Unfortunately, in these passages, Irigaray does not really elucidate what she understands to be 'subjective affects', although she briefly touches on sadness and joy (1996: 116). What I believe she is referring to, however, is that affect-charged acts such as moaning, lamenting and complaining place the other in the role of consoler or comforter. Other examples of affective communication would be insults and outbursts of rage. They are expressions of violence that force the other into a *passive* role or even render them speechless. What both alternatives of communication have in common is the loss of autonomy on one side, and, consequently, the loss of recognition of the other *as other*. The loss of autonomy comes about because the other has to give up her or his subjectivity and independence – the moment that they are forced into a new role. In the case of lamenting or complaining, the other is pushed to take on the role of comforter or consoler: a role that is never totally a free choice. In the case of tirades of insults or outbursts of rage the other becomes a victim of violence, in that they are reduced to an object and lose their status as a subject. Therefore, if the other is not comprehended in their radical otherness, then, in Irigaray's opinion, the problem is the leveling of difference or alterity.[3]

Irigaray's answer to the question of an alternative form of relating to one another lies in a request: to listen to the other. The French verb *écouter* can mean: listen to someone, overhear or eavesdrop on someone, or simply just hear someone.[4] But it all depends on *how* one listens to someone. Not every form of listening is, according to Irigaray, as aptly applicable. An example of inappropriate listening would be the type of listening that an adult engages in with a younger person. The older one, Irigaray tells us, listens to the younger one as if she or he knew the latter, who is measured according to the knowledge of the adult: 'The elder is supposed to know the younger, and only listens to him or her within the parameters of an existing science or truth' (1996: 116). When a three-year-old girl, in the course of learning about the animal world, spontaneously says 'dog' about a tiger, then the adult knows that she is mistaken. As a result, the term the toddler uses is measured according to the world of adults and their language competence. The adult's judgment in regard to the 'wrong' word uttered by the child stems from an established language, of which the child still has limited knowledge. That is why, according to Irigaray, it comes down to an unpleasant reduction: The other is reduced to my own existence or my own experience, to that which I know. Simultaneously there is an estrangement going on here: The other is alienated because she or he is confronted with a world that is not his or her own. Irigaray therefore speaks of the other being alienated into another 'pseudo-reality' (1996: 116).[5]

In contrast to the exchange-of-facts model of communication outlined above, Irigaray advocates a listening abstracted from the listening subject's own norms: 'I am listening to you not on the basis of what I know, I feel, I already am, nor in terms of what the world and language already are, thus in a formalistic manner, so to speak' (1996: 117). Strictly speaking, Irigaray suggests we refrain from our own knowledge, our own feelings and even our own self. Finally, she calls for us to listen to the other as if we knew nothing about them: 'I am listening to you as someone and something I do not know yet' (1996: 116). In simple terms this means not defining or judging the other using some sort of determining logic, such as assessments and statements. Predicative judgments in the form of logical statements such as 'X is p' are pre-empted by an acquired knowledge of the designated object: I *know* that the monitor in front of me is a monitor and that is why I call it a 'monitor'. Irigaray's intention with listening is something quite different. While I am listening, I am *not* directed at something known, but something unknown: '*I am listening to you* is to listen to your words as something unique, irreducible, especially to my own, as something new, as yet unknown' (1996: 116). In fact, it is questionable whether one can ever *hear* something if that which is heard is always already known.

The retraction, or rather the switching off of one's own knowledge in the perception of the world and the other, is comparable with the phenomenological method of the *époche*, which makes it its task, in the course of perceiving an object of perception, to suspend judgment in regard to acquired knowledge (Husserl 1983: § 32). There is also a parallel to the practice of psychoanalysis, since psychoanalysts are called upon not to impose their own knowledge onto the client. Wilfred Bion, for example, speaks of a 'capacity for forgetting' on the part of psychoanalysts:

> The capacity to remember what the patient has said needs to be allied to a capacity for forgetting so that the fact that any session is a new session and therefore an unknown situation that must be psycho-analytically investigated is not obscured by an already over-plentiful fund of pre-and misconception.
>
> (Bion 2004: 39)

Listening, then, according to Irigaray, does not consist of hearing what one knows. Rather, this listening is primarily characterized by a special kind of attentiveness, of being open to the meanings that may emerge. There is a particular 'attitude' that one needs to take on in regard to the other.[6] 'I am listening to you: I perceive what you are saying, I am attentive to it, I am attempting to understand and hear your intention' (1996: 116). This particular kind of attentiveness does not rely on the familiar but on the unexpected, on that which could still come about. In Irigaray's view, it conveys the emergence of a becoming (*devenir*), a growth (*croissance*) and a birth (*naissance*) (1992: 181, 1996: 117) on behalf of the other. We are dealing here with something that is alive, which in the case of an always-known cannot unfold its vitality. Irigaray's sense of listening also entails a certain openness in regard to the other and their existence: 'It is openness that nothing or no one occupies, or preoccupies – no language, no world, no God' (1996: 117). This does not so much involve what marks an individual subject or what they do, but it addresses the subject as such: 'It is thanks to silence that the other as other can exist or be, and the two be maintained' (2008: 5).

For Irigaray listening is a mode of communication whereby the other can unfold her or his freedom and, even more, come into existence. It offers the other the 'possibility of existence'. Above all 'it gives you a silent space in which to manifest yourself' (1996: 118). This clearly indicates Irigaray's conception of a different kind of 'communication'. While in a usual conversation information and data are exchanged, in this case everything revolves around the *existence* of the participants themselves. Thus, it is not information and data that are at the core but the subject itself.

The type of listening suggested by Irigaray is particular and incongruent with the present zeitgeist. In the practical everyday life of western society it is rarely applied, since this world has become too fast-paced and people are generally too focused on exerting their own will, following their own goals and imposing their opinions on others. The wish to be listened to and heard seems to be greater than the desire and capacity to listen to or hear someone else. It is here that Irigaray provides a commendable idea of autonomy which is less self-centered and more focused on the other's potential for autonomy, while not at odds with sustaining one's own subjectivity.

The meaning of the word 'silence'

To cultivate silence, listening is necessary. Listening is a prerequisite of silence, because the person who is listening is the one who is silent. The reverse is also true: only someone who is silent can attentively listen. Listening and being silent are thus closely linked, and both represent forms of communication. But in everyday life silence is mostly not considered a form of communication. In communication between two individuals silence is mostly interpreted, rather, as a refusal to engage in communication. Psychoanalysis takes a different view on this. Although in a psychoanalytical setting silence can be inferred as the refusal to speak, indicating an unconscious resistance on the part of the client, in psychoanalytical theory there are several meanings of silence (Akhtar 2009: 266). Besides silence as a form of resistance there is also silence as a form of non-verbal communication (Leira 1995), through which clients disclose themselves to the psychoanalyst.[7] In the colloquial expression 'a deafening silence' this meaning emerges in an idiomatic sense. Deafening silence is a silence that, in its non-speaking mode, speaks for itself. What kind of silence does Irigaray have in mind?

In the French original of her work, Irigaray continuously applies the French word *silence*. This has several meanings: it can mean the absence of noise, or the absence of words or information.[8] It can also describe a *state* or an *activity*. First, in the spatial sense, silence is a quiet place to think, a place where all is still, for example the quiet of the woods. Indeed, Irigaray does occasionally speak of a 'place of silence' (*lieu de silence*) (1997: 113, 2001: 62), which in my view could just as well be a 'place of stillness', where everything is still and where silence reigns.[9] Second, there is the activity of not speaking. We can view it as an activity because, strictly, not speaking is also a type of doing, even if only in the form of a negation.

As far as I can tell, Irigaray does not explicitly address the difference between silence as state and as activity. However, everything seems to point in the direction that both of these linguistic meanings play a role in her work. In the first instance, Irigaray relates the language of silence to non-speaking, intimately associated with her notion of listening as marked by the absence of speech. If we take into account that Irigaray was a practicing psychoanalyst, we might also be inclined to read silence as a matter of not speaking, having in mind the silent psychoanalyst carefully listening to the client. Completely in line with Irigaray, who views silence as an opportunity to bolster the other in their existence, in the psychoanalytical setting it is also about getting the client – through silence and listening – to talk and consequently become the subject.

However, silence is more than just something an individual subject has to achieve, by being silent. The already mentioned 'place of silence' does not seem to me to be simply a place where those present do not speak, but also a place where stillness reigns. Shifting focus away from the absence of speech, Irigaray claims that silence 'consists not at all in a lack of words, but in an almost tactile retouching of the spiritual in oneself, in a listening to the own breathing, appeased and attended' (2004: 167). In Asian philosophical traditions, such as Taoism, which Irigaray draws on in works such as *Between East and West* (2002 [1999]), this mode of silence or stillness plays a key spiritual role. While, in English, silence is the lack of sound, stillness is the state of being quiet. But the two meanings are interrelated and overlap. Stillness can only happen in the presence of silence, that is, when people stop talking.

Silence as a condition of love

But what does silence have to do with love? When Irigaray speaks of silence, it is not only about validating a new form of communication. For Irigaray such a new form of communication also serves another kind of *love*. According to her, silence is a condition of love between the sexes: 'The origin [...] of the love between us is silence' (2001: 62, cf. 2000: 106–7). To put it simply: Only those who can be silent can truly love. It is only in silence that love can really take place.

Undoubtedly, Irigaray, as a feminist difference theoretician, intends this not just in a general sense, but applies it specifically to the relationship between the sexes. In an interview where she is asked about her book *To Be Two* (2001) she claims: 'Silence is a way of respecting and acknowledging the fact that there's a difference between man and woman' (2000: 106). Hence, Irigaray reflects on silence in the service of an ethics of sexual difference.[10] Silence is, for her, a means of recognizing the other as other; it enables a loving relationship between a man and a woman since it maintains the subject status of both.[11] How can this be done? When you are silent and listen to the other, you offer the beloved other the opportunity to speak, and this means that the other gets the chance to become a subject. The person is no longer forced to listen to a speaking subject and thus to persevere in passivity. She or he turns from an object into a subject.

In order for love between the sexes to take place, Irigaray claims that silence must be generated, protected, and cultivated. This includes the protection of a 'place of silence' (2001: 62). A place of silence is not simply a place where stillness or silence can occur. Neither is it a quiet place for retreat, such as in the quiet solitude of a mountain landscape, where the sexes can meet calmly, removed from the hustle and bustle of everyday life. The silence, which Irigaray claims must be especially protected, takes place in the individual lovers themselves: 'I must protect the silence in me, and I must respect the silence of the other. Thus, silence is *two*: a two which cannot be reduced to the one or to the other, a two irreducible to one' (2001: 62). There are, then, at least two separate 'places' of silence, one in myself and one in the other. Furthermore, Irigaray speaks of a third silence. This is the silence which develops in the relationship between one and the other: 'Silence, therefore, is basic to the becoming of each man and each woman and to the becoming of their relationship. Silence is at least *three*' (2001: 62–63).

It is interesting and important to note that Irigaray speaks of not just two or three but *at least* three, since this calls to mind an earlier, similar and central thought that Irigaray had in regard to femininity. In *This Sex Which Is Not One* she describes woman as split in herself, that is, as plural. She even argues that, basically, one cannot even say of which parts the female sex consists: to some extent it is indeterminable: '*She is neither one nor two*. Rigorously speaking, she cannot be identified either as one person, or as two. She resists all adequate definition' (1985b: 26). In contrast to the male which is 'one', the female is the sex that is '*neither one nor two*'. She is, states Irigaray – alluding to the female vulvar lips – '*at least two*' (1985b: 26). The little phrase 'at least', which one finds in *This Sex Which Is Not One* as well as in *To Be Two*, points to a certain indeterminacy. 'At least' means that there *can* be more but not necessarily, and in case there is more we do not know exactly how much. If we do not know exactly how to proceed, then there is an indeterminable remainder. It is precisely for this reason that woman is 'resistant' to any kind of definition. Woman is, to a certain degree, an indeterminable gender and she should, according to my interpretation, thus remain, since only indetermination can prevent the problematic reduction to something determined. To the degree that woman evades definition, she can emerge as an autonomous and independent subject in her own right.[12] So, when Irigaray applies the adverbial phrase 'at least' to silence, it seems reasonable to assume that silence can be interpreted as a kind of *surplus*, which as such counts as a phenomenon which cannot be termed rationalistic or conceptual: it evades a precise definition or determination.

We can also not speak of a 'dialectic of silence' in the mode of Hegel's dialectics, whereby the silence of the individual can be contained in communal silence. The shared silence in the relationship between man and woman does not erase the difference between the silences of two subjects, nor the difference between the subjects themselves, as is the case, according to Irigaray, in Hegel (Irigaray 2001: 63). Rather, it is in the silence that the difference – and with it the alterity – of the 'silent' subjects remains. Finally, there is not *one* silence in which the sexes sublate each other, but 'at least *three*': one in me, on in the other, and one in the relationship. The risk of sublating the difference does not materialize in such silence, which assures that the singularity of the lovers is sustained. Here an inter-subjectivity materializes whereby the male and female subjects are not reduced to one another. 'You, who are you? You who are not nor ever will be me or mine' (Irigaray 1996: 119). Only if the one is not reduced to the other can the difference, strictly speaking, be maintained. In irreducibility lies the possibility of maintaining difference and with it the cultivation of alterity.[13]

Cultivating silence

Irigaray calls for a 'culture of silence', in particular in regard to love between the sexes. Such a culture of silence can in her view emerge in two ways: first, through cultivating the breath, as in the practice of yoga (2001: 64), and, second, in the 'practice of sexual difference' (2001: 65), which means all forms of ethical relationships between woman and man. But one might ask whether the cultivation of silence is an idealistic or utopian challenge. Irigaray herself will not let such allegations of 'utopian idealism' stand, objecting to them by saying 'that silence is a better guarantor of reality than is the concept' (2001: 66). Conceptual thinking is always tied to a reduction, since that at which it is directed is constrained by language.[14] The selectivity of language constantly brings exclusivity as a consequence: it aims at a meaning and at the same time excludes other meanings. The more formalistic the language, the more 'exclusive' it becomes. This leads to an artificial constriction of reality – or, as mentioned above, to a 'pseudo-reality'. In this way, conceptual thinking is always in danger of leveling difference. By talking to someone, for example, the other is reduced to a listener. Speech compromises the possibility of an autonomous existence for the other because while one talks, the other is forced to listen. In this case the silence of the other is imposed on the other, it is a negative silence. If someone gives a talk at a conference the audience is not free to speak at will, but must, out of respect, wait until the speech is over before having the opportunity to voice their opinion. In this way, the freedom of the listener is curtailed. Because even if the listener wants to speak, the cultural norm of being silent while listening to the talk, not disturbing the speaking person, stands contrary to such a desire. Even if the listener has a burning desire to speak, cultural norms dictate they have to wait for their turn in silence. If, alternatively, the speaking subject stops speaking and opens up a space of silence then, following Irigaray, a room of (two) subjects becomes possible. Hence, a culture of silence is necessary since only through such a culture can difference truly emerge – and difference is what constitutes a plural, democratic society or a community. If this difference is threatened or even extinguished through the idea of equality or a model of unity, according to Irigaray this puts society in danger. If we are all the same or equal, there is no diversity. And a society without plurality or variety is not a democracy.[15]

The call for a cultivation of silence is not only a matter of an immediate *practical* implementation by each and every individual. Rather, Irigaray's suggestions are always inextricably linked to a paraphrase of the western patriarchal culture. This means that they always ultimately revolve around a new interpretation of masculine culture in the field of the symbolic. That Irigaray deems such an interpretation possible is no secret. Certainly, it is questionable if the concrete implementation of silence and stillness is easy to achieve in a world where spoken words and voices demanding to be heard are ascribed such formidable power. However, it is unquestionable that such a world can, in principle, become the focus of a new definition or a redefinition.

Irigaray has demonstrated this over and over again in her lectures and philosophical reflections and invited her audience to participate in such a cultural reinterpretation.

Finally, that something is hard to implement does not necessarily imply that it can by no means be realized. We can indeed claim that although the call for a cultivation of silence is unusual, it is not unrealistic. It is unusual because there is no such tradition at the heart of western culture, and where silence is practiced this is generally not held in esteem. However, the fact that sub-cultures of silence do exist indicates that the call for a cultivation of silence is by no means unrealistic. The psychoanalytic practice of silence, inaugurated with Freud's 'technical rule' of 'evenly-suspended attention' (1912: 111), can be viewed as one such practice. Meditation and yoga are other examples of flourishing cultures of silence, which have travelled to the 'west' from an Asian cultural heritage where silence has long been valued as a central spiritual principle.

Silent love

In her contemplations on silence Irigaray repeatedly proclaims her ethics of sexual difference, whereby the other is recognized as truly other. As radical as she is, she claims that for such an ethics to be realized a revision is necessary at *all* levels of language, that is, also at the level of non-verbal communication. In this way, Irigaray extends her indispensable work on language. If we want to achieve a culture of two sexes, it is not enough to address language in its explicit, spoken expression. We have to delve into the unspoken as well. The silence that is marked by wordlessness, by the refraining from speech, becomes a means of a relationship between two lovers whereby they can encounter each other in their otherness. In that realm of silence they can meet without being reduced to one another, since objectification cannot exist in this silent realm. Silent love is the love of two subjects, who have left behind the subject-object scheme. It comprises an ethics of sexual difference through love.

As the term ethics indicates, this love is far removed from the question of sexual practices and desire; it is more of an ethical attitude toward the other. At its core this ethics comprises a feminist critique of patriarchy and a forceful analysis of the symbolic order in patriarchal societies. Yet, this does not mean it has no practical implications. Although Irigaray does not, in a normative way, call for lovers to keep silent and not speak with each other anymore, as if forbidden to use words, she invites us to think about the way we live our relationships with other human beings. Her ethics does not offer practical instructions on how to behave with others in real life; hence it remains for us to determine how silence (and what kind of silence) can foster love in an atmosphere of recognition of the other as other.

The cultivation of silence in the name of love is yet to emerge in our society. As Irigaray indicates, it is perhaps the key issue in our contemporary world: 'How can "I love you" be said in a different way? This is one of the most pertinent questions of our time' (1996: 129). Contrary to Irigaray, I believe that such a 'silent love' does not only work as a criticism of patriarchal love, in which woman in Irigaray's view does not yet exist. It comprises an ethical attitude relevant to all kinds of loving relationships – including, but not exclusive to, those based on sexual difference.

Notes

1 This is a revised and extended version of the article 'Schweigen und Stille. Zu Irigarays Vorschlag einer Kultivierung der sexuellen Differenz', published in *Texte: Psychoanalyse. Ästhetik. Kulturkritik 32(4)* 2012 and translated from German to English by Ida Černe.
2 For Irigaray autonomy is not just about acting on one's own authority or autonomously expressing one's opinion (free expression of opinion). The term 'autonomy' has to be taken literally. It is a compound of the Greek *autos* (self) and *nomos* (law) and literally means 'one who gives oneself one's own law'. In regard to Irigaray it means that the self (*autos*) is not measured according to another (male) norm (*nomos*), but according to itself.
3 For more on Irigaray's notion of difference, focusing on the idea of asymmetry, see Stoller (2005).
4 The English counterpart of the French verb *écouter* is *listen* (in contrast to *hear*, *entendre*) and that is how it is treated in the English translation of Irigaray's *J'aime à toi* (Irigaray 1996 [1992]).
5 Here Irigaray's proximity to the French phenomenologist Maurice Merleau-Ponty is evident. As Chair of the Institute for Child Psychology and Pedagogy at the Paris Sorbonne from 1949 to 1952, he advocated a phenomenology of the child, whereby the childlike language should stand on its own, with the aim of rehabilitating the world of children confronted by an adult world (Merleau-Ponty 2010). More recently, Eva Simms (2008) has contributed in her particular field of psychology to such a phenomenology of the child.
6 Here, there is also an affinity with phenomenology and psychoanalysis. The phenomenological method is based on a 'phenomenological attitude'. This attitude is, to a certain extent, an artificial attitude, because one has to consciously shift one's view: In the phenomenological attitude the phenomenologist no longer perceives the world in its immediate givenness but rather thematizes this givenness as it is presented to her or him in its immediateness. Put differently, the phenomenologist is not simply describing immediate experiences but rather reflects upon the 'immediateness' of experiences (for more on this see Stoller 2009). Furthermore, in psychoanalysis the analyst is encouraged to take on, to some extent, an 'artificial' attitude: the analyst is not allowed to relate to the client as in everyday life, but has to adhere to certain exceptional rules, a fundamental technique that Freud called the 'rule of abstinence' or 'evenly-suspended attention' (*gleichschwebende Aufmerksamkeit*) (1912: 111).
7 For the clinical and cultural aspects of silence, see Ronningstam (2006). Also, see the work of the German psychiatrist and philosopher Thomas Fuchs, who conceives of silence as 'indirect communication' (2004: 152–153).
8 See Larousse: Dictionnaires de français (n.d.) and CNRTL (Centre National de Ressources Textuelles et Lexicales) (n.d.).
9 In English *stillness* is differentiated from *silence*. The English standard translations of Irigaray's work mostly apply the English word *silence* for the French term *silence*. Only in a few cases in the study of Irigaray are both *silence* and *stillness* used (e.g. Hackenberg y Almansa 2013). In German *Stille* (*stillness*) is also clearly

distinguished from *Schweigen* (*silence*) (*schweigen* is also a verb, meaning being silent). For example, *silent night* translates into *stille Nacht* rather than *schweigende Nacht*. The English word 'silence' is somewhat broader than the German words *Schweigen* (which mainly means to not speak) and *Stille* (which is a kind of imposed quiet); silence can be a verb, a noun and an interjection ('Silence!' the teacher shouted), encompassing not only the absence of sound, but also the state of being surrounded by a lack of sound or noise. *Stille* is the closest word that comes to silence in the German language. I thank Ida Černe for this point.

10 Silence for Irigaray is only one way to promote such an ethics of sexual difference. Other possibilities are the establishment of a female imaginary, which Irigaray undertook in *This Sex Which Is Not One* (1985b), and the cultivation of breath, as thematized in *Entre Orient et Occident* (1999).

11 For Irigaray, *sexual* difference is the difference between woman and man. In her view this difference is primarily *ontological* rather than empirical and it is incomparable with other identity categories. For a critique of this ascription of primacy to sexual difference, see Deutscher (2002).

12 In my article 'The Indeterminable Gender' I sketch a new concept of gender by drawing on Irigaray's image of indeterminacy and indeterminability in conjunction with phenomenology (Stoller 2013). In Stoller (2011) I make a similar attempt in regard to the gendered experience of time.

13 On the meaning of irreducibility in Irigaray's ethic of sexual difference, see Stoller (2005).

14 Freud, in regard to writing down notes during a session, warned of an '*ostensible exactness*' (1912: 114), which could lead to problems such as a 'detrimental selection' (1912: 113). This seems to me to address a comparable problem.

15 In my book on Beauvoir, Irigaray and Butler I argue that plurality is based on difference and the possibility of differentiation (Stoller 2010, ch. 10, cf. 2013).

References

Akhtar, Salman (2009) *Comprehensive Dictionary of Psychoanalysis*. London: Karnac.

Bion, Wilfred R. (2004 [1962]) *Learning from Experience*. Oxford: Rowman & Littlefield.

Cixous, Hélène (1976) 'The Laugh of the Medusa', *Signs* 1(4): 875–893.

CNRTL (Centre National de Ressources Textuelles et Lexicales) (n.d.) 'Silence'. Available: www.cnrtl.fr/definition/silence (accessed 26 April 2015).

Deutscher, Penelope (2002) *A Politics of Impossible Difference: The Later Work of Luce Irigaray*. Ithaca NY and London: Cornell University Press.

De Vries, Roland J. (2013) *Becoming Two in Love: Kierkegaard, Irigaray, and the Ethics of Sexual Difference*. Eugene, OR: Pickwick.

Freud, Sigmund (1958 [1912]) 'Recommendations to Physicians Practising Psycho-Analysis', in J. Strachey (ed.) *The Standard Edition of the Complete Psychological Works of Sigmund Freud, Vol. XII*. London: Hogarth Press and the Institute of Psycho-analysis.

Fuchs, Thomas (2004) 'Zur Phänomenologie des Schweigens', *Phänomenologische Forschungen*. Hamburg: Felix Meiner.

Gunnarsson, Lena (2014) *The Contradictions of Love: Towards a Feminist-Realist Ontology of Sociosexuality*. London and New York: Routledge.

Hackenberg y Almansa, Sigrid (2013) 'The Distant ('*dis-tənt*) Stillness that is 'Breth', in E. A. Holmes and L. Škof (eds) *Breathing with Luce Irigaray*. London and New York: Bloomsbury.

Husserl, Edmund (1983) *Ideas Pertaining to a Pure Phenomenology and to a Phenom-enological Philosophy, First Book: General Introduction to a Pure Phenomenology.* Trans. F. Kersten. The Hague: Martinus Nijhoff.

Irigaray, Luce (1985a) *Speculum of the Other Woman*, trans. G. C. Gill. Ithaca, NY: Cornell University Press.

Irigaray, Luce (1985b) *This Sex Which Is Not One*, trans. C. Porter with C. Burke. Ithaca, NY: Cornell University Press.

Irigaray, Luce (1992) *J'aime à toi: Esquisse d'une félicité dans l'histoire.* Paris: Bernard Grasset.

Irigaray, Luce (1993) *An Ethics of Sexual Difference*, trans. C. Burke and G. C. Gill. Ithaca, NY: Cornell University Press.

Irigaray, Luce (1996) *I Love to You: Sketch for a Felicity Within History*, trans. A. Martin. New York and London: Routledge.

Irigaray, Luce (1997) *Être Deux*. Paris: Bernard Grasset.

Irigaray, Luce (1999) *Entre Orient et Occident*. Paris: Editions Grasset et Fasquelle.

Irigaray, Luce (2000) *Why Different? A Culture of Two Subjects. Interviews with Luce Irigaray.* L. Irigaray and S. Lotringer (eds), trans. C. Collins. New York: semiotext(e).

Irigaray, Luce (2001) *To Be Two*, trans. M. M. Rhodes and M. F. Cocito-Monoc. New York: Routledge.

Irigaray, Luce (2002) *Between East and West. From Singularity to Community*, trans. S. Pluháček. New York: Columbia University Press.

Irigaray, Luce (2004) *Luce Irigaray. Key Writings.* London and New York: Continuum.

Irigaray, Luce (2008) *Sharing the World.* London: Continuum.

Irigaray, Luce (2011) *Das Mysterium Marias*, trans. A. Dickmann. Hamburg: Les Éditions du Crieur Public.

Joy, Morny (2007) *Divine Love: Luce Irigaray, Women, Gender, and Religion.* Manchester: Manchester University Press.

Larousse: Dictionnaires de français (n.d.) 'Silence'. Available: www.larousse.fr/dic tionnaires/francais/silence/72720 (accessed 7 February 2017).

Leira, Torhild (1995) 'Silence and Communication: Nonverbal Dialogue and Therapeutic Action', *Scandinavian Psychoanalytic Review* 18: 41–65.

Merleau-Ponty, Maurice (2010) *Child Psychology and Pedagogy: The Sorbonne Lectures 1949–1952*, trans. T. Welsh. Evanston, IL: Northwestern University Press.

Miller, Shaun (2011) *The Problem of Love. From Sartre and Beauvoir to Irigaray.* Saarbrücken, Germany: Lambert Academic Publishing.

Postl, Gertrude (2009) 'Liebe im Kontext einer Politik der sexuellen Differenz', *Mitteilungen des Instituts für Wissenschaft und Kunst*, 3–4, 9–15. Special issue on 'Liebeskonzepte und Geschlechterdiskurs', S. Hochreiter and S. Stoller (eds).

Ronningstam, Elsa (2006) 'Silence: Cultural Function and Psychological Transformation in Psychoanalysis and Psychoanalytic Psychotherapy', *International Journal of Psychoanalysis* 87: 1277–1296.

Secomb, Linnell (2007) 'Irigaray: Re-directing the Gift of Love', in *Philosophy and Love: From Plato to Popular Culture.* Edinburgh: Edinburgh University Press.

Simms, Eva M. (2008) *The Child in the World. Embodiment, Time, and Language in Early Childhood.* Detroit, MI: Wayne State University Press.

Škof, Lenart (2015) *Breath of Proximity: Intersubjectivity, Ethics and Peace.* Dordrecht: Springer.

Stoller, Silvia (2005) 'Asymmetrical Genders: Phenomenological Reflections on Sexual Difference', *Hypatia* 20(2): 7–26. Special issue on 'Contemporary Feminist Philosophy in German', G. Postl (ed.).

Stoller, Silvia (2009) 'Phenomenology and the Poststructural Critique of Experience', *International Journal of Philosophical Studies* 17(5): 707–737.

Stoller, Silvia (2010) *Existenz – Differenz – Konstruktion. Phänomenologie der Geschlechtlichkeit bei Beauvoir, Irigaray und Butler.* Munich: Wilhelm Fink.

Stoller, Silvia (2011) 'Gender and Anonymous Temporality', in C. Schües, D. E. Olkowsky, and H. A. Fielding (eds) *Time in Feminist Phenomenology.* Bloomington and Indianapolis: Indiana University Press.

Stoller, Silvia (2012) 'Schweigen und Stille. Zu Irigarays Vorschlag einer Kultivierung der sexuellen Differenz', *Texte: Psychoanalyse. Ästhetik. Kulturkritik* 32(4): 85–100.

Stoller, Silvia (2013) 'The Indeterminable Gender', *Janus Head* 13(1): 17–34. Special issue on 'Interdisciplinary Feminist Phenomenology', E. Simms and B. Stawarska (eds). Available: www.janushead.org/13-1/Stoller.pdf (accessed 25 April 2015).

Toye, Margaret E. (2010) 'Towards a Poethics of Love: Poststructuralist Feminist Ethics and Literary Creation', *Feminist Theory* 11: 39–55.

10 Love, feminism and dialectics

Repairing splits in theory and practice

Lena Gunnarsson

Life offers a range of paradoxes and ontological tensions. Staying in control is often disempowering, while being vulnerable may empower us. Withholding what one has tends to deprive the withholder against their intentions, whereas giving is often a rewarding experience. How do we make sense of such paradoxes? The kind of analytical reasoning that has been the privileged method of grasping reality throughout the western history of thought[1] has difficulty making sense of ontological tensions of this kind, and is liable to see them as anomalies rather than constitutive features of reality. In this analytical mode of thought a phenomenon is defined by what it is not, meaning it cannot make sense of the ways that things often encompass their own opposite, as in the case where vulnerability means strength. By contrast, dialectical reasoning takes such ontological tensions to be constitutive features of reality which, therefore, needs to be epistemologically systematized.

In this chapter I foreground the constitutive role of ontological tensions[2] and elaborate on the bearings of this idea for the theorization of love and dominance, with specific focus on the patriarchal woman–man bond. My view of tension, and sometimes contradiction, as a constitutive feature of reality is underpinned by the dialectical critical realist ontology developed by Roy Bhaskar, as part of his broader philosophy of critical realism (Bhaskar 2008; Gunnarsson 2014, 2017b).[3] I apply this ontology to expand on Jessica Benjamin's analysis of male dominance, highlighting the central role of constitutive tension in her theorization of the patriarchal dynamic.

In relation to Benjamin as well as to the Sedgwickean/Kleinean 'reparative turn', I elaborate on the necessity of living-with-and-through rather than seeking to escape constitutive existential tensions, if we are to be able to live non-oppressively and sustainably with one another. I demonstrate how dialectics can account for the fact that life-enhancing impulses often underpin oppressive practices, where the latter can be seen as distorted or alienated expressions of the former. This theme underpins Benjamin's notion of 'redemptive critique', which I connect with Emmanuel Ghent's idea of the constructive longing for surrender as co-enfolded in the destructive tendency to accept or seek out submission. Finally I elaborate, partly in dialogue with Luce Irigaray's work, on the fundamental tension entailed by our concurrent inseparability *and* difference from others, teasing out the implications that this tension has for love and for how we can most effectively dissolve the contradictions currently permeating human bonds.

Dialectical critical realism

There is no room, nor need, to give an account here of dialectical thought as a whole, still less of all debates about it. The dialectical critical realist framework developed by the British philosopher Roy Bhaskar is a specific version of dialectics, which draws on Friedrich Hegel but comes closer to the Marxian take on dialectic in its pronounced realist standpoint that dialectical *thinking* is needed since *reality* is dialectically structured. Bhaskar defines dialectics as 'the art of thinking the coincidence of distinctions and connections' (2008: 180). This mode of thinking corresponds to a view of being as a stratified and differentiated whole, whose elements are both intra-connected and relatively independent from one another. The relations between different totalities and dimensions can thus be understood as different modes of *unity-in-difference*, 'whereby things have both points of identity with one another and points of divergence' (Gunnarsson 2017b: 116; Bhaskar 2008). The coincidence of distinction and inseparability may be constelled in a variety of ways, ranging from basic, existential tension between different aspects of a totality to the 'ontologically extravagant' phenomenon of *dialectical contradictions* (Bhaskar with Hartwig 2010: 193), characterized by 'historically accumulated splits between things that are fundamentally unified' (Gunnarsson 2017b: 116).

Humanity's relation of opposition to the nature that in fact sustains it is an example of a dialectical contradiction. Although this unsustainable combination of inseparability and exploitative separation is a product of human decisions and could be done away with, the dialectical realist perspective nevertheless highlights that it is enabled by and hooks onto a basic existential tension that we can *not* do away with: that entailed by the fact that humanity is paradoxically both different from and part of nature (Gunnarsson 2013; Soper 1995). Humans' relative autonomy from nature is what makes it possible for us to alienate ourselves from the needs of nature and exploit it for our own shortsighted purposes. At the same time, this separation can never challenge the fact that nature is the *de facto* ground of humanity, meaning our domination of nature is ultimately to our own detriment. It will be a central theme of this chapter that basic existential tensions may and often do accumulate into oppressive contradictions, but do not have to do so. In light of that, it becomes a crucial emancipatory task to (re)direct the energies and impulses produced by *inevitable* tensions in ways that do not produce the kind of *unnecessary* contradictions that currently structure the world.

In Bhaskar's ontology, dialectical relations in which (relative) autonomy coincides with unity exist on a range of different levels. For the purposes of this chapter, I will first enter this theme via the general figure of *dialectical totality* and then discuss it in terms of the more specific *self–other relation*. Some theorists are wary of invoking the term 'totality', presumably because it conveys a sense of totalitarianism if thought of in non-dialectical terms. Bhaskar's notion of dialectical totality is not at odds with plurality, fluidity and change, however; the borders of one totality are never absolute or fixed, but always in open-ended process. Also, where such borders are drawn depends on perspective, since any phenomenon in the world is always part of a range of different totalities, so that it can, paradoxically, be both inside and outside of the same totality, such as in the case of humanity being both part of nature and different from it. This relativity of distinctions and connections does not mean they are simply epistemological constructions, though. The reason why we need analytical distinctions to make sense of reality is because they relate to *ontological* differentiations, which despite their relativity and ambiguity have a reality beyond human perception (Gunnarsson 2014, 2017b).

The human self can be thought of as a dialectical totality with boundaries that are permeable and shifting, yet relatively stable and causally efficacious, and whose inside is composed of a complex set of sub-totalities which may both co-constitute and conflict with one another. Despite the relatively autonomous status of the self, as feminist theorists have been insisting, any self is also intrinsically relational in that it emerges[4] only by virtue of its relations with others. This means that just as nature is in a sense both inside and outside of humanity, others are both inside and outside of our own selves.

The paradox that our *independent* existence is *dependent* on others is at the heart of Hegel's famous master–slave dialectic (1977) and, as we shall see, Jessica Benjamin's feminist elaboration of it. Before presenting Benjamin's work, a word is needed about the strained relation between (Hegelian) dialectics and feminist theory more generally (Granberg 2013; Stone 2004). Magnus Granberg notes that whereas '[d]ialectics was once seen as the major alternative to positivist approaches; perhaps presently poststructuralism and its offshoots in gender, postcolonial and intersectional studies have usurped this position' (2013: 2). Peculiarly, to my mind, many poststructuralist feminists associate dialectics precisely with the kind of oppositional, closed system thinking that it in my view so effectively challenges (Braidotti 2011; Chanter 2010). It seems that this reading, largely inspired by French thinkers like Gilles Deleuze, is rooted in a conflation of dialectics as such with a specific, disputable (Jameson 2014; Stone 2004) interpretation of Hegel's dialectic that was dominant in particular in postwar France (Granberg 2013). The association of dialectics – or at least 'what we usually call dialectical' (Irigaray 1989: 32) – with an oppositional, often violent, logic also permeates the French school of 'difference feminism', as represented for example by Irigaray, whom I posit in this essay as a deeply dialectical thinker in that she foregrounds the mutual constitution of difference and unity (e.g. Irigaray 2002: 78).[5] Rather than going deeper in the complex debates about Hegel and dialectics here, it suffices to say that Bhaskar, Benjamin, and Irigaray alike all have some quarrels with Hegel's dialectic, but the latter is also a crucial ground from the point of which they develop their own theories, Bhaskar on a general level and Benjamin and Irigaray as regards the self–other dialectic.

Whereas radical difference is centered in Irigaray and similar works critiquing what they take to be mainstream dialectics, there is also a seemingly opposite tendency in non-dialectical poststructuralist thought to challenge binary thinking by playing down the reality of separateness and difference. The first tendency is mostly at work in theorizations of the self–other relation, while the focus on inseparability permeates more general ontological discussions. For instance, many new materialist feminists are suspicious of making distinctions *at all* between interrelated phenomena, such as epistemology/ ontology, nature/culture, subject/object. In a critique of the largely poststructuralist new materialist turn, Elmar Flatschart compares the latter's mode of challenging dualisms with the dialectical approach. Much like for new materialism, the aim of dialectics, states Flatschart, 'is to bring together subject and object; but unlike [new materialism], it does accept that in order to do so, both first have to be accepted in their relative separation' (2014: 10–11). Dialectics challenges dualisms at their root, precisely because it transcends what I see as *the most basic of dualisms, that between separateness and unity itself.* Entities like nature and humanity, subject and object, self and other are *both* (relatively) separate *and* (relatively) inseparable, and this tension needs to be theoretically harbored. As I elaborate upon below, impulses to overcome dualism by denying any of the poles in the dialectic of unity-*in*-difference are bound to reproduce dualism 'on a different, more abstract but also falsely disoriented level' (Flatschart 2014: 12). Without deepening my critique of poststructuralist thought here, I want to highlight that its common mode of challenging dualistic and atomistic thinking by emphasizing inseparability *at the cost of* separateness buys into the conceptual 'either/or' terrain of the dualistic-atomistic thinking it sets out to critique (for examples and critical elaboration, see Gunnarsson 2013, 2014, 2015a, 2017b).

Benjamin: from existential tension to oppressive contradiction

In the by now feminist classic *The Bonds of Love* (1988) psychoanalytical theorist Jessica Benjamin presents a theory of the psychological roots of male domination, which constitutes an innovative and compelling amalgam of Hegelian dialectics, Winnicottian object-relational theory and Frankfurt school theories of recognition (Benjamin 2013). Reading Hegel's master–slave dialectic through an object-relational psychoanalytical lens, Benjamin analyzes male domination as an *alienated kind of differentiation* based on attempts at circumventing existential tensions that are really uncircumventable. In her view, the process of becoming and being a self involves a tension between the two 'contradictory impulses [of] asserting the self and recognizing the other' (1988: 53). The paradox is that although these impulses are in a way contradictory to one another, they are also mutually constitutive poles in the same process of becoming a differentiated self. As Benjamin states, 'at the very moment of realizing our own independence, we are dependent on another to recognize it' (33), meaning any dualistic juxtapositions of independence and dependence is false.

Benjamin understands the current structure of male domination as linked to an inability to live with this tension between self-assertion and recognition on which human existence is premised. The current gender regime is based on a refusal of the condition that '[i]n order to exist for oneself, one has to exist for another' (Benjamin 1988: 53) and that, concomitantly, in order to exist for another one has to exist for oneself. This tension, which is really what gives life to selfhood, is repressed in a way that delegates one of its poles to men – self-assertion and independence – and the other – recognition and dependence – to women. The denial of dependence, the typically masculine way of avoiding tension in this regime, is liable to result in 'the transformation of the need for the other into domination of him' (54), inasmuch as controlling the other is a way of covering over the power that they inevitably have over us.

However, the control of the other can only go ever so far, for what we ultimately need from them, recognition, is something that can be bestowed only by someone outside of our control, with an existence *for-themself*; if I control them, their 'recognition' will have no value (cf. de Beauvoir 1989; Gunnarsson 2014, 2015b; Jónasdóttir 1994).

Ultimately this means that the suppressed reality of dependence is destined to re-emerge in one way or another. It also means that the need for differentiation, for renewed tension between self and other, will be repeatedly re-actualized, since the one whose recognition I need must be other to me in some way. Within the confines of male domination and gender polarity the re-actualization of dependence is likely to be dealt with by further attempts at control, combined with efforts to recreate differentiation and tension between self and other without having to really let go of the other. Benjamin states that the tension between self and other that is repeatedly broken down in the complementary economy of alienated male independence and female dependency must be continuously recreated 'through distance, idealization, and objectification', those alienated modes of differentiation that stand in for the genuine kind of differentiation that draws on rather than suppresses the fundamental tensions between self and other, independence and dependence, self-assertion and recognition. Such alienated attempts at recreating tension are doomed to break down again and again, though, 'unless and until the other makes a difference' (1988: 68), as *really* other rather than an extension of one's own needs.

If we look at the dialectic from the feminine side, as paradigmatically constellated, here existential tension is evaded via a denial of *in*dependence (Gunnarsson 2014; cf. de Beauvoir 1989). Subjecthood is instead sought by means of attachment to a strong, independent masculine subject, whose subjecthood is paradoxically premised on feminine objecthood. This solution is also endemically fragile, though, for the more a person makes themself into an object for an other, the less recognition they will in fact be able to offer this other on whom their own sense of self depends so acutely. One consequence of this paradoxical dynamic is that someone who erases their own needs and projects in an attempt to be lovable and loved, will often be met with dissatisfaction, as most clearly marked in some forms of violent couple dynamics.

As Benjamin argues throughout her work (1988, 1995, 1998), there is a tendency in western thought to conceive of relations between people in terms of an inevitable subject–object relation, in which the subject status of one is premised on the other's object status. It is in relation to this theme that she departs from what she takes to be Hegel's version of the master–slave dialectic, in which the tension between the needs for self-assertion and recognition is depicted as *bound* to break down. In her reading, the Hegelian dialectic offers no room for the possibility of *two* equal independent subjectivities, involved in a non-violent process of both asserting their own independence and recognizing the independence of the other as well as their own dependence on this independent other.[6] In contrast to this, for Benjamin the tendency of splitting the mutually constitutive poles of independence and dependence along gendered lines is but one historically specific way of dealing with this tension. The violent dialectic can be avoided if 'the real strain of acknowledging the other' (1998: 98) is accepted as part of one's own existence rather than seen as external obstacle. In my view, this process involves letting go of the idea of becoming a total(itarian) subject, embracing the fact that our subjecthood is constituted in dialectic with our position as *objects* shaped by forces beyond our control (cf. de Beauvoir 1947) and, with Benjamin, learning to 'appreciate the externality and aliveness of encountering uncontrollable otherness' (2006: 118).

Dialectics, necessity and redemptive critique

There are two central themes in Benjamin's theory that tie in with my reading of Bhaskar's dialectical ontology: (1) the foregrounding of tension as constitutive of life, meaning things that seem to contradict one another are often co-constitutive aspects of the same process; and (2) the process theorized by Benjamin whereby basic existential tensions take on an oppressive and unsustainable form characterized by split and polarization only when evaded. This latter theme can be related to Bhaskar's idea of the destructive and ultimately self-defeating character of practices that deny the conditions on which they really depend. Adapting somewhat Freud's 'reality principle' (Bhaskar 2008: 230), as I interpret it Bhaskar's work highlights that real freedom and empowerment cannot be based on a denial of the necessary constraints of being, but are entailed by living-with these constraints so that one can draw on the support and energy that they also entail. Seeking to escape the tensions on which our lives depend only makes them sharper; rather than disappearing they are pushed somewhere where they do not belong, split off from their source in a way that is bound to generate the kind of double-binds and knots (Bhaskar 2008: 56) that are characteristic of dialectical contradictions. As highlighted by dialectical critical realist Alan Norrie, projects based on this kind of suppression and split 'may work for a while, but reality has a habit of biting back' (2010: 106).

The need to act in accordance with life's necessities if one's aims are to be fulfilled is a theme that permeates Benjamin's work. Her vocabulary is replete with words signalling necessity, such as when she points to 'the contradictions that our *need* for the other's independent existence *demands* we bear' (1998: 98, emphasis added). The dialectical sophistication of her work lies very much in the way that she distinguishes necessary existential tensions from historically produced (unnecessary) contradictions, demonstrating that the latter do not automatically follow from the former, *while* acknowledging their intrinsic interconnections. Elsewhere (Gunnarsson 2013, 2014, 2015a) I argue that we cannot make sense of socially constructed power structures without pinpointing how they are anchored in the necessities of life. Although oppression is not an inevitable outcome of fundamental tensions in the human structure of needs, we can make sense of it only in relation to such basic constraints. From this follows that if we are to efficaciously challenge oppressive contradictions, we need to first understand and respect their connection to basic needs, in order to be able to direct the impulses they produce in more constructive directions. The dialectical theme of unity-in-difference and its challenge to 'either/or thinking' is crucial here, since it works against thinking about socially constructed orders as either pre-determined by pre-given necessities or having nothing at all to do with such basic constraints.

In a retrospective essay Benjamin thematizes the process of sifting out the vital needs and impulses buried under destructive practices in terms of a 'more complex path to liberation', premised on '[s]aving the baby while throwing out the bathwater' (2013: 4). She advocates a 'redemptive critique' drawing on the idea that 'behind the shameful, the abject, the fearful lie buried needs and longings' (3) and that 'ideals that take form in perverse and painful expression can be redeemed by understanding the desire and aspiration that lie beneath' (4). What is required is an 'exacting analytical work' of identifying and redeeming the constructive impulses that are distorted by their alienated mode of expression. Expressing concern over dualistic juxtapositions of victim and perpetrator, Benjamin stresses that in this more 'emotionally in touch' process of liberation women also need to be aware of their own part in reproducing structures of dominance, and points to the need for exploring 'how victims can perpetuate their own victimhood by becoming stuck in the complementarity of doer and done-to' (4). She suggests that the taboo on examining women's participation in their own subordination may be due to 'a fear of losing the moral edge' that can be claimed through victimhood (7). From a theoretical point of view, this taboo is enabled by the dialectical deficit in dominant modes of thought, inasmuch as non-dialectical either/or reasoning can only conceive of victims and perpetuators as dualistically positioned opposites, thereby precluding a conceptualization of the subordinate as *both* victim and co-player.

In her retrospective reflections Benjamin acknowledges her intellectual debt to Emmanuel Ghent, whose theory about masochism as an alienation (or 'perversion', in his terms) of the longing for surrender (Ghent 1990) was one important piece of groundwork on which her own thoughts built. In line with the idea of redemptive critique, Ghent posits that behind destructive urges to submission there is generally a constructive longing for *surrender*, that kind of letting go of one's defences that is necessary for being fully recognized for who one is. Entering into a submissive or masochistic position is on one level radically different from surrender, in that the former involves a negation of one's self, while the latter is liberatory of one's deeper self as well as a premise of the genuine intimacy that dominance precludes. At the same time, for Ghent submission can be viewed as 'something akin to distortion, corruption, diversion, misconstruction' of surrender (1990: 108), as its 'defensive mutant' (111), meaning the two are closely dialectically conjoined. Here we see at work the dialectical figure of two things, submission and surrender, being *both* opposite to one another *and* similar in a way that makes them likely to be confused, not only in imagination but in our real practices as well. Hence the importance of not simply rejecting masochistic tendencies as irrational (a position that is also likely to feed feminist denial of the existence of such tendencies), for what ultimately drive them are life-affirming impulses.

Whereas dialectics holds the world together by elucidating the connections between distinct aspects of reality in the face of the kind of splitting practices highlighted in the above section, it also has the opposite function of elucidating important distinctions between phenomena, which may be obscured by their entanglement in one another. The distinction between submission and surrender is an example, which, I think, has particular importance for feminists.[7] As shown in a study by psychoanalytical theorist and practitioner Lynne Layton (2004), it is not uncommon that women seek a way out of subordination and self-negation by warding themselves off from others and from their own vulnerability, in a way that denies them the empowering experience of love. Whereas Ghent discusses how someone can seek out submission when it is really surrender that is longed for, the reverse move of challenging subordination by refusing vulnerability and surrender is also a likely outcome of the fact, highlighted by Ghent (1990), that our dominant culture offers few resources for distinguishing between surrender and submission.

Layton conjectures that the reason why the heterosexual middle-class women that she meets in her clinical practice often take on what she calls 'defensive autonomy' is due to western culture's dualism between connection and autonomy, which makes it 'very difficult to be, for example, both dependent and independent, assertive and loving, feminine and competent' (2004: 32). Echoing Benjamin's work, she shows that inasmuch as these dualisms are false, these women do not really manage to achieve real autonomy by fending themselves off from others; 'the cultural dichotomization of relatedness and autonomy leaves neither pole functioning very well' (37). For instance, one of

Layton's clients experiences autonomy and relatedness as opposites, but in therapy their inevitable relatedness becomes clear in the way that her relational conflicts continuously disrupt her autonomous activities. On a broader cultural level, Layton highlights, this contradiction is expressed in the way that 'Western culture holds as an ideal the autonomous individual while it simultaneously creates people who are insecure, status craving, and dependency denying yet deeply dependent on the approval of others' (32–33).

The reparative turn and the issue of transformation

Layton is not alone cautioning against tendencies of challenging oppression by means of defensive strategies. Today at least certain groups of women are no longer confined to relationality, but are not only allowed but compelled to win an autonomous self. Inasmuch as femininity is still largely defined in terms of relationality, this has created new contradictions. In my understanding, the 'reparative turn' recently announced by feminist theorists (Feminist Theory 2014; Wiegman 2014) in the wake of an influential essay by Eve Kosofsky Sedgwick (2003a) draws on sensibilities similar to Layton's, although the reparative turn cautions against defensive strategies primarily on the level of critique rather than in our intimate lives. In her essay 'Paranoid Reading and Reparative Reading' Sedgwick argues that there is a striking similarity between paranoia – characterized by alertness to dangers and an impulse to reveal and anticipate them – and the virtues underpinning the critical tradition of thought, largely building on the work of the three 'masters of suspicion', Freud, Marx and Nietzsche. Drawing on Melanie Klein's (1946) psychoanalytical theory of the paranoid-schizoid and depressive positions, Sedgwick casts doubt on the potential of paranoid-critical practices to give us what we long for, that freedom and fulfilment whose relative absence in our lives is the reason why we critique society's disenabling character.

In Klein's theory the paranoid-schizoid position is what we are born into. Actualizing the dialectical theme, it is characterized by an inability to tolerate tension and ambivalence, resulting in a range of strategies premised on either/or notions: either I am powerful or powerless, either things are good or bad, and so forth. In this position the infant splits both itelf and the parent into mutually exclusive good and bad parts, unable to accept that the good and the bad are aspects of any entity (Klein 1946; Sedgwick 2003a, 2007). Here, then, emerges the mechanism of projecting onto the outside world those parts of oneself that are experienced as unacceptable. There are crucial affinities between Klein's and Benjamin's work, and the Benjaminian gender dialectic can be read in terms of the masculine projection of dependence onto the feminine and the feminine projection of independence onto the masculine, as complementary strategies of achieving non-ambiguous identity.

As we have seen, however, such splitting practices are ultimately unsustainable and self-defeating, in that they also tear apart the ground of one's own existence. This founds a deep self-interest to stop projecting and splitting.

In line with this, and against Freud, Sedgwick points out that '[i]t is not mainly "civilization" that needs the individual to be different from what she spontaneously is. The individual herself needs to be different, insofar as her intrinsic impulses conflict with one another' (2007: 633). This aligns with Bhaskar's reinterpretation of Freud's reality principle as inherent in our own co-relational constitution, rather than something forced upon us from the 'outside'. Any dualistic juxtaposition of the inside and the outside, the self and society, is in fact false. When the infant projects its 'bad' parts onto the parental object on which it depends, this hits back upon the infant. Their own goodness happens at the expense of the goodness of the parental object, and this will of course be a source of dread for the infant. Hence, the only way that the infant, and the adult, can achieve peace is by learning to tolerate that the good is 'contaminated' by the bad. The mourning to which this acceptance gives rise is the reason why Klein terms this position 'depressive'. The depressive element stands in a dialectical relation with satisfaction, though, in that it is the necessary platform from which to *repair* the split internal objects into wholes, which entail tension and ambivalence but are also 'more realistic, durable, and satisfying [...], available to be identified with, to offer and be offered nourishment and comfort in turn' (Sedgwick 2007: 637).

Although Sedgwick sees political commitment and critical thought as ultimately underpinned by reparative sensibilities, she notes that 'the propulsive energy of activism [...] tends to be structured very much in a paranoid/schizoid fashion: driven by attributed motives, fearful contempt of opponents, collective fantasies of powerlessness and/or omnipotence, scapegoating, purism, and schism' (2007: 638). Her scrutiny of the paranoid-critical stance can be read as an interrogation of to what extent the political-critical means we use to achieve transformation are in fact efficacious. She highlights that the vigilant mode of exposing ills that underpins much critical scholarship, in particular the queer theory of which she herself was a leading representative, does not itself remove those ills. In fact it is often quite the contrary, she states, drawing on Buddhist insights that highlight the circular logic whereby 'trying to remedy [an oppressive mechanism], or even in fact articulate it, simply adds propulsive energy to that very mechanism' (2007: 635). To continue this Buddhist theme, which permeates Sedgwick's later work (2003b, 2007; Sedgwick with Snediker 2008), we can also think of the non-productive character of (paranoia-leaning) critique in terms of how its outsmarting, one-upmanship elements (Love 2010) lock reality inside pre-conceived schemes, which screen the critic off from the energy of the here-and-now, disempowering her in a way that also makes her transformative interventions less efficacious.

In my experience, many feminist and other progressive modes of critique and activism pay too little attention to whether what they do in fact helps create the change wanted. If it feels morally right to direct anger and blame at a group or person perceived as having done wrong, it seems that we often do not care if our angry stance is transformative or not: if the other does not change it is their problem, not ours. It *is* our problem, though, since we are interested in change. As I state elsewhere, I think we need to be better at 'disentangling the moral issue of who is to blame, of who *should* change, from what will *actually* effectuate change' (Gunnarsson 2015b: 330, emphasis in original; cf. Gunnarsson 2017a).

In love it seems more obvious than in other arenas that adopting the attitude typical of the paranoid critique will not take us far in delivering the mutuality and fulfilment we are after. Engaging in heterosexual love as a feminist woman can be experienced as extremely conflict-ridden: it is difficult to combine a critical stance towards male power, based on the revelatory practice of identifying injustices that are not apparent at first sight because of their normalized and naturalized status, with the openness, vulnerability, and trust that love requires (Gunnarsson 2017a). Here, the ability to harbour tension and ambivalence could hardly be more crucial. In an essay on heterosexual love in patriarchy, Virginia Held states that

> [i]n trying to live with a recognition of the importance of both fighting and loving, women will have to accept a kind of schizophrenic existence. An integrated stance toward the world is a distant goal to be sought, a luxury they cannot yet afford.
>
> (1976: 182)

This can be related to Heather Love's comment that we ought not read Sedgwick's reparative turn as suggesting we replace the paranoid position with a reparative one; these positions should rather be seen as mutually co-productive and 'the oscillation between them [as] inevitable' (2010: 239). Perhaps what we need is a forgiving, accepting, reparative, rather than paranoid, stance towards our very paranoia. Such an interpretation would be faithful to the Buddhist perspective that inspired Sedgwick, according to which ills are not removed by being *opposed* but tend to dissolve if met with the kind of loving attention that is based on apprehending that the 'good' is always co-enfolded in the 'bad'. This perspective also aligns with Bhaskar's later spiritual writings (2000, 2002a, 2002b; Gunnarsson 2014), in which he does acknowledge the constitutive role of tension and difference, but holds the cohering power of love and trust to be ontologically prior, harbouring tensions in its embrace.

In the pulse of now

There is a crucial temporal dimension to the paranoid/reparative theme. Sedgwick highlights that for the paranoid 'there must be no bad surprises' and this imperative creates a 'unidirectionally future-oriented vigilance' (2003a: 130), aimed at anticipating bad news before it happens. She notes that the problem with this orientation is that it tends to depend on being defensive towards anything new and surprising, so that good surprises are blocked out as well. In my reading the paranoid is actually as much locked up in the past as in the future. It is in light of past experiences that the paranoid pre-conceives the future, meaning that although past and future are opposite to one another on one level, on another level they are dialectically unified.

This temporal motif ties in with insights from mystical spiritual traditions, which foreground the liberatory potentials of immediate intimacy with the now. Bhaskar highlights that it is only if we are attentively in touch with the present that we can act with power in the world, effectively drawing on the life forces. He goes as far as stating that '[a]ny received belief, any repetitive pattern of thought or action, will inevitably divide/separate/split/alienate, and perpetuate the state of dilemmatic being which is characteristic of an alienated world' (2002a: 32–33), emphasizing the importance of 'unthinking' (2002a: 145) in order to connect with the power of now. This theme is also present in Luce Irigaray's later work, which, similarly to Bhaskar, Ghent and Sedgwick, draws inspiration from mystical-spiritual modes of knowing. Being specifically concerned with the self–other relation, Irigaray highlights that '[s]ilencing what we already know' is a condition of being able to 'let the other appear, and light ourselves up through this entry into presence irreducible to our knowledge' (2002: 165; cf. Stoller this volume).[8]

Bhaskar's dialectic foregrounds the ways in which the world is both unified and differentiated. In his spiritual writings (2000, 2002a, 2002b) he becomes more practically oriented, presenting techniques for drawing on our interconnectedness with the world so as to be able to ride its waves. As I see it, being in/with the pulse of now is precisely that point where being is unified, dissolving gaps between self and other, subject and object, interior and exterior, and so forth. The reason why intimacy with the now is 'that platform from which we alone can truly initiate change' (Bhaskar 2002a: 32) is precisely because it is only in the now that we are forcefully connected with the world. In a sense, we cannot of course but be in this now and cannot but be one with the world. However, when our attention is diverted by congealed memories and presumptions, we cannot draw fully on this connection.

To return to the theme of tensions, this kind of unification with the now is no closed or un-tensed unity. It is premised on being-in the tensed process of life, which is characterized by movement and transformation. The constitutive tension that must be harboured here is that between being and becoming, which are two equally real aspects of our existence: in order to *be* something in a stable and coherent sense, we need to be-with the movement of life.[9] If we think that we have arrived once and for all, life will in a sense continue without us. This is valid for our relation to life as a whole; more specifically it pertains to our relation to loved others.

Just as 'then' is dialectically co-enfolded in 'now', 'there' is co-enfolded in 'here', to add a spatial dimension to this ethics of presence. This helps make sense of why connecting with – affecting and being affected by – that which is in a sense external to us is premised on connection with ourselves; if we grasp outwards towards the other, we cannot connect our own interior with theirs.

In Bhaskar's understanding, the paradox that turning inwards to connect with our own constitutive reality intensifies our connection with what is 'outside' of ourselves, is explained by the fact that the unity of being operates precisely at the level of the 'fine-structure or deep interior' of being, which we can most easily access through ourselves (Bhaskar 2002a: 188, 2002b; Gunnarsson 2011b, 2014). He highlights that current social conditions tend to reinforce the hiatus between selves and their world, while obscuring their ultimate inseparability. This condition disempowers us, since it is only when we are really in touch with the world, including other people, that we can act efficaciously upon/in/with it. However, no matter how alienated we are from our 'surroundings', it remains the case that essentially and inexorably we *are* not split from them, since they are the conditions of our existence. Making efficacious use of our agency in order to change these conditions crucially involves reclaiming our intrinsic tie to them.

The need for 'intimacy with oneself' as the premise of intimacy with others is a crucial theme in Irigaray's work on love (2002: 150, 1996). She argues that if we are to restore a loving relation between people (and between women and men in particular), we need to inhibit impulses to reach out towards the other in an unmediated fashion and instead foster a culture of turning inwards, for it is only by 'being faithful to our own Being' (2002: 157) that we can really put ourselves in relation with others. Irigaray is deeply dialectical in emphasizing that any unity that does not respect difference is a false unity, and in her challenge of dualistic juxtapositions of self-love and other-love.

The typical patriarchal constitution of feminine and masculine selves can be thought of as based on the projection of aspects of one's own constitution outside of oneself, as a means of avoiding tension within oneself and achieving an allegedly un-conflicted identity. Paradoxically, the flipside of this projective move is that the self that it constitutes will be extremely dependent on the outside for being whole. The masculine self, in its paradigmatic form, projects the reality of dependence outside of himself, only to then express his own inescapable dependence in an alienated and often violent form, by controlling what is outside. 'It is always to an outside-of-oneself that man first grants Being', states Irigaray in a critique of such projective modes. 'He thus becomes the effect of what he has regarded or constructed external to him' (2002: 93). For Irigaray, as for Bhaskar, this externalizing tendency, which they see as internal to western modernity, is ultimately deadening (cf. Brennan 2004), since it cuts us off from the life energy generated by the tensions of our own constitutive ground. Whereas turning away from others in the defensive way, which requires that one suppresses parts of oneself, stands in the way for connection, turning inwards in a way that embraces what we really are is a dialectical premise for reaching out to others.

The self that is constructed in opposition to other selves and the world, yet dependent on them in an acute and more or less instrumentalized way, is often referred to as the 'ego' (Bhaskar 2002a, 2002b; Brennan 2004; Ghent, 1990). Inasmuch as the reality of the ego self is 'premised on denying aspects of what is in fact its reality' (Gunnarsson 2014: 149), its surface of connection is bound to be limited. We typically think of the ego as that kind of masculinized self that denies dependence; however, the feminine self that suppresses her own immutable *in*dependence is in fact also an ego self (Gross 1993). Similar to the masculine self, she is cut off from aspects of her own constitutive reality, in a way that prevents her from fully bringing herself into relation with that on which she experiences herself to depend so badly.

Ghent reflects on the fact that the notion of surrendering one's self has traditionally been differently received in the west and the east and suggests that this is related to different views of the self. Whereas in the west it is commonplace to equate the ego with the self and therefore cherish its sustenance, in the eastern tradition of thought there is a notion of the self that lies beneath the ego, whose flourishing is hampered by the latter's defensive constructions. The self that has no problem being distinct and particular, while unbounded and intrinsically interconnected, is that more basic self that for Ghent is the 'ultimate direction' of surrender, 'one's sense of wholeness, even one's sense of unity with other living beings' (1990: 111). It is also undoubtedly what Irigaray refers to when invoking 'that place of ours where life still lives, still palpitates' (2002: 93), 'the groundless ground of the co-belonging of human being to itself and to its world' (90). Bhaskar calls it the 'ground-state' (2002a: x) or the 'transcendentally real self' (2002b: 91; cf. Brennan 2004).

To many, the 'inaction' (Bhaskar 2000: 60) involved in surrendering to what is, looks suspiciously similar to passivity and compliance. It is quite the contrary, though, for channelling one's attention towards connecting with the fine structure of being is bound to reflect itself in actions that express fidelity to the dignity at the core of one's own as well as others' being. However, current society offers few resources for distinguishing the disempowering vulnerability entailed by subordination from the empowering vulnerability and openness required in surrender. This is further complicated by the fact, highlighted by Benjamin in a passage that discusses surrender in relation to Klein's depressive position, that '[t]he very distinction between passivity and surrender only becomes possible when fear of passivity is lifted' (2004: 55).[10] Since we live within a structure in which vulnerability often equals trauma, it is difficult to create the 'awareness that strength derives not from denial but from acknowledging helplessness, damage, and the overwhelming of the psyche by suffering' (Benjamin 2013: 55). The gender regime that delegates in perverted form helplessness to women and strength to men can only be challenged in conjunction with a challenge of the structural, cultural and psychological pitching of dependence and vulnerability against independence and strength.

Closing words

In this chapter I have shed light on the relation between love and dominance, so as to point towards ways of transforming our modes of bonding into genuinely loving relations based on respect for the irreducibility and uncontrollability of the other. This endeavour was guided by my dialectical approach, which regards tensions as ontologically constitutive and protects both against splitting – in theory as well as practice – interrelated aspects of being from one another and against the creation of false unities of things that cannot be reduced to one another.

Against strong social constructionism, my claims have been underpinned by a realist perspective that regards socially formed power structures as necessarily drawing on basic tendencies in the human situation. The structural splits and contradictions between women and men, self and other, autonomy and relatedness can be remedied, but only if we first understand how they draw their power from tensions at the ground of existence and find ways of dealing with these tensions that sustain rather than hamper life. Other people's independent existence both constrains and constitutes our own independent selves; the task is to live in and through such ontological tensions, instead of tearing up the tissue of being in efforts to escape them. Realism, then, does not only concern what *is*; it also has implications for how we need to live if we are to have our intentions sustainably fulfilled. There is no shortcut to truly enriching relations with others; the only way there is via our own tension-ridden constitution.

It seems to be a universal human impulse to engage in the suppression of tension, as illustrated in Klein's depiction of the paranoid-schizoid position, and I think it is important to acknowledge this destructive tendency if we are to be able to hamper its effects. As Ghent states, accepting paradox and tension 'presupposes a high degree of maturity' (1992: 155). The good news is that there are also things about the human constitution that work as a conatus against the defensiveness against tension: as shown throughout this chapter, the suppression of constitutive tension is ultimately self-defeating, since it splits us off from parts of reality on which we really depend. This reality principle creates a conatus to give up engaging in the kinds of suppressions that underpin dominance and submission.

Perhaps somewhat belatedly, I am now ready to present a definition of love: Love is the act of enhancing life in a way that does not pitch one life against another but keeps different life impulses in sustainable tension. It involves respecting the necessary structure of life and living with and through its constitutive tensions, rather than vainly seeking the kind of closed harmony, unity and identity that cannot harbour differentiation, tension, and change.

Apart from the fact that tension is *desirable* in that it generates life, it is also *inescapable*. We do, however, encounter yet another ontological ambiguity in the dynamic whereby accepting the reality of tension in a way cancels it. It is here, in the continuous movement of being one with the tensed process of life, that the blissful unification experience can be achieved in a *sustainable* and *non-oppressive* way. It is also from this platform of attentive intimacy with life's deep processual structure that transformation can happen nonviolently and relatively effortlessly, since we can then balance life's tensions as soon as they arise rather than when they have accumulated into more dualistic and multiplied forms.

Inasmuch as we cannot altogether separate the contradictions that structure the current social order from our own constitution, in this particular context the loving act of living with and through one's constitutive tensions is particularly demanding. In my view, we must take responsibility for how structural contradictions are part of ourselves and act upon them from there, rather than simply projecting their dualistic play of forces out in the world so as to relieve ourselves from the distress they cause. This is no easy task for the oppressed, who rightly feel that they have carried enough burdens. However, inasmuch as it is only ourselves that we can immediately affect, focusing on mitigating dualisms in oneself is often a more powerful way of breaking with the circular logic of contradictions than attempting to get others to change (Gunnarsson 2017a). There is a need to resist the temptation to seek instant freedom from the oppressive tensions we resent, since a simple repudiation of the negative is likely to enhance the violent dialectic underpinning these contradictions. Being ready to harbour – and mourn – painful tensions not of our own making is a premise of being a channel of love unmuddied by resentment. By virtue of love's nature of radiating in ever-widening circles, this is bound to help dissolve contradictions in others too, enabling the deep change we need so badly.

Notes

1 See Morgan (2007) on analytical reasoning as necessary in a basic sense yet too heavily depended on within western philosophy.
2 'Ontological tension' here simply refers to tensions *in being*. It is not restricted to fundamental existential tensions, i.e. those necessary tensions built into existence as such, but includes tensions generated by human practices. Similarly, in my use 'constitutive tension' refers not only to basic, existential tensions but to all kinds of tensions that are building blocks of reality as currently organized. See Lawson (2015) for a critical realist conception of ontology generally and social ontology specifically.
3 See Gunnarsson (2011a, 2013, 2014) for an introduction of the philosophy of critical realism and arguments in favor of its usefulness for feminist theory.
4 See Gunnarsson (2013, 2014) for an elaboration on the phenomenon of *emergence*.
5 'The unity of the being as human', writes Irigaray, 'remains open and leaves each term its specificity and autonomy' (2002: 78).
6 This reading of Hegel contrasts with for example Simone de Beauvoir's interpretation, which holds Hegel's work to offer a space for the possibility of *mutual* recognition (1989; Lundgren-Gothlin 1996).
7 In a critique of Catharine MacKinnon's work, Drucilla Cornell implicitly addresses the difference between surrender and subordination, when stating that MacKinnon fails to distinguish between 'the vulnerability and risk to the self involved in eroticism' and the 'feminine position of "being fucked"' (1999: 153).
8 This process seems to have similarities with what Rosi Braidotti terms 'dis-identification' (2008: 17).
9 Here I differ from poststructuralist accounts that tend to emphasize the reality of *becoming* at the cost of *being*, in a way that pits one against the other (e.g. Braidotti 2002; Grosz 2011; see Gunnarsson 2013).

10 Ghent suggests that resignation be thought of as 'the impersonator of acceptance, where the maturity involved in accepting paradox is not well developed' (1992: 155).

References

Benjamin, Jessica (1988) *The Bonds of Love: Psychoanalysis, Feminism, and the Problem of Domination.* New York: Pantheon Books.

Benjamin, Jessica (1995) *Like Subjects, Love Objects: Essays on Recognition and Sexual Difference.* New Haven and London: Yale University Press.

Benjamin, Jessica (1998) *Shadow of the Other: Intersubjectivity and Gender in Psychoanalysis.* New York: Routledge.

Benjamin, Jessica (2004) 'Deconstructing Femininity: Understanding "Passivity" and the Daughter Position', *The Annual of Psychoanalysis* 32: 45–57.

Benjamin, Jessica (2006) 'Two-Way Streets: Recognition of Difference and the Intersubjective Third', *Differences* 17(1): 116–146.

Benjamin, Jessica (2013) 'The Bonds of Love: Looking Backward', *Studies in Gender and Sexuality* 14(1): 1–15.

Bhaskar, Roy (2000) *From East to West: Odyssey of a Soul.* London: Routledge.

Bhaskar, Roy (2002a) *Meta-Reality. The Philosophy of Meta-Reality: Creativity, Love and Freedom.* London: Sage.

Bhaskar, Roy (2002b) *Reflections on Meta-Reality: Transcendence, Emancipation and Everyday Life.* London: Sage.

Bhaskar, Roy (2008) *Dialectic: The Pulse of Freedom*, 2nd edn. London: Routledge.

Bhaskar, Roy with Mervyn Hartwig (2010) *Formations of Critical Realism: A Personal Perspective.* London: Routledge.

Braidotti, Rosi (2002) *Metamorphoses: Towards a Materialist Theory of Becoming.* Cambridge: Polity Press.

Braidotti, Rosi (2008) 'In Spite of the Times: The Postsecular Turn in Feminism', *Theory, Culture and Society* 25(6): 1–24.

Braidotti, Rosi (2011) *Nomadic Subjects: Embodiment and Sexual Difference in Contemporary Feminist Theory.* New York: Columbia University Press.

Brennan, Teresa (2004) *The Transmission of Affect.* Ithaca, NY: Cornell University Press.

Chanter, Tina (2010) 'Antigone's Liminality: Hegel's Racial Purification of Tragedy and the Naturalization of Slavery', in K. Hutchings and T. Pulkkinen (eds) *Hegel's Philosophy and Feminist Thought: Beyond Antigone?* Basingstoke: Palgrave Macmillan.

Cornell, Drucilla (1999) *Beyond Accommodation: Ethical Feminism, Deconstruction and the Law.* Lanham, MD: Rowman & Littlefield.

de Beauvoir, Simone (1947) *Pour une morale de l'ambiguïté.* Paris: Gallimard.

de Beauvoir, Simone (1989) *The Second Sex.* New York: Vintage.

Feminist Theory (2014) 'Special Section: The Time of Reparation – in Dialogue with Robyn Wiegman', 15(1): 39: 3–49.

Flatschart, Elmar (2014) 'Matter That Really Matters? "New" Materialism and "Old" Dialectical Theory of Society'. Available: https://www.academia.edu/5897539/Matter_that_really_matters_New_Materialism_and_old_dialectical_theory_of_society (accessed 16 September 2015).

Ghent, Emmanuel (1990) 'Masochism, Submission, Surrender: Masochism as a Perversion of Surrender', *Contemporary Psychoanalysis* 26(1): 108–136.

Ghent, Emmanuel (1992) 'Paradox and Process', *Psychoanalytic Dialogues* 2(2): 135–159.

Granberg, Magnus (2013) 'A Contextual Analysis of Deleuze's Critique of Dialectics'. Unpublished paper, Mid-Sweden University.

Gross, Rita M. (1993) *Buddhism after Patriarchy: A Feminist History, Analysis, and Reconstruction of Buddhism*. Albany: State University of New York Press.

Grosz, Elizabeth (2011) *Becoming Undone*. Durham, NC: Duke University Press.

Gunnarsson, Lena (2011a) 'A Defence of the Category "Women"', *Feminist Theory* 12 (1): 23–37.

Gunnarsson, Lena (2011b) 'Love – Exploitable Resource or "No-Lose Situation"? Reconciling Jónasdóttir's Feminist View with Bhaskar's Philosophy of Meta-Reality', *Journal of Critical Realism* 10(4): 419–441.

Gunnarsson, Lena (2013) 'The Naturalistic Turn in Feminist Theory: A Marxist-Realist Contribution', *Feminist Theory* 14(1): 3–19.

Gunnarsson, Lena (2014) *The Contradictions of Love: Towards a Feminist-Realist Ontology of Sociosexuality*. London and New York: Routledge.

Gunnarsson, Lena (2015a) 'Breaking Intellectual Taboos with Roy by My Side', *Journal of Critical Realism* 14(2): 121–124.

Gunnarsson, Lena (2015b) 'Nature, Love and the Limits of Male Power: 2013 Cheryl Frank Memorial Prize Lecture', *Journal of Critical Realism* 14(3): 325–332.

Gunnarsson, Lena (2017a) 'Hetero-Love in Patriarchy: An Autobiographical Substantiation', *Hypatia* 32(1): 187–192.

Gunnarsson, Lena (2017b) 'Why We Keep Separating the "Inseparable": Dialecticizing Intersectionality', *European Journal of Women's Studies* 24(2): 114–127.

Hegel, Georg W. F. (1977) *Phenomenology of Spirit*. Oxford: Oxford University Press.

Irigaray, Luce (1989) 'Sorcerer Love: A Reading of Plato's Symposium, Diotima's Speech', *Hypatia* 3(3): 32–44.

Irigaray, Luce (1996) *I Love to You: Sketch of a Possible Felicity in History*. London: Routledge.

Irigaray, Luce (2002) *The Way of Love*. London: Continuum.

Jameson, Fredric (2014) *The Hegel Variations: On the Phenomenology of Spirit*. London and New York: Verso.

Jónasdóttir, Anna G. (1994) *Why Women Are Oppressed*. Philadelphia, PA: Temple University Press.

Klein, Melanie (1946) 'Notes on Some Schizoid Mechanisms', *International Journal of Psycho-Analysis* 27: 99–110.

Lawson, Tony (2015) 'A Conception of Social Ontology', in S. Pratten (ed.) *Social Ontology and Modern Economics*. New York: Routledge.

Layton, Lynne (2004) 'Relational No More: Defensive Autonomy in Middle-class Women', *The Annual of Psychoanalysis* 32: 29–42.

Love, Heather (2010) 'Truth and Consequences: On Paranoid Reading and Reparative Reading', *Criticism* 52(2): 235–241.

Lundgren-Gothlin, Eva (1996) *Sex and Existence: Simone de Beauvoir's The Second Sex*. London: Athlone Press.

Morgan, Jamie (2007) 'Analytical Problematic', in M. Hartwig (ed.) *Dictionary of Critical Realism*. London and New York: Routledge.

Norrie, Alan (2010) *Dialectic and Difference: Dialectical Critical Realism and the Grounds of Justice*. London and New York: Routledge.

Sedgwick, Eve Kosofsky (2003a) 'Paranoid Reading and Reparative Reading: Or, You're So Paranoid, You Probably Think This Essay Is about You', in *Touching Feeling: Affect, Pedagogy, Performativity*. Durham,. NC: Duke University Press.

Sedgwick, Eve Kosofsky (2003b) 'Pedagogy of Buddhism,' in *Touching Feeling: Affect, Pedagogy, Performativity*. Durham, NC: Duke University Press.

Sedgwick, Eve Kosofsky (2007) 'Melanie Klein and the Difference Affect Makes', *South Atlantic Quarterly* 106(3): 625–642.

Sedgwick, Eve Kosofsky, with Michael D. Snediker (2008) 'Queer Little Gods: A Conversation', *The Massachusetts Review* 49(1/2): 194–218.

Soper, Kate (1995) *What Is Nature? Culture, Politics, and the Non-Human*. Oxford and Cambridge: Blackwell.

Stone, Alison (2004) 'Going Beyond Oppositional Thinking? The Possibility of a Hegelian Feminist Philosophy. Review of Kimberly Hutchings, *Hegel and Feminist Philosophy*', *Res Publica* 10(3): 301–310.

Wiegman, Robyn (2014) 'The Times We're in: Queer Feminist Criticism and the Reparative "Turn"', *Feminist Theory* 15(1): 4–25.

Index

Note: Page numbers in *italics* denote references to Figures.